Finland

WORLD BIBLIOGRAPHICAL SERIES

General Editors:
Robert G. Neville (Executive Editor)
John J. Horton

Robert A. Myers   Hans H. Wellisch
Ian Wallace   Ralph Lee Woodward, Jr.

John J. Horton is Deputy Librarian of the University of Bradford and was formerly Chairman of its Academic Board of Studies in Social Sciences. He has maintained a longstanding interest in the discipline of area studies and its associated bibliographical problems, with special reference to European Studies. In particular he has published in the field of Icelandic and of Yugoslav studies, including the two relevant volumes in the World Bibliographical Series.

Robert A. Myers is Associate Professor of Anthropology in the Division of Social Sciences and Director of Study Abroad Programs at Alfred University, Alfred, New York. He has studied post-colonial island nations of the Caribbean and has spent two years in Nigeria on a Fulbright Lectureship. His interests include international public health, historical anthropology and developing societies. In addition to *Amerindians of the Lesser Antilles: a bibliography* (1981), *A Resource Guide to Dominica, 1493-1986* (1987) and numerous articles, he has compiled the World Bibliographical Series volumes on *Dominica* (1987), *Nigeria* (1989) and *Ghana* (1991).

Ian Wallace is Professor of German at the University of Bath. A graduate of Oxford in French and German, he also studied in Tübingen, Heidelberg and Lausanne before taking teaching posts at universities in the USA, Scotland and England. He specializes in contemporary German affairs, especially literature and culture, on which he has published numerous articles and books. In 1979 he founded the journal *GDR Monitor*, which he continues to edit under its new title *German Monitor*.

Hans H. Wellisch is Professor emeritus at the College of Library and Information Services, University of Maryland. He was President of the American Society of Indexers and was a member of the International Federation for Documentation. He is the author of numerous articles and several books on indexing and abstracting, and has published *The Conversion of Scripts and Indexing and Abstracting: an International Bibliography*, and *Indexing from A to Z*. He also contributes frequently to *Journal of the American Society for Information Science*, *The Indexer* and other professional journals.

Ralph Lee Woodward, Jr. is Professor of History at Tulane University, New Orleans. He is the author of *Central America, a Nation Divided*, 2nd ed. (1985), as well as several monographs and more than seventy scholarly articles on modern Latin America. He has also compiled volumes in the World Bibliographical Series on *Belize* (1980), *El Salvador* (1988), *Guatemala* (Rev. Ed.) (1992) and *Nicaragua* (Rev. Ed.) (1994). Dr. Woodward edited the Central American section of the *Research Guide to Central America and the Caribbean* (1985) and is currently associate editor of Scribner's *Encyclopedia of Latin American History*.

VOLUME 31

Finland

Revised Edition

J. E. O. Screen

Compiler

CLIO PRESS

OXFORD, ENGLAND · SANTA BARBARA, CALIFORNIA
DENVER, COLORADO

British Library Cataloguing in Publication Data

Screen, J. E. O. (John Ernest Oliver), 1939-
Finland. – Rev. ed. – (World bibliographical series; v. 31)
1. Finland – Bibliography
I. Title
016.9′4897

ISBN 1–85109–265–X

ABC-CLIO Ltd.,
Old Clarendon Ironworks,
35A Great Clarendon Street,
Oxford OX2 6AT, England.

––––––––––

ABC-CLIO Inc.,
130 Cremona Drive,
Santa Barbara,
CA 93117, USA.

Designed by Bernard Crossland.
Typeset by Columns Design Ltd., Reading, England.
Printed and bound in Great Britain by Bookcraft (Bath) Ltd., Midsomer Norton.

THE WORLD BIBLIOGRAPHICAL SERIES

This series, which is principally designed for the English speaker, will eventually cover every country (and some of the world's principal regions and cities), each in a separate volume comprising annotated entries on works dealing with its history, geography, economy and politics; and with its people, their culture, customs, religion and social organization. Attention will also be paid to current living conditions – housing, education, newspapers, clothing, etc. – that are all too often ignored in standard bibliographies; and to those particular aspects relevant to individual countries. Each volume seeks to achieve, by use of careful selectivity and critical assessment of the literature, an expression of the country and an appreciation of its nature and national aspirations, to guide the reader towards an understanding of its importance. The keynote of the series is to provide, in a uniform format, an interpretation of each country that will express its culture, its place in the world, and the qualities and background that make it unique. The views expressed in individual volumes, however, are not necessarily those of the publisher.

VOLUMES IN THE SERIES

Contents

Contents

Contents

Contents

Contents

Contents

Introduction

Finland became a member of the European Union on 1 January 1995. This marked a fundamental change in Finnish policy which would have been inconceivable without the dissolution of the Soviet Union. Finland's character as a Western European democracy, with a capitalist economy, survived its defeat by the Soviet Union during the Second World War and the country was never occupied by the Red Army or turned into a Soviet satellite. However, Finland prudently and skilfully pursued a foreign policy line of friendship and cooperation with the Soviet Union that aimed to ensure Finland's national self preservation by means of acknowledging Soviet interests and expectations. This had the consequence of limiting Finland's freedom of movement in foreign affairs. The Treaty of Friendship, Cooperation and Mutual Assistance which Finland had to conclude with the Soviet Union in 1948 created a relationship in matters of security which could be held to compromise the neutrality to which Finland aspired. In time the term 'Finlandization' was coined, somewhat unfairly, to signify a relationship that was leading gradually to a country's subordination to the Soviet Union. The term was always strongly opposed by the Finns but Finland's international position nevertheless remained less independent than was desirable.

Only in October 1989 did President Gorbachev of the Soviet Union formally recognize Finland's neutrality without reservation. Only in the autumn of 1990 did Finland declare that certain restrictive clauses of its peace treaty of 1947 with the wartime allies were of no effect. Only in January 1992 – after the collapse of the Soviet Union – was the Treaty of Friendship, Cooperation and Mutual Assistance replaced by a very different treaty, with no military obligations, between Finland and the Russian Federation. The way had become clear for Finland's long-sustained and important relationship with the countries of Western Europe to take a new form.

Finland's security relationship with the Soviet Union did not prevent the rapid re-establishment and further development of strong economies ties with the West. Indeed, Finland's Western trade played an important part in its postwar recovery. Finnish timber, paper and other wood products remain vital exports to Western Europe and the country's long-term economic interests have dictated increasingly close association with the Western economic blocs. The pace of that association was, however, delayed by the need to pay heed to Soviet reactions. Moreover, long-term trading agreements with the Soviet Union helped Finland, until the late 1980s, to secure an export market for manufactured goods that remained stable when Western economies were in recession. The Soviet Union supplied Finland with much-needed gas and oil. Finland thus proceeded cautiously and adroitly in its West European economic policy. It became associated with the European Free Trade Area in the 1960s but sought full membership only in 1986. Finland concluded a trade agreement with the European Economic Community in 1973 but at the price of granting the same favoured trading position to the Soviet Union and the COMECON countries that it granted to members of the Common Market.

With the 1990s the pace of association was able to quicken. In May 1992 Finland joined the European Economic Area. In March 1992 it had applied to join the European Community and negotiations about its membership began in February 1993. Against the background of the collapse of trade with the former Soviet Union, which coincided with a Western recession to produce a massive depression in Finland with nineteen per cent unemployment, Finland set itself on a new course of European integration.

Finland's older historic ties are with Scandinavia. It formed part of Sweden until 1809 when, as the result of war, it was annexed by the Russian Empire and constituted an autonomous grand duchy. That autonomous status was to develop during the 19th century and it facilitated both the formation of the Finnish nation and the country's transition to independence as the result of the Russian revolutions of 1917. Finland's Scandinavian heritage is reflected in its system of government and administration, laws, egalitarian social structure, welfare state (albeit under pressure), high standard of living, and its Lutheran religion. Such traditions place Finland firmly among the Western democracies. From the 1950s it became possible for Finland to develop its links with Scandinavia through the Nordic Council. Its links to the West have now been broadened and deepened through membership of the European Union.

The Finns decided to join the European Union as the result of a national referendum in October 1994 in which the vote in favour of membership was fifty-seven per cent. Urban Finland (where the bulk of the population now lives although many retain links with the countryside) voted yes and rural Finland no; younger people tended to vote yes. Business was resoundingly in favour. What Finns expect from membership of the European Union is unclear. Membership is undoubtedly perceived in many quarters as a valuable counterbalance to a revived Russia. Finland has, however, secured acceptance of its military non-alignment within the European Union and not joined NATO, although it has entered the Partnership for Peace programme and become a Western European Union observer. Finland has not relaxed the preparedness of its highly efficient defence forces.

A topic in the referendum debate and a matter of current concern in Finland is the preservation of the Finnish identity, not only in an integrating Europe (which may pose the threat of 'Finlandization' from the West) but also in an increasingly internationalized world. What is the future for a nation of five million people on the northern periphery of Europe? Fortunately, Finland is still a remarkably homogeneous society. Most of the inhabitants are Finnish speakers. The Swedish-speaking minority (5.8 per cent of the population) is different in language alone and its position is legally protected and uncontroversial. The Lapps have been a more vociferous minority than their numbers would warrant (some 5,300, of whom fewer than 2,000 claim Lapp as their mother tongue). However, they should now be satisfied with their recently-granted cultural autonomy. Finland has one of the smallest percentages of foreigners of any country in Europe (1.2 per cent) and has practised a prudent policy on immigration. Although the political and social consensus that prevailed until the late 1980s is no longer so obvious, reactions to the recent recession have shown a remarkable willingness among the Finnish people to face up to harsh realities and pull together in a crisis, though that willingness has been increasingly under strain as the high level of unemployment caused by the recession has con-tinued. Investment in high technology and higher education is generally accepted policy. Large numbers of Finnish students are sent to study abroad, a development which is reducing Finland's isolation and will surely increase its competitiveness in the international market place. Perhaps in this respect there is a risk to shared Finnish identity through the emergence of an internationalized élite.

According to surveys of public opinion, however, Finns remain refreshingly content to be Finns: patriotism and national feeling are strong. They have much of which they can be justifiably proud. Most obvious to foreigners are the high quality of Finnish products and the excellence of Finnish design, art, music and literature. Athletes and, more recently, motor racing drivers have played their part in making

Finland better known. International acclaim of Finnish culture has been fostered by a discreet but active policy to promote it abroad. If there is in Finland a greater willingness to question received national ideas, and even the workings of the constitution, there is also a greater self confidence. Perhaps because of this it has become a little easier to get to know the often enigmatic Finns. They remain, however, reserved as well as sincere. There can be an endearing cussedness about them which one hopes will bring them safely through the trials of the ERM and European Union politics as it has secured their successful survival in the unpromising geographical and geopolitical environment of their homeland.

The bibliography

Fifteen years have passed since the compilation of the first edition of this bibliography and, as is apparent from the preceding paragraphs, much in relation to Finland has changed. Nevertheless, librarians are urged to retain the first edition. The editorial requirements of the World Bibliographical Series – to include material in print where possible and to carry over only a small proportion of entries from the first edition – have led to a winnowing of some works that have not lost their significance. In particular some of the first edition's introductory and guide books, histories, encyclopaedias, writings on foreign relations and on the arts retain value either in their own right or as a reflection of Finland at the time of their publication.

Perhaps the most remarkable contrast between the present and the early 1980s is the vast increase in translations of Finnish literature, both from Finnish and – relatively even more – from Swedish. The existence of a strong representative selection of contemporary literature (reflected in this bibliography) is due to the work of the Finnish Literature Information Centre and to the editors of *Books from Finland* and their circle of translators. More Finnish scholarly work generally is being published in English. This is particularly noticeable in history and the social sciences, while architecture and music continue to attract wide attention.

As a selection of material primarily in the English language, the bibliography inevitably reflects what is actually available in English. Some sections are thus leaner than others. Despite attempts to be systematic in the work of compilation, there is always an element of chance in what is discovered, and some worthwhile material has undoubtedly been missed or proved impossible to locate. The most recently-published material is not always available in libraries. Some sections of the bibliography are more strictly representative than others; for example, there are many more specialized language glossaries than those actually included. The collection of material ceased in September 1996.

The arrangement of material presents problems. An alphabetical order of authors or titles, rigidly applied, can be unhelpful in that it can separate related items and only the determined user may find the best work if it comes at the end of a chapter. In many cases, therefore, I have tried to put the most highly recommended works at the beginning of chapters or sections. Arrangement by author (or title in the case of edited works) will be found but a chronological arrangement has been followed where appropriate. Thus travel accounts are arranged by date of publication. History, art, architecture and music are arranged by period except for biographies and memoirs in the history and architecture sections which are arranged alphabetically by person. In some sections the most recent material comes first, as in those about elections and for literary anthologies, while in those on the economy and industry material of current concern precedes references of historical interest. Many of the volumes in the series 'The History of Learning and Science in Finland' are gathered in a single section, arranged in alphabetical order of the science or discipline. Periodicals relating to particular sections usually come at the end of those sections. Sub-headings have been used liberally to guide the reader through particular chapters.

There is a single index of authors, titles and subjects, as was the case in the first edition. The letters å, ä and ö are filed as a, a and o, for the convenience of users who do not know their locations in the Finnish and Swedish alphabets, while Finnish users should also note that v and w are treated as separate letters. Place-names in Finland have been cited in the language of the publication in question; thus Helsinki is used in Finnish- and Helsingfors in Swedish-language publications. In the case of publications in more than one language, the first-cited place-name has been used.

Readers wishing to buy books published in Finland should note the postal addresses of two large bookshops: Akateeminen Kirjakauppa, P.O. Box 128, FIN-00101 Helsinki; and Suomalainen Kirjakauppa, P.O. Box 2, FIN-01641 Vantaa. Books published by the Finnish learned societies may be ordered from Tiedekirja, Kirkkokatu 14, FIN-00170, Helsinki.

Use of the Internet is highly developed in Finland and much information is available that way. A convenient starting point for information about Finland is Virtual Finland http://www.vn.fi/vn/um/index.html, produced by the Finnish Ministry of Foreign Affairs Press and Cultural Department Information Services Unit.

Introduction

Acknowledgements

It is a pleasure to acknowledge the help of many friends and colleagues in the compilation work. Miss Marja-Leena Rautalin, Director of the Finnish Literature Information Centre, arranged for me to visit Finland to collect material and the School of Slavonic and East European Studies gave me leave of absence for that visit. Professor Esko Häkli, Director of Helsinki University Library, Ms Erja Tikka of the Embassy of Finland in London, Mr Tom Geddes and Mrs Barbara Hawes of the British Library have helped in various ways: my thanks to them all.

J. E. O. Screen

Introductory Works

General

1 **Finland: a country study.**
Edited by Eric Solsten, Sandra W. Meditz. Washington, DC: Library
of Congress, Federal Research Division, 1990. 2nd ed. xxxiii + 444p.
15 maps. bibliog. (Area Handbook Series, DA Pam 550-167).
A general introduction to Finland covering society and its environment (e.g. history,
geography, social structure, minorities, religion, education, welfare, living
conditions), the economy, government and politics, and national security. Gives some
statistics. Excellent bibliography (p. 373-420), mostly of English-language material,
supplemented by some comments on sources at the end of each chapter. Users of this
admirable handbook must keep in mind that the research for it was completed in
December 1988.

2 **Facts about Finland.**
Helsinki: Otava, 1996. 4th ed. 190p. map. bibliog.
Provides lots of basic information about the country, its government, history, foreign
policy, social security, education, culture, media and sport, with some guidance for the
visitor.

3 **Finfo: Finnish Features.**
Helsinki: Ministry for Foreign Affairs, 1981- . maps.
Originally a loose-leaf publication entitled *Finnish Features* providing short and
reliable articles on numerous aspects of Finland, from geography to shipbuilding, and
from education to national parks. Published since 1995 on a more regular basis as
Finfo: Finnish Features, while maintaining the same spread of topics and good
quality. A good first stop for information about Finland. The Ministry of Foreign
Affairs Press and Cultural Department Information Services Unit also produces
'Virtual Finland', an excellent source of information about Finland on the Internet
with the address http://www.vn.fi/vn/um/index.html[.]

1

4 Finland: a cultural outline.

Veikko Kallio, translated by Peter Herring.   Porvoo, Finland; Helsinki: Werner Söderström, 1994. 214p.

A general survey of Finnish cultural history from the middle ages to the present. Originally published in 1989 as *Finland: cultural perspectives*.

5 An experience of Finland.

W. R. Mead.   London: Hurst, 1993. xii + 164p.

This is an intensely personal account of the author's involvement with Finland which began in the late 1930s. Geography, history, economic life and the arts all have a place in a book both scholarly and poetical. Those who know nothing of Finland will learn a vast amount from it; those who already know something will savour its richness with deep appreciation. The author, a geographer, is the doyen of British scholars concerned with Finland.

6 Finland in a changing Europe.

W. R. Mead.   *Geographical Journal*, vol. 157, no. 3 (November 1991), p. 307-15.

A stimulating review, both historical and contemporary, of 'Finland in Europe' and 'Europe in Finland', reflecting on the elements in the society and economy of Finland which are common to Europe or distinctive to Finland.

7 Finland.

W. R. Mead.   London: Benn, 1968. 256p. maps. bibliog.

Remains useful background reading, containing a sound geographical base, a good deal of history and enough economics and culture to give the reader a lively picture of the development of the modern nation. There is a discursive bibliographical appendix.

8 Image of Finland in the year zero.

Jörn Donner, Martti Häikiö.   Helsinki: [Ulkoasiainministeriö], 1991. [i] + 105p. 2 maps. (Ulkoasiainministeriön julkaisuja [Publications of the Ministry for Foreign Affairs], 8:91).

'The purpose of this book is to sketch out the new international challenges that Finnish identity faces in the new situation' [after the Cold War] (p. 1). The authors take a deliberately subjective look at various aspects of Finnish life and at how Finland presents itself and is regarded abroad. No cows are too sacred to be slain and the result is a stimulating (if occasionally repetitive) look at modern Finland.

9 The Finns and their society: a national survey of opinions and attitudes, 1995.

Helsinki: Centre for Finnish Business and Policy Studies, 1995. 26p.

The sixth national attitude survey to be published by the Centre. Reflects the impact of the recession of the early 1990s, showing popular concern over the future of the welfare state and strong criticism of political parties and the way the Finnish democratic system functions. Patriotism and national feeling, however, remain strong.

10   **Indicators of the Finnish society, 1995/96.**
Helsinki: Centre for Finnish Business and Policy Studies, 1995. 47p.
Useful tables and brief comments on such topics as the significance of foreign trade,
Finland's exports by industry, growth of the GDP, inflation, women in the labour
market, taxation and attitudes towards Finland's policy in the European Union.
Compiled annually since 1991/92 by a private 'think tank' sponsored by various
Finnish business organizations.

Austerity and prosperity: perspectives on Finnish society.
See item no. 221.

Kerro Suomesta 5 kielellä. Englanti, ruotsi, saksa, ranska, venäjä. (Tell
about Finland in five languages. English, Swedish, German, French,
Russian.)
See item no. 520.

Picture books

11   **Finland: land of natural beauty.**
Editor-in-chief Rainer Palmunen.   Helsinki: Reader's Digest, 1989.
303p. maps.
An excellent and attractive richly-illustrated book about rural Finland, region by
region, from the coasts, through the lakeland, to Kainuu, Koillismaa and Lapland.
Includes much on wildlife, plants and forests.

12   **Finland: the land of a thousand lakes.**
Stefania Belloni, English text by Brian Williams.   Narni Terni, Italy:
Plurigraf, 1995. 96p. map.
An attractive picture book with information of use to the tourist.

13   **Picture Finland.**
Maarit Niiniluoto. Picture editor: Peter Sandberg. English translation:
Tim Steffa.   Helsinki: Otava, 1993. 2nd ed. 95p.
A hundred photographs, with some explanatory text, evoking what Finland is like. By
no means confined to idyllic rural landscapes.

14   **Finland 2000. English, Deutsch, suomi.**
Raimo Suikari.   Espoo, Finland: RKS Tietopalvelu, 1996. 96p. map.
An attractive picture book about Finland with some text (in English, German and
Finnish) and some factual information in an appendix.

For children

15 **My Finnish workbook.**
Nigel Allenby Jaffé, Margaret Allenby Jaffé. Skipton, England: Folk
Dance Enterprises, 1988. 35p. 2 maps.

This is a very good little book about Finland for children although the geographical
'tour' of the country is better than the brief history. There are a couple of pages on
music and dancing, one on customs and several illustrating folk costumes. Things to
do (hence the workbook of the title) include two recipes, performing a song and
simple dance, finding places on the map and sewing a cross-stitch reindeer. Those not
up to sewing can assemble a small cardboard cut-out reindeer instead.

Geography

Finland as part of the Baltic region

16 **Norden: man and environment.**
   Edited by Uuno Varjo, Wolf Tietze, on behalf of Geographical Society
   of Northern Finland and the Department of Geography, University of
   Oulu.   Berlin; Stuttgart, Germany: Borntraeger, 1987. xvi + 535p.
   maps. bibliog.

A substantial textbook covering the historical geography of the Scandinavian
countries, the seas, the geology and geomorphology, climate and hydrology,
biogeography and climate, population and settlement, primary occupations,
manufacturing and services, social geography and regional geography.

17 **An historical geography of Scandinavia.**
   W. R. Mead.   London: Academic Press, 1981. xviii + 313p. maps.
   bibliog.

On Denmark, Finland, Iceland, Norway and Sweden. Takes cross-sections of
Scandinavia at c.1250, c.1650, c.1750, c.1850 and c.1900, following the political
outline, the distribution of population and settlement, the use of resources and
communications, and looking at how the available means served changing human
ends.

General geography

18 **A geography of Finland.**
Kalevi Rikkinen. Lahti, Finland: University of Helsinki Lahti
Research and Training Centre, 1992. 144p. maps. bibliog.
A basic textbook of Finnish geography which pays particular attention to the
geography of the regions of Finland.

19 **Finland's landscapes and urban and rural milieus.**
Edited by Pentti Alalammi. Helsinki: National Land Survey;
Geographical Society of Finland, 1994. 234p. maps. bibliog. (Atlas of
Finland, 350).
This part of the fifth edition of the *Atlas of Finland* (item no. 30) has been published
in Finnish, Swedish and English. It is a study of the Finnish landscape and of
settlement, arranged by area, and with excellent photographs.

20 **National landscapes.**
Elias Härö, Mikko Mansikka. Editor: Lauri Putkonen. Translation:
Timothy Binham. [Helsinki]: Ministry of the Environment, Land Use
Department, 1994. 2nd ed. 64p. map. bibliog.
An attractive and informative large-format work, containing descriptions and pictures
(old and new) of twenty-seven locations throughout Finland which are held to be
representative of national landscapes. The areas chosen include natural scenery, river
valleys and waterways, built environments and cultivated lands. They show the
characteristic features of Finland and how the land has been used for the Finns'
livelihood.

21 **Fennia.**
Helsinki: Geographical Society of Finland, 1889- .
A series comprising lengthy works on the geography of Finland in all its aspects and
now written in English. Two or three issues per year.

Special aspects of geography

Political geography

22 **Political geography around the world VIII. The rise and fall of Finnish geopolitics.**
Anssi Paasi. *Political Geography Quarterly*, vol. 9, no. 1 (January 1990), p. 53-65.
Examines the development and content of Finnish political geography and in particular the development of geopolitical thinking and its social and historical contexts in Finland and internationally. The 'rise and fall' of the title relate to the idea of a Greater Finland, which was significant in the 1930s and early 1940s.

23 **Territories, boundaries and consciousness: the changing geographies of the Finnish-Russian border.**
Anssi Paasi. Chichester, England; New York: Wiley, 1996. xxi + 353p. maps. bibliog. (Belhaven Studies in Political Geography).
A theoretically-based book on the political geography of the Finno-Russian border from the 19th century to the present. Considers how the Finns defined themselves and their border with Russia. Also takes as a case-study at the local level the consequences for the border area of Värtsilä that was divided by the new frontier during the Second World War.

24 **The East-West interface in the European North.**
Edited by Margareta Dahlström, Heikki Eskelinen, Ulf Wiberg. Uppsala, Sweden: Nordisk Samhällsgeografisk Tidskrift, 1995. [ii] + vi + 155p. 8 maps. bibliog.
Ten studies of 'cross-border interaction' in the Baltic and more particularly the Barents region, adopting historical, political or economic approaches to the subject. Finnish contacts with St Petersburg and attitudes in northern Finland to the frontier with Russia are of particular significance here but the looming role of Russia in the region generally is of greater importance.

Land emergence

25 **Finland: daughter of the sea.**
Michael Jones. Folkestone, England: Dawson; Hamden, Connecticut: Archon, 1977. 247p. maps. (Studies in Historical Geography).
A study of land emergence, which is one of the physical phenomena of Finland, in its human and legal as well as physical respects.

Winter and climate

26 **Winter in Finland.**
W. R. Mead, Helmer Smeds. London: Evelyn; New York: Praeger, 1967. 144p. maps. bibliog.
Winter exerts a profound influence on all aspects of life and work in Finland. This book is a scholarly consideration of the problems posed by winter in Finland and the solutions adopted to deal with them.

27 **The climate of Finland in relation to its hydrology, ecology and culture.**
Reijo Solantie. Helsinki: Finnish Meteorological Institute, 1990. 130p. maps. bibliog. (Finnish Meteorological Institute Contributions, 2).
This Helsinki University thesis demonstrates how essential a factor climate is for many areas of ecology and human activities. It shows that the regional divisions applicable to climate in Finland apply, with small modifications, to botany, zoology, the national economy, settlement history, archaeology, linguistics, agriculture, forestry and building technology, and are also important for understanding folk culture and the relationship between man and the environment.

Regional geography: the Åland islands

28 **The Åland islands.**
W. R. Mead, S. H. Jaatinen. Newton Abbot, England: David & Charles, 1975. 183p. 4 maps. bibliog.
Describes the geography and history of the Åland islands, paying particular attention to the development of society and the economy and to the problems confronting these 'fortunate islands'.

Maps and atlases

General and national atlases

29 **Fennia. Suuri Suomi-kartasto. Kartverk över Finland. Finland in maps. Finnischer Atlas.**
Helsinki: Weilin & Göös, 1979. 224p. maps.
At 1:250,000 this is a large-scale atlas, comprising the fine maps published by the National Board of Survey, and as such it still deserves attention. The atlas also includes a gazetteer of 9,000 places, town plans, and information about the availability of maps at other scales.

30　**Suomen kartasto. Atlas över Finland. Atlas of Finland.**
　　Helsinki: National Land Survey and Geographical Society of Finland,
　　1976-94. 5th ed. 45 fascicules. maps. bibliog.

This new edition of the *Atlas of Finland* has maps and figures in Finnish, Swedish and English. The accompanying articles are in Finnish but Swedish and English translations are available as enclosures. It is an excellent national atlas which covers the mapping of Finland, the land, geology, climate, waters, animals and nature protection, land use and ownership, settlement, environment, population, economic activity, agriculture, forestry, industry, construction, energy, commerce and services, transport and tourism, society, administration, planning, social activities, education, science and culture, living conditions and social policy, landscape and the environment. The final part (numbered 350) on the landscape and settlement is published separately in Finnish, Swedish and English (see item no. 19).

31　**Atlas de Finlande.** (Atlas of Finland.)
　　Helsinki: Société de Géographie de Finlande, 1899. 2 vols. maps.

This is the first of an excellent series of national atlases published by the Geographical Society of Finland, of which the older volumes retain considerable value since they measure the changing circumstances of Finland, both physical and human. The maps cover climate, vegetation, population, schools, agriculture, industry, transport and communications, prehistoric finds, historic frontiers, and reproductions of the maps of Olaus Magnus (1539) and Andreas Bureus (1626). The introductory material to the atlas volume includes statistics of area and population by administrative division. The atlas was published in two editions, one in French, the other in Finnish and Swedish. The text volume, published separately in Finnish, Swedish and French (the last being in the series *Fennia* [see item no. 21], vol. 17), gives full comments and explanations of the maps individually.

32　**Atlas de Finlande, 1910.** (Atlas of Finland, 1910.)
　　Helsinki: Société Géographique de Finlande, 1911. 3 vols. maps.

This is a greatly expanded version of the 1899 atlas. The atlas itself was published in a single edition, with captions in Finnish, Swedish and French; the text was published separately in each language, the last as *Fennia*, vol. 30. Volume 1 of the text provides a detailed explanation of twenty-three maps covering the land, water, meteorology, flora, vegetation, fauna and forests of Finland, while volume 2 explains twenty-seven maps covering population, agriculture, industry, languages, education, towns, etc.

33　**Suomen kartasto. Atlas of Finland. Atlas över Finland. 1925.**
　　Geographical Society of Finland.　Helsinki: Otava, 1925-29. 2 vols.
　　maps.

Detailed explanation of the maps on the same lines as the 1910 atlas but with additional coverage of mining, industry, foreign trade, shipping, banking, cooperation, postal services, education, health, boundaries, etc. The atlas was published in a single edition, with its captions in Finnish, Swedish and English; the text appeared in separate editions in each of those languages, the English as *Fennia*, vol. 48.

34   **Suomen kartasto. Atlas of Finland. Atlas över Finland. 1960.**
     Geographical Society of Finland and University of Helsinki Department
     of Geography.   Helsinki: Otava, 1960-62. 2 vols. maps.
     Follows a similar pattern of coverage to the 1925 atlas but with less detailed notes.

Atlases and maps for motorists

35   **Autoilijan Suomi-kartasto.** (The motorist's atlas of Finland.)
     [Helsinki]: Valitut Palat, 1994. [343 + 1]p.
     An atlas of Finland for the motorist with maps at the scale of 1:200,000 except for the
     north of the country where they are at 1:400,000. Also includes street plans of towns
     and an index of places as well as 'a hundred sights to see' in Finland. Finnish-
     language text only.

36   **GT tiekartasto Suomi-Finland. Vägatlas. Road atlas. Strassenatlas.**
     1:200000/1:400000.
     Helsinki: Karttakeskus, 1996. 3rd enl. ed. 287p. maps.
     Regularly updated road atlas of Finland at the scale of 1:200,000, with index sheets at
     1:400,000. The index lists 50,000 names.

37   **GT Suomen tiekartta. Vägkarta över Finland. Road map of Finland.**
     Finnische Strassenkarte.
     Helsinki: Karttakeskus, 1991-95. 19 sheets.
     Gives topographical as well as road information. The scale is 1:200,000. Regularly
     revised.

38   **Autoilijan tiekartta. Bilistens vägkarta. Motoring road map.**
     Auto-Strassenkarte. Suomi. Finland. Finnland. 1:800 000.
     Helsinki: Karttakeskus, 1996.
     An annually-issued map covering Finland and the north of Sweden and Norway at a
     scale of 1:800,000 on one sheet, printed on both sides. Explanations are in Finnish,
     Swedish, English and German.

Regional atlases

39   **Atlas över Skärgårds-Finland. Saaristo-Suomen kartasto. Atlas of**
     the archipelago of southwestern Finland.
     Helsinki: Nordenskiöld-Samfundet i Finland, 1960. 2 vols. maps.
     Published by the Nordenskiöld Society of Finland, this is a very detailed study of a
     comparatively small but characteristic region of Finland. The atlas is in two parts: 1,
     General features: natural history, human geography and history; and 2, Typical
     villages: natural vegetation, crops, land tenure and settlement. The captions to the

maps are in Swedish, Finnish and English, but the detailed explanations in volume 2 (the text to the atlas) are in Swedish only.

Historical atlases

40 **Suomen historian kartasto. Atlas of Finnish history.**
Edited by Eino Jutikkala. Porvoo, Finland; Helsinki: Werner Söderström, 1959. 2nd rev. ed. 83p. maps. (Suomen tiedettä [Finnish Science], 2).
Introduction and captions in Finnish and English. Includes maps on population and settlement, ecclesiastical and civil administrative divisions, military campaigns, farming, industry, trade, towns, communications and schools.

41 **Scandinavian atlas of historic towns.**
[Odense, Denmark]: Danish Committee for Urban History; Odense University Press, 1977. Vols. 1-2.
Volume 1: *Finland: Turku-Åbo*, by Eino Jutikkala. 10p. maps; volume 2: *Finland: Borgå-Porvoo*, by Eino Jutikkala. 11p. maps. These first two fascicules, of an atlas intended to comprise fifteen, are devoted to Finland. For Turku there is a reproduction of a coloured map (1:5,000) showing the town in 1741-43 and a reproduction of a plan on the same scale for 1808 on which occupations have been plotted. For Porvoo there is a reproduction of a coloured map (1:2,500) from 1792, a plan on the same scale showing occupations in 1694-96, and another showing buildings in the 1830s. The texts include maps showing the towns as well as their localities, and describe the history and development of the towns as well as describing the maps themselves. The text of the atlas is in English, Finnish and Swedish. For the new series of the Atlas, see item no. 42.

42 **Scandinavian atlas of historic towns. New series.**
[Helsinki]: Finnish Historical Society; [Odense, Denmark]: Odense University Press, 1990. Vol. 1.
Kokkola-Gamlakarleby, by Eino Jutikkala and Marjatta Hietala. 23p. maps. bibliog. Follows the same pattern as the first series (see item no. 41), with reproductions of maps and plans and the text of the atlas in Finnish, Swedish and English. No more parts are planned.

Historical maps

43 **Finland defined: a nation takes shape on the map.**
Erkki Fredrikson. Jyväskylä, Finland; Helsinki: Gummerus, 1994. 125p. maps. bibliog.
Uses some 100 maps to show how the mapping of Finland has changed over five centuries. An attractive and useful volume.

44 **Vanhoja Suomen karttoja. Old maps of Finland.**
Isak Gordin. Helsinki: Kustannuskilta, 1973. 2nd rev. ed. 111p. maps.

A handsome volume which comprises forty-seven pages of reproductions of printed maps and charts showing Finland and dating from between 1482 and 1799. The brief annotations and introductions are in Finnish and English. The book gives an excellent impression of the development of the cartographers' image of Finland.

45 **Vanhojen karttojen Suomi: historiallisen kartografian vertaileva tarkastelu. Finland in old maps.** (A comparative examination of historical cartography.)
Harri Rosberg. Jyväskylä, Finland: Gummerus, 1984. 144p. maps.

Reproduces 130 maps, both manuscript and published, from the mid-16th century onwards, showing how cartographic design has changed. Brief summary in English.

Glossaries and gazetteers

46 **Finland. Official standard names approved by the United States Board on Geographic Names.**
Washington, DC: US Government Printing Office, 1962. vi + 556p. map. (Gazetteer No. 62).

About 39,800 entries for places and features in Finland, the map scale of the name coverage being approximately 1:400,000. There is a glossary of generic terms.

47 **A glossary of Finnish map terms and abbreviations.**
A. E. Palmerlee. Cleveland, Ohio: Micro Photo Division, Bell & Howell Company, 1968. [iv] + iii + 50p.

An expansion of a glossary originally compiled in 1959. Covers geological as well as topographical and administrative terms. Also has some Lapp words (designated as such) and some archaisms. Comprises some 1,200 terms and abbreviations.

48 **Svenska ortnamn i Finland.** (Swedish place-names in Finland.)
Edited by Kurt Zilliacus, Ulla Ådahl-Sundgren. Helsingfors: Forskningscentralen för de inhemska språken, 1984. 4th ed. 112p. (Forskningscentralen för de inhemska språken. Skrifter [Research Centre for the Languages of Finland. Publications], 2).

A list of Swedish-language place-names in Finland, giving their location (by district) and corresponding Finnish names, where these exist. Index of Finnish names with Swedish equivalents.

**Fennia. Suuri Suomi-kartasto. Kartverk över Finland. Finland in maps.
Finnischer Atlas.**
See item no. 29.

GT tiekartasto Suomi-Finland. Vägatlas. Road atlas. Strassenatlas.
See item no. 36.

Travel and Tourism

Older descriptions and guidebooks

49 **Travels through Sweden, Finland, and Lapland, to the North Cape in the years 1798 and 1799.**
    Joseph Acerbi.   London: printed for Joseph Mawman, 1802. 2 vols. map.

Giuseppe Acerbi (1773-1846) was born near Mantua. His *Travels* describes the journey in Scandinavia which he undertook with the son of a rich banker from Brescia. Crossing from Stockholm to Turku via the Åland islands, he continued to Vaasa, Oulu and Kemi and into Lapland. His account and observations are very readable and remain full of interest, particularly the material on Lapland.

50 **Travels in various countries of Europe, Asia and Africa. Part the third: Scandinavia.**
    Edward Daniel Clarke.   London: Cadell & Davies, 1819-23. 2 vols. 11 maps.

Edward Daniel Clarke (1769-1822), a Cambridge mineralogist, was a notable traveller who visited Scandinavia in 1799-1800. 'Section the first' includes Lapland and Ostrobothnia; 'Section the second' is mainly concerned with a journey from Stockholm to St Petersburg via the Åland islands, Turku, Helsinki and Viipuri (Vyborg). Clarke did not travel without experiencing danger. His style is attractive, his observations careful and still significant.

51 **Sergejevin Suomi.** (Sergeev's Finland.)
    Edited by Jouni Kuurne.   Helsinki: Museovirasto, 1994. 96p. bibliog.

In 1811 the Russian military surveyor and artist Gavril Sergeevich Sergeev painted or drew sixty-four superb watercolours and sketches of newly-conquered Finland. They lay unknown in the Russian Military History Archives until 1991. This volume (in Finnish) reproduces them, providing a fresh (if sometimes romanticized) picture of early 19th-century Finland. The text is available separately in English: *Sergejevs*

Finland. Gavril Sergeyev and Finland. Finliandiia v akvareliakh Sergeeva, edited by
Jouni Kuurne (Helsinki: Museovirasto, 1995. 52p.).

52 Handbook for northern Europe, including Denmark, Norway, Sweden, Finland and Russia. Part I: Denmark, Norway and Sweden. Part II: Finland and Russia.

John Murray. London: John Murray, 1848-49. New ed. 2 vols. 7 maps.
Part II, section IV: Finland, p. 349-78.

A fascinating guide for travellers in the pre-railway age of Finland. 'Nervous people
have no business to travel to Finland' (p. 371), although 'the living in Finland we
found very tolerable' (p. 356).

53 Finland in the nineteenth century.

Helsinki: Tilgmann, 1894. 367 + ixp. 3 maps.

An extensive and richly illustrated survey of Finland at the end of the 19th century,
which pays attention to scholarship and literature as well as to the country, the people
and politics. It reflects throughout the aspirations of the emergent Finnish nation.

54 Through Finland in carts.

Mrs Alec Tweedie. London: Black, 1897. [xii] + 366p. map.

This lively account by an intrepid and perceptive lady traveller was a great
commercial success (it was frequently reprinted) and it remains entertaining.

55 Letters from Finland, August, 1908-March, 1909.

Rosalind Travers. London: Kegan Paul, Trench, Trübner, 1911.
xi + 404p. map.

The author's exceptional knowledge of Finland and Finnish politics makes this book
still worth reading as more than a travel account.

56 Russia with Teheran, Port Arthur, and Peking: handbook for travellers.

Karl Baedeker. Leipzig, Germany: Baedeker, 1914. lxiv + 590p.
40 maps. Reprinted, London: Allen & Unwin; Newton Abbot, England:
David & Charles, 1971. [ii] + lxiv + 590p. 40 maps.

Part IV, 'The Grand Duchy of Finland' (p. 197-246), provides a mine of information
on Finland as it was at the end of the autonomy period: indispensable for the nostalgic
tourist or the historian. Reprinted as *Baedeker's Russia 1914*.

57 Finland: the country, its people and institutions.

Helsinki: Otava, 1926. 598 + [i] + viip. 7 maps.

This large work by various eminent Finns covers all aspects of the country and of
Finnish life and culture. As an account of the newly-independent state, and as an
expression of its self-confidence, the book retains considerable value.

Guides

58 **Finland.**
Edited by Doreen Taylor-Wilkie.   [Hong Kong]: APA Publications,
1992. 302p. 12 maps. (Insight Guides).
Colourfully-illustrated guidebook by several authors containing information about
Finnish history, culture and life as well as descriptions of places and sights to see.
There is also a section on practical information for the traveller.

59 **The visitor's guide to Finland.**
Hannes Lange.   Ashbourne, England: Moorland Publishing; Edison,
New Jersey: Hunter Publishing, 1987. 240p. 8 maps.
A short introduction on the country is followed by several routes for the motorist
through the different parts of Finland. Concludes with some practical advice for
tourists.

60 **Finland: a travel survival kit.**
Markus Lehtipuu, Virpi Mäkelä.   Hawthorn, Australia: Lonely Planet,
1993. 374p. maps.
Practical guide, giving plenty of information in an easy to follow form. Arranged
principally by area of the country.

61 **Finland.**
Reinhard Rode.   [Hong Kong]: APA Publications, 1995. 104p. 6 maps.
(Insight Compact Guides).
Small-format guide, with a good deal of information and pleasing illustrations.

62 **Finland.**
In: *The Baltic Sea: Germany, Poland, the Baltic States, Russia, Finland,
Sweden and Denmark.*   RCC Pilotage Foundation, compiled by Barry
Sheffield, edited by Oz Robinson.   St. Ives, England: Imray, Laurie,
Norie & Wilson, 1992, p. 107-34.
A general introduction to the Baltic for yachtsmen, followed by specific information
on each country set out in a standard way. Contains charts, both general and detailed
(e.g. Helsinki approaches), and details for each port of such matters as approach,
anchorages, berthing, formalities, yachting services and communications. Also
mentions lake harbours.

63 **Finland handbook 1996.**
Helsinki: Comma Finland and Finnish Tourist Board, 1996. 184p. maps.
An annual sales guide produced for the travel trade by the Finnish Tourist Board and
available only to the travel trade. Gives information about travel to Finland, events,
tourist attractions, towns and cities, accommodation, activities and tours as well as
travel to and within Finland. Comprehensive and extremely useful. Try to see it at
your travel agent's.

64   **Finland: budget accommodation and holiday villages. 1996.**
     Helsinki: Finnish Tourist Board and Comma Finland, 1996. 56p. map.
An annually-published guide to hostels and summer hotels, camp-sites and holiday
villages. Information in English, Swedish, German, French and Italian.

65   **Finland hotels. 1996.**
     Helsinki: Finnish Tourist Board and Comma Finland, 1996. 46p. map.
An annually-published list of Finnish hotels with information in Swedish, English,
German, French and Italian.

66   **[Pamphlets].**
     Helsinki: Finnish Tourist Board.
The Finnish Tourist Board publishes a number of pamphlets each year which provide
essential and accurate information on their subjects. Those on hotels and budget
accommodation have been listed separately (item nos. 64-65). There are separate
brochures for summer and winter visits, giving information about places and regions
of interest. There is also a good map (giving distances) together with useful basic
information about visiting Finland. Pamphlets and information (including lists of
British tour operators offering holidays to Finland) may be obtained from the Finnish
Tourist Board UK Office, 3rd Floor, 30-35 Pall Mall, London SW1Y 5LP. The
Board's office in the United States of America is: Finnish Tourist Board, PO Box
4649, Grand Central Station, New York, NY 10163-4649.

Finland: the land of a thousand lakes.
See item no. 12.

Suomen kulkuneuvot. Finlands kommunikationer. (Finnish transport.)
See item no. 398.

Kansallispuistoissa. Exploring Finland's national parks.
See item no. 426.

**Living in Finland: a practical guide for international students and
trainees.**
See item no. 442.

Berlitz Finnish phrase book.
See item no. 521.

Regions

67   **Helsinki and Southern Finland.**
Oxford: Berlitz, 1995. 8th ed. 128p. 9 maps. (Berlitz Pocket Guides).
Good for its genuinely pocket size. Gives some practical information as well as hints on what to see. The geographical coverage is wider than the title suggests: there is a section on Lapland.

68   **Finnish cities: travels in Helsinki, Turku, Tampere and Lapland.**
Philip Ward.   Cambridge; New York: Oleander Press, 1987.
xvi + 228p. 12 maps.
A narrative guide which offers a rather wider coverage of Finland than the title suggests. Contains useful practical information but is especially good on architecture, museums and art galleries. The illustrations and maps are disappointingly grey.

Helsinki, Espoo, Kauniainen, Vantaa: an architectural guide.
See item no. 697.

Tapiola: a history and architectural guide.
See item no. 705.

Prehistory, Archaeology, Ethnography and Genealogy

Prehistory and archaeology

69 **Finland.**
Ella Kivikoski. London: Thames & Hudson; New York: Praeger, 1967. 204p. maps. bibliog. (Ancient Peoples and Places, 53).
This, still the only comprehensive scholarly work in English on Finland's prehistory, is an adaptation of the author's *Suomen esihistoria* (The prehistory of Finland) (Porvoo, Finland: Werner Söderström, 1961) which is a standard, though now dated, work on Finnish archaeology.

70 **Studies on the chronology, material culture and subsistence economy of the Finnish Mesolithic, 10,000-6000 b.p.**
Heikki Matiskainen. Helsinki: Suomen Muinaismuistoyhdistys, 1989.
XII + 370-90 + 19-34 + 77-98 + 5-34 + 1-97p. maps. bibliog. (Iskos, 8).
A collection of five articles (three in German and two in English) forming a thesis on the subject.

71 **Ancient hillforts of Finland: problems of analysis, chronology and interpretation with special reference to the hillfort of Kuhmoinen.**
J.-P. Taavitsainen. Helsinki: Suomen Muinaismuistoyhdistys, 1990.
294p. maps. bibliog.
The hillfort at Kuhmoinen (in Häme, 70 km NNW of Lahti) dates from between the second quarter of the 11th century and the end of the 13th and beginning of the 14th centuries. It would have constituted a base for the protection of local people against hostile raiding parties until Häme became part of Sweden. There is little in English on Finnish prehistory and early medieval history and embedded in this scholarly archaeological study are important insights into the settlement and culture of the time.

72 **Archaeology in Finland before 1920.**
Carl Axel Nordman.   Helsinki: Societas Scientiarum Fennica, 1968.
82p. bibliog. (The History of Learning and Science in Finland
1828-1918, 14a).
One of a valuable series of books on the history of Finnish scholarship.

Finland: people, nation, state.
See item no. 96.

**The history of the Åland people. I:1. From the Stone Age to Gustavus
Wasa.**
See item no. 170.

Early Finnish art from prehistory to the Middle Ages.
See item no. 647.

Ethnography

General

73 **Suomen kansankulttuurin kartasto. Atlas der finnischen
Volkskultur. Atlas of Finnish folk culture. 1. Aineellinen kulttuuri.
Materielle Kultur. Material culture.**
Edited by Toivo Vuorela.   Helsinki: Suomalaisen Kirjallisuuden Seura,
1976. 151p. maps. bibliog. (Suomalaisen Kirjallisuuden Seuran
toimituksia [Publications of the Finnish Literature Society], 325).
This, and volume 2 (item no. 74), are essential works for the study of ethnography in
Finland. The eighty-four maps on material culture show the distribution of crafts, tool
production, and types of buildings, furniture, tools, etc. The explanatory data is given
in German or English (as well as Finnish), with German predominating.

74 **Suomen perinneatlas. Suomen kansankulttuurin kartasto. 2. Atlas
of Finnish ethnic culture. 2. Folklore.**
Matti Sarmela.   Helsinki: Suomalaisen Kirjallisuuden Seura, 1994.
259 + [80]p. maps. bibliog. (Suomalaisen Kirjallisuuden Seuran
toimituksia [Publications of the Finnish Literature Society], 587).
Extensive introductions and detailed explanations of ninety-nine maps relating to the
traditions of Finnish ethnic culture, grouped according to the following themes: life
and death; marriage; annual feasts; village youth; shamans; sorcerers and witches;
environment narratives; and songs in the archaic metre. The list of contents and the
symbols on the maps are given in English as well as Finnish.

75 **Pioneers: the history of Finnish ethnology.**
Edited by Matti Räsänen. Helsinki: Suomalaisen Kirjallisuuden Seura,
1992. 213p. bibliog. (Studia Fennica. Ethnologica, 1).

Papers by various authors assess the contribution of Finnish ethnographers to the
study of the Finno-Ugrian peoples in the Russian Empire, the shift in emphasis in
Finnish ethnographical scholarship after 1917 to the study of Finnish culture,
especially agrarian culture, and the significance of ethnology in the history of Finland,
for example in the shaping of national culture by means of folk culture.

76 **Trends in Finnish ethnology.**
Edited by Veikko Anttila, translated by Susan Sinisalo. Helsinki:
Suomalaisen Kirjallisuuden Seura, 1985. 163p. maps. bibliog. (Studia
Fennica. Review of Finnish Linguistics and Ethnology, 30).

Contains four articles which demonstrate the movement of Finnish ethnological
studies from agrarian culture to the structure of the local community: Veikko Anttila,
'Tourula – a small community'; Jukka Pennanen, 'Evolution in culture change'; Nils
Storå, 'Adaptive dynamics and island life'; and Outi Tuomi-Nikula, 'The cultural-
ecological aspect of culture change'.

77 **Ethnology in Finland before 1920.**
Toivo Vuorela. Helsinki: Societas Scientiarum Fennica, 1977. 79p.
bibliog. (The History of Learning and Science in Finland 1828-1920,
14b).

A concise history of its subject, concentrating on Finno-Ugric ethnology and the
scholars and collectors in that field, but not neglecting Finland's general ethnologists.

Sananjalka: Suomen kielen seuran vuosikirja. (Yearbook of the Finnish
Language Society.)
See item no. 473.

The *ryijy*-rugs of Finland: a historical study.
See item no. 667.

The Finno-Ugric collections at the National Museum of Finland.
See item no. 754.

Seurasaari. Kuvakirja ulkomuseosta. The Open-Air Museum in pictures.
See item no. 755.

Costume and fashion

78 **Rahwaan puku: näkökulmia Suomen kansallismuseon kansanpukukokoelmiin. Folk costume: a survey of the Finnish National Museum folk costume collection.**
Ildikó Lehtinen, Pirkko Sihvo.   Helsinki: Museovirasto, 1984. 208p. 22 maps. bibliog.
Not parallel texts in Finnish and English, as one might assume from the title, but there is a short English summary (p. 206-08) and the captions to the fine illustrations are in English as well as Finnish. Considers Finnish women's costumes, their head-dresses and jewellery, and (more briefly) men's costume.

79 **Muodin vuosikymmenet. Dress and fashion 1810-1910. Suomen Kansallismuseo. National Museum of Finland.**
Sirkka Kopisto.   Helsinki: National Board of Antiquities, 1991. 176p. bibliog.
The book is based on the collections of the National Museum of Finland and shows how international trends in fashion influenced the country from Empire style to art nouveau. Chiefly on women's fashion. Picture captions and brief summary in English.

Folk medicine

80 **Snakefat and knotted threads: a short introduction to traditional Finnish magic.**
K. M. Koppana.   Helsinki: Mandragora Dimensions, 1990. [ii] + 87p. bibliog.
About the shaman, or more particularly the folk healer, and a selection of folk medicine cures (snake fat being used against snake bites and knotted threads for strains and sprains) and of spells. The publisher offers 'pagan books in English' and the book is intended to be practical as well as magical.

Genealogy

81 **Find your roots: the adventures of William and Matti in the world of genealogy.**
[Turku, Finland: Institute of Migration, 1992.] 32p.
Pamphlet issued to accompany the 'Find Your Roots Exhibition', which was linked to the celebrations in 1992 of the seventy-fifth anniversary of Finland's independence. The two fictitious characters of the title, an American Finn and his distant Finnish relative, are used to demonstrate the sources available for finding genealogical information in Finland.

History

Finland as part of the Baltic region

82 **Northern Europe in the early modern period: the Baltic world, 1492-1772.**
David Kirby. London; New York: Longman, 1990. xii + 443p.
4 maps. bibliog.

83 **The Baltic world, 1772-1993: Europe's northern periphery in an age of change.**
David Kirby. London; New York: Longman, 1995. viii + 472p.
4 maps. bibliog.

These volumes provide a fine survey of the history of the countries around the Baltic Sea and contain much on Finland. Based on the most recent research, Kirby's works pay attention to economic, social and intellectual developments as well as to political history and the interaction of northern Europe with the rest of the world.

84 **The Baltic world.**
Matti Klinge. Helsinki: Otava, 1994. 176p. map. bibliog.

This brief history of the countries around the Baltic Sea, from ancient times to the present, considers economic, social and cultural developments as well as political events. It sets Finland in its Baltic context.

85 **Dictionary of Scandinavian history.**
Edited by Byron J. Nordstrom. Westport, Connecticut; London: Greenwood Press, 1986. xix + 703p. bibliog.

A generally reliable handbook, particularly good on biographies of Finnish statesmen, on political parties and on the Civil War (1918) and Finland's conflicts during the Second World War. Some unevenness of coverage between the Scandinavian countries was probably inevitable given the limitations of space and the expertise of the individual contributors, though there are surprising inconsistencies, such as the absence of an entry for Finnish newspapers. Information about Finland is often embedded in broader entries. It is odd to see the Finnish language included under 'Languages: Scandinavian'. Cross references may promise more than they yield; e.g. a reference from Finnish Employers' Federation to the Swedish Employers' Federation produces only a note that the Finnish equivalent was founded in 1907. Many entries have useful bibliographies and there is also a brief general bibliography.

86 **Finland's place in Viking-Age relations between Sweden and the Eastern Baltic/Northern Russia: the numismatic evidence.**
Tuukka Talvio. *Journal of Baltic Studies*, vol. 13, no. 3 (Fall 1982), p. 245-55.

Considers in particular coin hoards from the 9th to the 12th century and notes that a comprehensive survey of the chronological structure of the hoards and other finds is lacking. The relative scarcity of finds in Finland appears to reflect the country's isolated position in regard to trade.

87 **The presentation of Baltic and Finnish affairs within the tsarist government in the 18th and 19th centuries.**
Osmo Jussila. *Journal of Baltic Studies*, vol. 16, no. 4 (Winter 1985), p. 373-82.

A comparison between the methods by which Finnish affairs and Baltic affairs were dealt with by local and Russian central authorities. Concludes that only Finland made the decisive step towards autonomy.

88 **Russification in the Baltic provinces and Finland, 1855-1914.**
Edited by Edward C. Thaden. Princeton, New Jersey: Princeton University Press, 1981. xiii + 497p. 2 maps. bibliog.

A key collective work on russification in the Baltic borderlands of the Russian Empire between 1855 and 1914, covering both Russian attempts to integrate the nationalities and the nationalities' resistance. C. Leonard Lundin is author of the part devoted to Finland but attention should also be paid to Thaden's section on Russian policies in general and, for comparative purposes, to the sections on the Baltic Germans, Latvians and Estonians.

89 **The Baltic parallel: reality or historiographical myth? The influence of the tsarist government's experience in the Baltic provinces on its Finnish policy.**
Robert Schweitzer. *Journal of Baltic Studies*, vol. 15, no. 2/3 (Summer-Fall 1984), p. 195-215.

Argues that there was no parallel between Russian policy towards the Baltic provinces and Finland and suggests some reasons why the Russian government showed so little consistency in its borderlands policy. A useful comparative survey.

90 **Finland and the Baltic provinces: elite roles and social and economic conditions and structures.**
Edward C. Thaden. *Journal of Baltic Studies*, vol. 15, no. 2/3 (Summer-Fall 1984), p. 216-27.
A comparative article on the leader classes (nobles, clergy and burghers) in Finland and the Baltic provinces, on the consequences of the emergence of nationalist leaders, and on the alienation felt by the middle class and by workers where the major centres were controlled by Swedish or German elites (in Finland and the Baltic provinces respectively).

91 **Scandinavia during the Second World War.**
Edited by Henrik S. Nissen, translated by Thomas Munch-Petersen. Oslo: Universitetsforlaget; Minneapolis, Minnesota: University of Minnesota Press, 1983. x + 407p. 12 maps. bibliog.
Adopts an integrated, rather than a country by country, approach to the subject. The chapters by the two Finnish authors, Martti Häikiö and Ohto Manninen, are of particular interest since they cover, *inter alia*, the Winter War and the beginning of the Continuation War (1941-44, the 'continuation' of the Winter War with the Soviet Union).

92 **Scandinavian Economic History Review.**
Odense, Denmark: Odense University Press for Scandinavian Society for Economic and Social History and Historical Geography, 1953- . three issues per year.
Comprises articles and reviews on the economic history of the Scandinavian countries and also an annual 'Select bibliography of contributions to economic and social history appearing in Scandinavian books, periodicals and year-books' (from 1967). '*Scandinavian Economy History Review* and *Economy and History*. Bibliography 1953-1989', a list of contents, was published in 1990.

93 **Scandinavian Journal of History.**
Oslo: Scandinavian University Press, 1976- . quarterly.
Published under the auspices of the Historical Associations of Denmark, Finland, Norway and Sweden, to provide an opportunity for Nordic scholars 'to present to a wider international audience their investigations and the background evidence for their standpoints'. An important source of up-to-date work in English on Finnish history.

The emergence of the Finnish multi-party system: a comparison with developments in Scandinavia, 1870-1920.
See item no. 277.

General histories

94 A history of Finland.
Eino Jutikkala, Kauko Pirinen.   Porvoo, Finland; Helsinki: Werner Söderström, 1996. 5th rev. ed. 485p. 5 maps.
Originally published in 1962, and revised for this edition, this is largely a political history by two distinguished Finnish historians. Although it goes (extremely briefly) to the present, it is strongest on the period to the end of the Second World War.

95 Historical dictionary of Finland.
George Maude.   Lanham, Maryland; London: Scarecrow Press, 1995. [ii] + xxiii + 357p. map. bibliog. (European Historical Dictionaries, 8).
The author has provided a helpful and yet personal 'first stop' for information about the history of Finland. The book is primarily on the political history of modern Finland but earlier periods are not neglected. Contains a chronology and an overview of the geography, population and history of Finland. The dictionary (p. 15-270) is alphabetically arranged and the entry words enable the non-specialist to follow up specialized terms encountered in other sources (e.g. Arms caching, Zavidovo). The selected bibliography (p. 271-356) is not confined to recent work and gives an excellent impression of the literature available (primarily in English) on Finnish history broadly interpreted.

96 Finland: people, nation, state.
Edited by Max Engman, David Kirby.   London: Hurst; Bloomington, Indiana: Indiana University Press, 1989. xviii + 254p. 6 maps. bibliog.
All but one of these valuable essays, by a distinguished group of Finnish and British scholars from different disciplines, were originally published in a special issue of *Historisk tidskrift för Finland* (see item no. 107) to mark the seventieth anniversary of Finland's independence. Topics include prehistory, history, international relations, culture and society. There is a helpful 'Note on books in English on Finnish history and politics'.

97 A brief history of Finland.
Matti Klinge.   Helsinki: Otava, 1994. 10th ed. 167p.
A useful introduction by a leading Finnish historian.

98 A short history of Finland.
Fred Singleton.   Cambridge; New York: Cambridge University Press, 1989. xii + 211p. 2 maps. bibliog.
A convenient introduction for the general reader although not abreast of recent Finnish historical scholarship, particularly on the 19th century.

99   **The political history of Finland 1809-1966.**
      L. A. Puntila.   Helsinki: Otava, 1974; London: Heinemann, 1975.
      248p. 2 maps.
A translation of a standard work by a former professor of political history in the
University of Helsinki.

100   **Finland in the twentieth century.**
      D. G. Kirby.   London: Hurst, 1984. reprint. x + 253p. map. bibliog.
By a British historian specializing in Finland, and originally published in 1979, this is
an important study and interpretation of Finnish history from the 1870s to the 1970s,
paying attention to economic and social developments as well as to politics. The
concluding chapter on 'The Kekkonen era' surveys Finnish foreign policy after 1944,
politics and society in the 1960s and 1970s, and examines the then state of Finland.
The work embodies the results of Finnish and foreign research and has a good
bibliography.

101   **A brief history of modern Finland.**
      Martti Häikiö.   Lahti, Finland: University of Helsinki Lahti Research
      and Training Centre, 1992. 133p. map. bibliog. (Profiles of Finland – a
      Study Program).
A valuable introductory history which concentrates on the period after 1956, though
earlier history, particularly the years 1920-55, is not neglected. Not merely on the
political aspects of the 'Age of Kekkonen', who dominated the period most closely
covered, but looks also at the growing prosperity of Finland and at its movement
towards the new Europe that was emerging after 1987.

102   **Finland after 1917.**
      Seppo Zetterberg. English translation: Malcolm Hicks.   Helsinki:
      Otava, 1991. 176p. 3 maps.
Useful short introduction to the history of Finland since independence. Good
illustrations.

103   **Let us be Finns – essays on history.**
      Matti Klinge.   Helsinki: Otava, 1992. 2nd ed. 168p.
The common themes of these essays are Finland's place in the history and culture of
the Nordic countries on the European periphery and the development of Finland's own
national identity and culture.

104   **Transformation of ideas on a periphery: political studies in Finnish
      history.**
      Edited by Jukka Kanerva, Kari Palonen.   Helsinki: Finnish Political
      Science Association, 1987. 151p. bibliog. (Books from the Finnish
      Political Science Association, 6).
Seven essays on Finnish intellectual history concerning how ideas from the 'centre'
(meaning in practice Germany) have been received and adapted in the 'periphery' of
Finland. The pieces by Ilmari Susiluoto on the political science of Rudolf Holsti

(foreign minister in 1919-22 and 1936-38) and on the *Realpolitik* of presidents J. K. Paasikivi and Urho Kekkonen deserve mention.

105 **Quellenkunde zur Geschichte Finnlands.** (Sources for the history of Finland.)
Toivo J. Paloposki. Wiesbaden, Germany: Harrassowitz, 1988. 145p. bibliog. (Veröffentlichungen des Osteuropa-Institutes München. Reihe: Geschichte, Band 55).

Originally published in Finnish, this is an authoritative and informative guide, in German, to the archival sources for Finnish history.

106 **Historiallinen aikakauskirja.** (Historical Journal.)
Helsinki: Suomen Historiallinen Seura & Historian Ystäväin Liitto, 1903- . quarterly.

An historical journal in Finnish containing articles on Finnish and general history, reviews and information about historians and their profession in Finland.

107 **Historisk tidskrift för Finland.** (Finnish Historical Journal.)
Helsingfors: Historiska föreningen, 1916- . quarterly.

An historical journal in Swedish, with articles, reviews, news of historical associations, archives and conferences, and an annual selected bibliography of books and articles on the history of Finland.

Suomen historian kartasto. Atlas of Finnish history.
See item no. 40.

Scandinavian atlas of historic towns.
See item no. 41.

Scandinavian atlas of historic towns. New Series.
See item no. 42.

Frost or microbes.
See item no. 190.

Austerity and prosperity: perspectives on Finnish society.
See item no. 221.

State, culture and the bourgeoisie: aspects of the peculiarity of the Finnish [*sic*].
See item no. 224.

Revue Internationale d'Histoire Militaire: Edition Finlandaise.
(International Review of Military History: Finnish Edition.)
See item no. 308.

Finnish neutrality.
See item no. 329.

Folklore and nationalism in modern Finland.
See item no. 551.

A select list of books and articles in English, French and German on Finnish politics in the 19th and 20th century.
See item no. 795.

A select list of books and articles in English, French and German on Finnish politics in the 19th and 20th century. Volume II: Publications 1968-89.
See item no. 796.

Medieval and modern periods to 1917

Middle ages

108 **Quotidianum fennicum. Daily life in medieval Finland.**
Edited by Christian Krötzl, Jaakko Masonen. Krems, Austria: Gesellschaft zur Erforschung der materiellen Kultur des Mittelalters, 1989. 103p. bibliog. (Medium aevum quotidianum [Daily life in the Middle Ages], 19).
Not really on daily life, this is a wide-ranging look at Finland in the middle ages, comprising seven articles (four in German, one in Italian and two in English), covering questions of church structure, illness, witchcraft and – in a broad way – cultural influences on Finland and the directions from which they came.

109 **Finland in Russian sources up to the year 1323.**
Heikki Kirkinen. *Scandinavian Journal of History*, vol. 7, no. 4 (1982), p. 255-75.
Concentrates on source materials concerning the names of the Finnish tribes of Suomi, Häme and Karelia.

110 **The progress of settlement in Finland during the late middle ages.**
Eljas Orrman. *Scandinavian Economic History Review*, vol. 29, no. 2 (1981), p. 129-43.
Shows how the number of farms in Finland increased during the late middle ages although there were variations between provinces. Exceptional desertion of farms occurred in the 1420s-30s but this phenomenon was minimal compared with other Scandinavian countries.

The history of the Åland people. I:1. From the Stone Age to Gustavus Wasa.
See item no. 170.

Township and territory: a study of rural land use and settlement patterns in Åland c. A.D. 500-1500.
See item no. 171.

Suomen vanhat linnat. The castles of Finland.
See item no. 671.

17th-18th centuries

111 "Envious are all the people, witches watch at every gate": Finnish witches and witch trials in the 17th century.
Marko Nenonen. *Scandinavian Journal of History*, vol. 18, no. 1 (1993), p. 77-91.
There was a high incidence of witchcraft trials in Finland, proceedings forming part of the authorities' religious and social policy aimed at controlling the customs of their subjects and maintaining religious conformity.

112 Notions of a Finnish national identity during the period of Swedish rule.
Erkki Lehtinen. *Scandinavian Journal of History*, vol. 6, no. 4 (1981), p. 277-95.
Surveys Finnish national feeling and identity from the sparse sources of the middle ages to awareness of the coming of the national idea among Henrik Gabriel Porthan and his contemporaries at the end of the 18th century.

The extended family in the Finnish Karelia. The family system in Ruokolahti 1750-1850.
See item no. 173.

Sveaborg, Viapori, Suomenlinna: the island fortress off Helsinki. Linnoituksen rakennushistoria. Fästningens byggnadshistoria. An architectural history.
See item no. 703.

Autonomy period (1809-1917)

113 **Finland and Russia, 1808-1920, from autonomy to independence: a selection of documents.**
Edited by D. G. Kirby.   London: Macmillan, 1975; New York: Barnes & Noble, 1976. xiv + 265p. map. bibliog. (Studies in Russian and East European History).

Over 150 documents in translation, mostly from Finnish sources, on one of the central themes of Finnish history: the development of relations between Finland and Russia. Brief but good editorial comment.

114 **Finland and Poland in the Russian Empire: a comparative study.**
Edited by Michael Branch, Janet Hartley, Antoni Mączak.   London: School of Slavonic and East European Studies, University of London, 1995. xi + 311p. bibliog. (SSEES Occasional Papers, 29).

Contains the subsequently revised papers from a conference held in 1989. A convenient source of scholarly opinion on Finland's relationship with Russia between 1809 and 1917 in respect of the constitution and government, the economy, culture, military affairs and the migration of Finns to Russia.

115 **Finland and Europe: international crises in the period of autonomy, 1808-1914.**
Juhani Paasivirta, translated from the Finnish by Anthony F. Upton and Sirkka R. Upton, edited and abridged by D. G. Kirby.   London: Hurst, 1981. xii + 270p. map. bibliog.

This major study examines the way Finland was viewed abroad in connection with international crises and events and what sort of interest Finland aroused there. It also considers how different social and occupational groups in Finland reacted to major international crises during the time the country formed part of the Russian Empire. For a continuation see item no. 135.

116 **Nationalism in modern Finland.**
John H. Wuorinen.   New York: Columbia University Press, 1931. x + 303p. bibliog.

This major study of the development of Finnish and Swedish-Finnish nationalism in Finland up to 1920 remains worth reading.

117 **Integration without revolution: the Finns.**
Miroslav Hroch.   In: *Social preconditions of national revival in Europe: a comparative analysis of the social composition of patriotic groups among the smaller European nations.*   Miroslav Hroch. Cambridge: Cambridge University Press, 1985, p. 62-75. map.

A chapter on 19th-century Finland in a book which analyses the social structure of national movements in various parts of Europe. Deals particularly with the role of officials, students, clergy, the free professions and teachers, the urban character of the national movement and the geographical areas in which it was concentrated.

118 **Finland's progress to national statehood within the development of the Russian Empire's administrative system.**
Osmo Jussila. In: *Nationality and nationalism in Italy and Finland from the mid-19th century to 1918.* Helsinki: Suomen Historiallinen Seura, 1984, p. 91-103. bibliog. (Studia Historica, 16).
Concise statement of how Finland's autonomous administration was organized as part of the framework of an extended Russian Empire which had a regional administrative system. This pattern of administration changed as the Empire's ministerial administrative system grew stronger and more uniform, provoking conflict with Finland at the end of the 19th century.

119 **Initiation of the Finnish people into nationalist thinking.**
Aira Kemiläinen. In: *Nationality and nationalism in Italy and Finland from the mid-19th century to 1918.* Helsinki: Suomen Historiallinen Seura, 1984, p. 105-20. (Studia Historica, 16).
Concise summary of the development of nationalist thinking by the Finns, considering the nationalism of the Finnish autonomous state, national feeling for Finland, and national feeling of Swedish speakers towards Swedish nationalism in Finland.

120 **The British assault on Finland, 1854-1855: a forgotten naval war.**
Basil Greenhill, Ann Giffard. London: Conway Maritime Press, 1988. xviii + 366p. 6 maps. bibliog.
An account of the little-known naval campaigns fought by the British, with some French assistance, in the Baltic during the Crimean War. The Russian fortress of Bomarsund on the Åland islands was destroyed and that of Sveaborg (off Helsinki) bombarded.

121 **Deprivation and disease: mortality during the Great Finnish Famine of the 1860s.**
Kari J. Pitkänen. Helsinki: Finnish Demographic Society, 1993. 176p. 12 maps. bibliog. (Publications of the Finnish Demographic Society, 14).
During the famine years of 1866-68 Finland's population of 1.8 million fell by more than 100,000. This detailed study shows that economic deprivation, 'nutritional stress' and social dislocation were closely associated as causes of the severe mortality of that period.

122 **The Russian government and the Finnish Diet: a study of the evolution of political representation, 1863-1914.**
Osmo Jussila. In: *Governments, ethnic groups and political representation.* Edited by Geoffrey Alderman, in collaboration with John Leslie and Klaus Erich Pollmann. Aldershot, England: Dartmouth; New York: New York University Press, for the European Science Foundation, 1993, p. 167-99. bibliog. (Comparative Studies on Governments and Non-dominant Ethnic Groups in Europe, 1850-1940, vol. IV).

Describes how the provincial diet of Finland was developed by the Finns into a representative, national parliament, and how this evolution came into conflict with developments in Russia, particularly the new representative state council and the duma.

123 **The rise and fall of the Russo-Finnish consensus: the history of the "Second" Committee on Finnish Affairs in St. Petersburg (1857-1891).**
Robert Schweitzer. Helsinki: Hallintohistoriakomitea; Edita, 1996. 262p. bibliog. (Hallintohistoriallisia tutkimuksia [Studies on administrative history], 23).

One of a series of studies on the administration of Finland during the autonomy period. The second Committee on Finnish Affairs was designed as a check on the Russian Governor-General of Finland and it acted as a means of establishing consensus over Finno-Russian relations until the Russian authorities ceased to accept that a body of Finns could provide the Emperor with final advice on Finnish matters.

124 **The historical background of the February Manifesto of 1899.**
Osmo Jussila. *Journal of Baltic Studies*, vol. 15, no. 2/3 (Summer-Fall 1984), p. 141-47.

Argues that the February Manifesto, usually regarded as the most significant aspect of russification in Finland, was not really a major change but rather a codification of the existing order under which Russian officials participated in Finnish legislation.

125 **Constitutionalist insurgency in Finland: Finnish "passive resistance" against russification as a case of nonmilitary struggle in the European resistance tradition.**
Steven Duncan Huxley. Helsinki: Finnish Historical Society, 1990. xii + 284p. bibliog. (Studia Historica, 38).

A stimulating reinterpretation, by a political scientist, of the period of russification in Finland at the beginning of the 20th century.

126 **Finland and the Russian duma.**
Osmo Jussila. *Journal of Baltic Studies*, vol. 19, no. 3 (Fall 1988), p. 241-48.

A useful summary of the background to the legislation – opposed by Finns – concerning Finland's representation in successive Russian dumas between 1905 and 1910.

33

127 **The British conception of the Finnish 'race', nation and culture, 1760-1918.**
Anssi Halmesvirta. Helsinki: Finnish Historical Society, 1990. 324p. map. bibliog. (Studia Historica, 34).
Places the terms used in Britain to describe Finland and the Finns in the context of cultural and political discussion and developments in the period covered.

128 **Ritualization of daily life: life of the gentry at Ratula manor in Artsjö (Finnish Artjärvi) around 1900.**
Bo Lönnqvist. *Ethnologia Europaea: Journal of European Ethnology*, vol. 18, no. 2 (1988), p. 93-116.
Describes the physical milieu and life styles at the turn of the century. Evocative illustrations.

Territories, boundaries and consciousness: the changing geographies of the Finnish-Russian border.
See item no. 23.

The presentation of Baltic and Finnish affairs within the tsarist government in the 18th and 19th centuries.
See item no. 87.

Russification in the Baltic provinces and Finland, 1855-1914.
See item no. 88.

The Baltic parallel: reality or historiographical myth? The influence of the tsarist government's experience in the Baltic provinces on its Finnish policy.
See item no. 89.

Finland and the Baltic provinces: elite roles and social and economic conditions and structures.
See item no. 90.

Helsinki of the Czars. Finland's capital: 1808-1918.
See item no. 172.

The extended family in the Finnish Karelia. The family system in Ruokolahti 1750-1850.
See item no. 173.

Imperial borderland: Bobrikov and the attempted russification of Finland, 1898-1904.
See item no. 175.

J. K. Paasikivi: a pictorial biography.
See item no. 184.

F. A. Seyn: a political biography of a tsarist imperialist as administrator of Finland.
See item no. 185.

Migration from Finland to Russia during the nineteenth century.
See item no. 205.

The Finns in St Petersburg.
See item no. 206.

Migration from Finland to North America in the years between the United States Civil War and the First World War.
See item no. 208.

History of the Finnish temperance movement: temperance as a civic religion.
See item no. 247.

The Finnish army, 1881-1901: training the rifle battalions.
See item no. 310.

The Republic, 1917-39

Revolution and Civil War

129 **The Finnish Revolution, 1917-1918.**
Anthony F. Upton.   Minneapolis, Minnesota: University of Minnesota Press, 1980. [vii] + 608p. 7 maps. bibliog. (Nordic Series, 3).
Detailed account and perceptive analysis of the events of 1917-18: the political and social crises in Finland that accompanied the Russian Revolution, the coming of the revolution to Finland, the declaration of independence, the seizure of power by the Finnish Reds in January 1918, the ensuing Civil War and the immediate aftermath of the White (non-socialist) victory.

130 **State and revolution in Finland.**
Risto Alapuro.   Berkeley, California; London: University of California Press, 1988. xiv + 315p. 10 maps. bibliog.
Analyses the formation of the Finnish state and the political, social and economic factors involved, together with the reasons for the abortive revolution of 1917-18. Concludes that in respect of class relations, state structures and political organization Finland differed from the other regions between Russia and the rest of Europe.

131   **In time of storm: revolution, civil war and the ethnolinguistic issue in Finland.**
Pekka Kalevi Hamalainen.   Albany, New York: State University of New York Press, 1979. xvii + 172p. bibliog.

An examination, by an American historian, of 'the relationship of the critical revolutionary and civil war period, the Red and White cleavages and confrontation, and the causes and nature of the war itself to a major theme in nineteenth- and twentieth-century Finnish history – the ethnolinguistic juxtaposition of Finland's Finnish- and Swedish-speaking populations'. Considerable 'Selected bibliography'.

132   **Finland's War of Independence.**
J. O. Hannula.   London: Faber & Faber, 1939. 2nd ed. 229p. 13 maps.

A military history of the Finnish Civil War of 1918 written from the White standpoint by a Finnish officer who had previously produced a larger Finnish work on the subject. Useful as an account of operations.

The memoirs of Marshal Mannerheim.
See item no. 180.

Mannerheim, Marshal of Finland.
See item no. 181.

Marshal Mannerheim and the Finns.
See item no. 183.

Implementing humanitarian law applicable in armed conflicts: the case of Finland.
See item no. 295.

Cold will: the defence of Finland.
See item no. 303.

Finland at peace and war, 1918-1993.
See item no. 304.

1920s-30s

Political geography around the world VIII. The rise and fall of Finnish geopolitics.
See item no. 22.

Territories, boundaries and consciousness: the changing geographies of the Finnish-Russian border.
See item no. 23.

Four Finns: political profiles.
See item no. 174.

The bells of the Kremlin: an experience in communism.
See item no. 186.

'Karelian fever': the Finnish immigrant community during Stalin's purges.
See item no. 207.

The prohibition experiment in Finland.
See item no. 248.

The emergence of the Finnish multi-party system: a comparison with developments in Scandinavia, 1870-1920.
See item no. 279.

Diplomatic history

133   **Finland in British politics in the First World War.**
Eino Lyytinen.   Helsinki: Suomalainen Tiedeakatemia, 1980. 219p.
map. bibliog. (Annales Academiae Scientiarum Fennicae, Ser. B, 207).
'It is the main contention of this study that the British government was prepared to accept the new political constellation in the Baltic area, i.e. the disruption of the Russian Empire and the independence of Finland in early 1918, although the official recognition had to wait until the spring of 1919. The Finnish Civil War, the German intervention and the negative attitude of the United States government were responsible for this postponement' (p. 4).

134   **The victors in World War I and Finland: Finland's relations with the British, French and United States governments in 1918-1919.**
Juhani Paasivirta.   Helsinki: Finnish Historical Society, 1965. 198p.
bibliog. (Studia Historica, 7).
'This work examines Finland's relations with the British, United States and French governments during the closing stage of World War I and the period immediately after the war' (p. 5). Based particularly on United States and Finnish archives.

135   **Finland and Europe: the early years of independence, 1917-1939.**
Juhani Paasivirta, edited and translated by Peter Herring.   Helsinki: Finnish Historical Society, 1988. 555p. bibliog. (Studia Historica, 29).
A significant survey of Finnish foreign policy and international relations, covering trade, cultural and sporting links as well as political relations, and including an examination of how Finland's position was regarded by its neighbours and the great powers. A sequel to item no. 115.

136   **The Aland [*sic*] islands question: its settlement by the League of Nations.**
James Barros.   New Haven, Connecticut; London: Yale University Press, 1968. xiii + 362p. map. bibliog.
Describes the origin of the dispute between Finland and Sweden over the sovereignty of the Åland islands and the role of the League of Nations in its subsequent settlement during the period 1917-21.

The Right

137   **Finland.**
Anthony F. Upton.   In: *European fascism.*   Edited by S. J. Woolf. London: Weidenfeld & Nicolson, 1968, p. 184-216.
A very good survey of the growth and decline of fascism in Finland, pointing out that it owed its strength to local, native roots and not to the ideology of international fascism.

138   **From White to Blue-and-Black: Finnish fascism in the inter-war era.**
Lauri Karvonen.   Helsinki: Finnish Society of Sciences and Letters, 1988. 115p. 5 maps. bibliog. (Commentationes Scientiarum Socialium, 36).
Although Finnish democracy never succumbed to fascism in the interwar period, fascist pressures did influence Finnish politics. This study emphasizes the Civil War of 1918 as the precondition of Finnish fascism, which was a political movement aiming at total victory over the Reds rather than a socio-economic movement.

139   **Three generations: the extreme right wing in Finnish politics.**
Marvin Rintala.   Bloomington, Indiana: Indiana University Press, 1962. [viii] + 281p. bibliog. (Indiana University Publications. Russian and East European Series, 22).
An important study of the Finnish extreme right during the period 1918-39. The concept of political generation is used to illuminate, *inter alia*, the ideal of Greater Finland, the Lapua Movement (which aimed to eradicate communism in Finland), the influence of the army and the Civil Guards (a volunteer military organization), and the influence of the Academic Karelia Society (a Finnish nationalist and russophobic organization of students and teachers).

Communism

140 **Communism in Finland: a history and interpretation.**
John H. Hodgson. Princeton, New Jersey: Princeton University Press, 1967. xi + 261p. bibliog.
A major account and evaluation of communism in Finland from the rise of socialism to the election of 1945.

Women

141 **Women's voluntary associations in Finland during the 1920s and 1930s.**
Anne Ollila. *Scandinavian Journal of History*, vol. 20, no. 2 (1995), p. 97-107.
Although held to be a quiet period in the history of the Finnish women's movement, the 1920s and 1930s were a time of great expansion (particularly in rural areas) for such organizations as the Farm Women's Association, the Lotta Svärd (an auxiliary defence organization) and the Martta Organization (which concentrated on domestic economics).

The Second World War

The War in general

142 **Neither Stalin nor Hitler: Finland during the Second World War.**
Jukka Tarkka. Helsinki: Otava, 1991. 111p. 7 maps.
A handy account of Finland's wars between 1939 and 1945 written from the political and diplomatic standpoints.

143 **Finland in the Second World War.**
C. Leonard Lundin. Bloomington, Indiana: Indiana University Press, 1957. ix + 303p. map. bibliog.
This book concentrates on Finland's relations with Germany and the Soviet Union and is frank in its discussion of Finnish involvement in war in 1941 and of Finnish war aims. Its impact in Finland was less than that of Upton's *Finland in crisis* (see item no. 154) but it started the debate on Finnish involvement in the war in 1941 and covers a longer period than Upton's book.

Scandinavia during the Second World War.
See item no. 91.

Four Finns: political profiles.
See item no. 174.

Finland and the great powers: memoirs of a diplomat.
See item no. 176.

The memoirs of Marshal Mannerheim.
See item no. 180.

Mannerheim, Marshal of Finland.
See item no. 181.

Marshal Mannerheim and the Finns.
See item no. 183.

J. K. Paasikivi: a pictorial biography.
See item no. 184.

The bells of the Kremlin: an experience in communism.
See item no. 186.

Implementing humanitarian law applicable in armed conflicts: the case of Finland.
See item no. 295.

Cold will: the defence of Finland.
See item no. 303.

Finland at peace and war, 1918-1993.
See item no. 304.

Revue International d'Histoire Militaire: Edition Finlandaise. (International Review of Military History.)
See item no. 308.

Revue Internationale d'Histoire Militaire. (International Review of Military History.)
See item no. 309.

Finnish neutrality.
See item no. 329.

Finland's war years 1939-1945: a list of books and articles concerning the Winter War and the Continuation War, excluding literature in Finnish and Russian.
See item no. 794.

The Winter War (November 1939-March 1940)

144 **Finland 1939-1940.**
Anthony F. Upton. London: Davis-Poynter, 1974. 174p. 3 maps.
bibliog. (The Politics and Strategy of the Second World War).
The best short account of the Winter War in English, well written and based on a
sound understanding of the sources. Good selective bibliography.

145 **Finland survived: an account of the Finnish-Soviet Winter War,
1939-1940.**
Max Jakobson. Helsinki: Otava, 1984. 2nd enl. ed. xxvi + 281p. map.
bibliog.
Describes the diplomatic background to the Winter War, the attitude of the great
powers to the war, and the diplomatic activity of the Finnish government during the
war. This is the same text as the 1961 edition, *The diplomacy of the Winter War: an
account of the Russo-Finnish War, 1939-40* (Cambridge, Massachusetts: Harvard
University Press) but with a new introduction by the author.

146 **The Winter War: Finland against Russia, 1939-1940.**
Väinö Tanner. Stanford, California: Stanford University Press, 1957.
x + 274p. map.
Tanner, a leading Finnish Social Democrat politician, described in this book the
negotiations in Moscow in which he took part before the outbreak of the Winter War,
and then Finland's efforts to make peace with the Soviet Union, efforts which he led
as foreign minister in the government formed after the war had begun.

147 **The white death: the epic of the Soviet-Finnish Winter War.**
Allen F. Chew. East Lansing, Michigan: Michigan State University
Press, 1971. xi + 313p. 16 maps. bibliog.
This book concentrates mainly on military operations and is more detailed than other
accounts in English. It is well thought of in Finnish military circles.

148 **A frozen hell: the Russo-Finnish Winter War of 1939-1940.**
William R. Trotter. Chapel Hill, North Carolina: Algonquin Books of
Chapel Hill, 1991. xv + 283p. 14 maps. bibliog.
A readable account of the military side of the Winter War, which is somewhat coy
about its Finnish sources.

149 **The appeal that was never made: the Allies, Scandinavia and the
Finnish Winter War, 1939-40.**
Jukka Nevakivi. London: Hurst, 1976. [xii] + 225p. map. bibliog.
A considered historical study of Allied politics and plans during the Winter War
which has made use of British, Swedish, Norwegian, Finnish and French archives. The
author sees Finland as only an object in the policy making of the great powers.

150 **Great Britain, the Soviet Union and Finland at the beginning of the Second World War.**
Patrick Salmon.   In: *The Baltic and the outbreak of the Second World War*.   Edited by John Hiden, Thomas Lane.   Cambridge; New York: Cambridge University Press, 1992, p. 95-123.
Excellent account of British policy towards Finland before and during the period of the Winter War, including the possibility of allied military intervention to assist the Finns in their fight against the Soviet Union.

151 **The volunteers: the full story of the British volunteers in Finland, 1939-41.**
Justin Brooke.   Upton-upon-Severn, England: Self Publishing Association, 1990. 236p. bibliog.
The Soviet invasion of 1939 prompted various volunteer movements to help Finland. This is the extraordinary story of the British volunteers, who included 227 men who enlisted for military service and actually reached Finland, though too late to fight in the Winter War and certainly in no state of training to do so. There were also volunteer RAF ground crew, firemen, nurses and the Friends' Ambulance Unit. The demobilization and repatriation of the volunteers caused great problems.

152 **America and the Winter War, 1939-1940.**
Travis Beal Jacobs.   New York; London: Garland, 1981. xvi + 265p. 4 maps. bibliog. (Modern American History).
A Columbia University thesis on United States policy towards Finland during the Winter War, based on American documents and published material in English. Notes how American concern over totalitarian aggression in Europe was offset by fear of being drawn into a conflict there.

153 **The Soviet decision for war against Finland, 30 November 1939.**
D. W. Spring.   *Soviet Studies*, vol. 38, no. 2 (April 1986), p. 207-26.
Argues that having entered the Nazi-Soviet pact, the Soviet leaders needed to demonstrate that, like Germany, they could impose their will on smaller powers. This overcame Soviet reluctance to embark on military operations against the Finns.

1941-45

154 **Finland in crisis, 1940-41: a study in small-power politics.**
Anthony F. Upton.   London: Faber & Faber, 1964; Ithaca, New York: Cornell University Press, 1965. 318p. 5 maps. bibliog.
One of the most significant and crucial periods of Finnish history lies between the end of the Winter War with the Soviet Union in March 1940 and the resumption of hostilities following the German invasion of the USSR in June 1941. Upton's book did not claim to be a definitive account of Finnish policy during this period but it has been a seminal work on the subject. Hitherto Finnish scholars had argued that Finland had drifted willy-nilly into war in 1941; Upton's argument that Finland was a willing

participant in German plans to attack the Soviet Union, which initially aroused intense controversy in Finland, has subsequently been proved right and become accepted historical orthodoxy.

155 Finland, Germany, and the Soviet Union, 1940-1941: the Petsamo dispute.
H. Peter Krosby. Madison, Wisconsin; London: University of Wisconsin Press, 1968. xvii + 276p. map. bibliog.

The question of the ownership and exploitation of the nickel mines in the Finnish territory of Petsamo caused great difficulties for the Finns in 1940-41 since it exposed them to British, German and Soviet pressure. Finnish nickel proved a vital means of obtaining German support against Soviet demands and Krosby argues that the Petsamo question served as an accurate barometer of Finland's relations with Germany in 1940-41.

156 Finland's entrance into the Continuation War.
Mauno Jokipii. *Yearbook of Finnish Foreign Policy*, vol. 5 (1977), p. 8-19.

A carefully documented article by a leading Finnish military historian on how Finland became involved in the Continuation War of 1941-44 with the Soviet Union, the 'continuation' being of the Winter War.

157 American foreign policy and the Finnish exception: ideological preferences and wartime realities.
R. Michael Berry. Helsinki: Suomen Historiallinen Seura, 1987. 492p. bibliog. (Studia Historica, 24).

Looks at the period of the Second World War and the transition to the Cold War. A valuable study 'of how and why American and Finnish ideological preferences came to terms with the exigencies of power politics and how these accommodations affected the wartime American-Finland relationship' (p. 9). Gives weight to the influence on American foreign policy of US efforts to foster an international order based on principles of political and economic liberalism with which Americans associated Finland. Exceptionally well indexed.

158 Finland and the holocaust: the rescue of Finland's Jews.
Hannu Rautkallio, translated from the Finnish by Paul Sjöblom. New York: Holocaust Library, 1987. xiii + 268p. bibliog.

Provides the necessary background about the settlement of Jews in Finland (mostly as time-expired Russian soldiers during the autonomy period). As a result of the removal of political disabilities relating to Jews in 1917, the small number of Finnish Jews became well integrated in society. As such they, and a small number of Jewish refugees from Central Europe, were protected by the Finnish government despite German pressure. A balanced, unemotional account of the subject.

159   **The black market in Finland and Sweden.**
Sven Sperlings, Hannu Takala, Johnny Wijk.   *Scandinavian Studies in Criminology*, vol. 10 (1989), p. 69-89.
On the period of the Second World War, covering the regulatory system, the black market and the infringement of the regulations, together with the government's response. The black market in Finland was accepted and even the authorities learned to live with it.

160   **Treaty of Peace with Finland, Paris, 10th February 1947.**
London: HM Stationery Office, 1948. 123p. map. (Cmd. 7484. Treaty Series, no. 53 [1948]).
The full text (in English, Russian, French and Finnish) of the peace treaty between the USSR, the United Kingdom, other allies, and Finland.

The Republic after 1944

161   **Finland: myth and reality.**
Max Jakobson.   Helsinki: Otava, 1987. 159p. map.
This perceptive analysis, by a leading Finnish diplomat, of Finland's progress 'from survival to success', from the Second World War to the prosperity and stability of the 1980s, stresses the influence of international developments.

162   **Finland's search for security through defence, 1944-89.**
Risto E. J. Penttilä.   Basingstoke, England; London: Macmillan, 1991. viii + 209p. map. bibliog.
Based on an Oxford University doctoral thesis, this important book examines the defence component of Finland's security policy from the armistice of 1944 to the time of Gorbachev. Penttilä shows how Finland responded to the Soviet threat to its continued independence and by pursuing a policy of reconciliation gradually built up a position of neutrality backed by armed forces whose doctrine and equipment were gradually modernized.

163   **Between East and West: Finland in international politics, 1944-1947.**
Tuomo Polvinen, edited and translated by D. G. Kirby and Peter Herring.   Minneapolis, Minnesota: University of Minnesota Press, 1986. xi + 363p. 2 maps. bibliog. (Nordic Series, 13).
Derived from a major Finnish study of Finland in international politics between 1941 and 1947, this book discusses the political and military aspects of the relations of the victorious allies in the Second World War with defeated Finland and the emergence of a new Finnish foreign policy aimed particularly at mutual trust with the Soviet Union.

164 **Finland.**
Anthony F. Upton. In: *Communist power in Europe, 1944-1949.*
Edited by Martin McCauley. London: Macmillan, 1977, p. 133-50.
The volume examines the events of 1944-49, concentrating on the activities of the
various communist parties. Upton's chapter on Finland suggests that the communists
in Finland did not fail to seize power in 1948 – as they did in all other East European
countries within the Soviet sphere of influence – because they did not intend to do so.
Stalin could get what he wanted more advantageously in Finland through the
conservative J. K. Paasikivi, who was first prime minister and then president, than
through the Finnish Communist Party.

165 **Finnish-Soviet relations 1944-1948. Papers of the Seminar
organized in Helsinki, March 21-25, 1994, by the Department of
Political History, University of Helsinki, in cooperation with the
Institute of Universal History, Russian Academy of Sciences,
Moscow.**
Edited by Jukka Nevakivi. Helsinki: Department of Political History,
University of Helsinki, 1994. 248p. (Department of Political History,
University of Helsinki. Research Reports).
Thirteen papers by Finnish and Russian scholars on a crucial period of modern Finnish
history, some topics being considered both from the Finnish and Russian viewpoints,
the former in particular being based on newly-accessible material in former Soviet
archives.

166 **A decisive armistice 1944-1947: why was Finland not sovietized?**
Jukka Nevakivi. *Scandinavian Journal of History*, vol. 19, no. 2
(1994), p. 91-115.
An important article for its use of Soviet archives, particularly the papers of A. A.
Zhdanov, chairman of the Allied Control Commission in Helsinki, 1944-47.
Concludes that Finland avoided sovietization because the Russians wanted to save
Finland from a full-scale war with Germany in order to mobilize its industry intact to
produce goods for war reparations.

167 **Finland and the Cold War.**
Jukka Nevakivi. *Scandinavian Journal of History*, vol. 10, no. 3
(1985), p. 211-24.
A review of research on Finland's international relations as affected by the Cold War.

168 **Self-restraint as containment: United States' economic policy,
Finland, and the Soviet Union, 1945-1953.**
Jussi Hanhimäki. *International History Review*, vol. 17, no. 2 (May
1995), p. 287-305.
Describes the cautious policy of the United States towards Finland immediately after
the Second World War. This policy had the effect of accommodating the Finno-Soviet
relationship while allowing Finland to retain its trade connections with the West.

169   **Soviet policy toward Finland and Norway, 1947-1949.**
      Maxim Korobochkin.   *Scandinavian Journal of History*, vol. 20, no. 3
      (1995), p. 185-207.
Based primarily on Soviet Foreign Ministry files, this article reveals both the caution
and the flexibility of Soviet policy towards Finland and Norway. That policy, it is
argued, was basically defensive.

Four Finns: political profiles.
See item no. 174.

The memoirs of Marshal Mannerheim.
See item no. 180.

Mannerheim, Marshal of Finland.
See item no. 181.

Marshal Mannerheim and the Finns.
See item no. 183.

J. K. Paasikivi: a pictorial biography.
See item no. 184.

**State, culture and the bourgeoisie: aspects of the peculiarity of the
Finnish [*sic*].**
See item no. 224.

Political elite action: strategy and extremes.
See item no. 265.

Regions

The Åland islands

170   **The history of the Åland people. I:1. From the Stone Age to
      Gustavus Wasa.**
      Matts Dreijer, translated from the Swedish by Jocelyn Palmer.
      Stockholm: Almqvist & Wiksell International, 1986. 561p. maps.
A pioneering and comprehensive work on the prehistory and medieval history of the
Åland islands, by the former official archaeologist of Åland. The Swedish original was
published in 1983.

171 **Township and territory: a study of rural land-use and settlement patterns in Åland c. A.D. 500-1550.**
Birgitta Roeck Hansen. Stockholm: Almqvist & Wiksell International, 1991. 186p. maps. bibliog. (Acta Universitatis Stockholmensis. Stockholm Studies in Human Geography, 6).
Shows that settlement in Åland has been continuous since the late Iron Age but with great variations within the area studied. Sees Åland as a peripheral part of Sweden and predominantly influenced by Sweden although since the middle ages influences have come from the east as well as the west.

Åland islands: a strategic survey.
See item no. 327.

Helsinki

172 **Helsinki of the Czars. Finland's capital: 1808-1918.**
George C. Schoolfield. Columbia, South Carolina: Camden House, 1996. xix + 308p. bibliog. (Studies in Scandinavian Literature and Culture).
An attractive account of the history of Helsinki from the arrival of the Russian army in 1808 to the liberation of the city from the Red insurrection in 1918. Contains much on cultural life.

Karelia

173 **The extended family in the Finnish Karelia. The family system in Ruokolahti 1750-1850.**
Elina Waris. *Scandinavian Journal of History*, vol. 20, no. 2 (1995), p. 109-28.
Describes the family community as a workforce, particularly for burn-beating farming and forest clearance.

Biographies and memoirs

Collective

174　**Four Finns: political profiles.**
　　Marvin Rintala.　Berkeley, California: University of California Press,
　　1969. [ix] + 120p.
This book compares and analyses the political careers of four major Finnish leaders:
Gustaf Mannerheim (a conservative soldier who was twice head of state); Väinö
Tanner (a social democrat who held numerous ministerial appointments); K. J.
Ståhlberg (a liberal constitutional lawyer and the republic's first president); and J. K.
Paasikivi. Rintala concludes that of these Paasikivi (a conservative banker and
president in 1946-56) 'expressed the highest aspirations of the Finnish people'.

**Transformation of ideas on a periphery: political studies in Finnish
history.**
See item no. 104.

Individual

175　**Imperial borderland: Bobrikov and the attempted russification of
　　Finland, 1898-1904.**
　　Tuomo Polvinen, translated from the Finnish by Steven Huxley.
　　London: Hurst, 1995. ix + 342p. map. bibliog.
General Nikolai Bobrikov was appointed governor-general of Finland in 1898 with the
aim of reducing the country's autonomous status and drawing it closer to the rest of
the Russian Empire. The measures of russification which he introduced provoked great
hostility in Finland and in 1904 Bobrikov was assassinated. Polvinen's book is a
scholarly assessment of Russian policy towards Finland and of Bobrikov's role in
implementing it.

176　**Finland and the great powers: memoirs of a diplomat.**
　　Georg Achates Gripenberg.　Lincoln, Nebraska: University of
　　Nebraska Press, 1965. xx + 380p.
Georg Achates Gripenberg (1890-1975) was successively Finnish envoy to London,
the Vatican and Stockholm during the Second World War. His memoirs, based on his
diaries, give an important, inside picture of Finnish policies and attitudes.

177　**Urho Kekkonen: a statesman for peace.**
　　Edited by Keijo Korhonen.　Helsinki: Otava, 1975. 186p.
President Kekkonen's reputation, by no means uncontroversial during his long period
of office (1956-82), has been subject to revisionist scrutiny since the late 1980s. This
book, with its Cold War title, antedates such revisionism but contains an important
series of articles in which a number of Finnish and Scandinavian authorities examine

his influence and ideas relating to various aspects of Finnish foreign policy and international relations.

178 **President Mauno Koivisto on the Finnish political scene.**
Martti Häikiö, Pertti Pesonen. Helsinki: Ministry for Foreign Affairs, 1992. 62p. bibliog.
A summary of President Koivisto's career (his terms of office as president ran from 1982 to 1994) and his contribution to Finnish politics and constitutional development.

179 **Pitkä linja. Mauno Koivisto: valtiomies ja vaikuttaja. The long perspective. Mauno Koivisto: statesman.**
Edited by Keijo Immonen. Helsinki: Kirjayhtymä, 1993. 386p.
Five articles (each in Finnish and English) on different aspects of the public life of Mauno Koivisto, who served as president of the republic for two terms, from 1982 to 1994. The articles cover Koivisto's career in banking and politics, his relationship as president with the government, his contribution to foreign policy and the way in which his presidency has been regarded from abroad, notably from Sweden. Koivisto's presidency saw a deliberate shift towards an increased role for both government and parliament at the expense of the president's very considerable constitutional powers. His presidency also coincided with the collapse of the Soviet Union, the establishment of an untrammelled Finnish neutrality and moves to join the European Union. Although a longer perspective is needed for a balanced assessment of Koivisto, this book is a useful beginning.

180 **The memoirs of Marshal Mannerheim.**
Carl Gustaf Emil Mannerheim. London: Cassell, 1953; New York: Dutton, 1954. xi + 540p. 5 maps.
Baron Gustaf Mannerheim was one of the dominating personalities in Finland during the period from 1918 to 1946, a soldier with a keen political sense and, at times, great influence on national policy. His *Memoirs*, abridged in English, convey his interpretation of modern Finnish history while discreetly revealing little of himself.

181 **Mannerheim, Marshal of Finland.**
Stig Jägerskiöld. London: Hurst, 1986. x + 210p. 5 maps. bibliog.
A distillation of the important eight-volume biography published by Jägerskiöld in 1964-81. An admiring portrayal of Mannerheim, reluctant to recognize that he was possessed of prejudices and sometimes fallible.

182 **Mannerheim: the years of preparation.**
J. E. O. Screen. London: Hurst, 1993. 2nd impression. xiii + 159p. 5 maps. bibliog.
Describes Mannerheim's early life and service as an officer in the imperial Russian army before he returned to Finland and achieved fame as the victor in the Civil War of 1918. Both the survey of the development of writing about Mannerheim and the good bibliography are updated in this new impression of the 1970 original edition.

183 **Marshal Mannerheim and the Finns.**
Oliver Warner. London: Weidenfeld & Nicolson, 1967. 232p. map. bibliog.
This is the only biography of Mannerheim by an Englishman which covers the whole of his life. Warner succeeds very well in portraying the character of the man.

184 **J. K. Paasikivi: a pictorial biography.**
Uuno Tuominen, Kari Uusitalo. Helsinki: Otava, 1970. 101p.
Despite its title, this book is not simply made up of pictures. It has a reasonable text which gives an outline assessment of the life and work of Juho Kusti Paasikivi (1870-1956), the Finnish banker and statesman whose lasting achievement was the establishment of good relations between Finland and the Soviet Union after the Second World War.

185 **F. A. Seyn: a political biography of a tsarist imperialist as administrator of Finland.**
Pertti Luntinen. Helsinki: Finnish Historical Society, 1985. 343p. bibliog. (Studia Historica, 19).
Definitive biography of the conscientious servant of Russian imperialism who was governor-general of Finland from 1909 to 1917. Although personally no villain, he was hated by the Finns for his russification policies.

186 **The bells of the Kremlin: an experience in communism.**
Arvo Tuominen, edited by Piltti Heiskanen, translated by Lily Leino. Hanover, New Hampshire; London: University Press of New England, 1983. xvi + 333p.
Arvo Tuominen (1894-1981) was an active Finnish communist, first in Finland and then in the Soviet Union in the 1920s-30s, where he was a confidant of the Finnish communist leader Otto Ville Kuusinen. This book of memoirs (derived from several which Tuominen wrote in the 1950s and 1970s) concentrates on events in Russia but also throws light on the activities of the Finnish Communist Party. Tuominen broke off his ties with Moscow in November 1939, when in Sweden, and returned to Finland in 1955.

A president's view.
See item no. 330.
Landmarks: Finland in the world.
See item no. 332.
Foreign policy standpoints 1982-92: Finland and Europe.
See item no. 333.

Population

Statistics and general studies

187 **Väestörakenne 1994. Befolkningens sammansättning. Population structure.**
Helsinki: Statistics Finland, 1995. 152p. (Väestö. Befolkning. Population, 1995:8).
Contains statistics of the structure of the population of Finland in 1994: size of population, division into urban and rural areas, sex, age structure, marital status, mother tongue, citizenship and country of birth. Some explanatory material is given in English as well as the headings of all the tables.

188 **Cultural minorities in Finland: an overview towards cultural policy.**
Edited by Juha Pentikäinen, Marja Hiltunen. Helsinki: Finnish National Commission for Unesco, 1995. 2nd rev. ed. 238p. maps. bibliog. (Publications of the Finnish National Commission for Unesco, 66).
A most valuable account of minorities in Finland, on their numbers, legal status and cultural position. Covers the Swedish-speaking minority, the Karelians in Finland, the Lapps, Gypsies, Jews and Tatars, as well as emigration and immigration, including the Ingrians, Russians, refugees and asylum seekers, together with the ethnic and social structure of the immigrant population.

189 **Ethnicity and nation-building in the Nordic world.**
Edited by Sven Tägil. London: C. Hurst, 1995. ix + 333p. 13 maps. bibliog.
Chapters of particular interest are: Helge Salvesen, 'Sami Aednan: four states – one nation? Nordic minority policy and the history of the Sami' (p. 106-44), on the Lapps; Einar Niemi, 'The Finns in Northern Scandinavia and minority policy' (p. 145-78), on

the Finns in northern Norway and Sweden; Max Engman, 'Finns and Swedes in Finland' (p. 179-216), a most useful historical survey of the relations between Swedish- and Finnish-speakers (see item no. 194); and Max Engman, 'Karelians between East and West' (p. 217-46), on Karelians in Finland and in Russian Eastern Karelia, covering their history and present condition.

190   **Frost or microbes.**
Eino Jutikkala.   *Scandinavian Economic History Review*, vol. 41, no. 1 (1993), p. 73-79.
Considers the reasons for the demographic crises in Finnish history. Concludes that epidemics and scarcity of food worked in parallel to cause crises and even catastrophic mortality.

191   **End of Finnish population growth.**
Jarl Lindgren.   *Yearbook of Population Research in Finland*, vol. 29 (1991), p. 99-113.
Demographic trends are leading to the population of Finland ageing, but rather slowly. By 2030 twenty-five per cent of the population will be over sixty-five.

192   **Population development in Finland in the 1980s.**
Marketta Ritamies.   *Yearbook of Population Research in Finland*, vol. 29 (1991), p. 114-26.
Emphasizes fertility, mortality and migration. During the 1980s the downward trend in fertility and mortality ceased and migration stabilized. The population structure aged.

193   **Yearbook of Population Research in Finland.**
Helsinki: Population Research Institute, 1946- . annual.
Published as *Väestöliiton vuosikirja* (Yearbook of the Finnish Population and Family Welfare League) from 1946 to 1956 (vols. 1-5), the yearbook concentrates on demographic developments, population and family welfare policy. From vol. 11, 1969, the yearbook has been published entirely in English. It contains articles, surveys and reviews, not exclusively on Finland. There are regular bibliographies of Finnish population research and population data for the 20th century.

Deprivation and disease: mortality during the Great Finnish Famine of the 1860s.
See item no. 121.

Austerity and prosperity: perspectives on Finnish society.
See item no. 221.

Small states in comparative perspective: essays for Erik Allardt.
See item no. 222.

Family formation and structure in Finland.
See item no. 225.

Finland Swedes

194 **Finns and Swedes in Finland.**
Max Engman. In: *Ethnicity and nation-building in the Nordic world.*
Edited by Sven Tägil. London: C. Hurst, 1995, p. 179-216.
Although this chapter deals with the relationship between Finns and Finland Swedes
in Finland, it provides a valuable survey of the Finland Swedish population, its
numbers, social structure, political organization, the status of the Swedish language
and the special position of the Åland islands.

195 **The case of the Swedish ethnic group in Finland, 1850-1940.**
Tore Modeen. In: *Ethnic groups and language rights.* Edited by
Sergij Vilfan, Gudmund Sandvik, Lode Wils. Aldershot, England:
Dartmouth; New York: New York University Press, for the European
Science Foundation, 1993, p. 251-67. bibliog. (Comparative Studies on
Governments and Non-dominant Ethnic Groups in Europe, 1850-1940,
vol. III).
On the language rights of the Finland Swedes, considering particularly the language
legislation affecting access to administrative and judicial authorities.

196 **Upper class life over three generations: the case of the Swedish
Finns.**
J. P. Roos, Barbara Roos. *Oral History: the Journal of the Oral
History Society,* vol. 12, no. 1 (Spring 1984), p. 25-39.
Based on interviews with upper-class Finland Swedes, the youngest generation being
in its thirties. Claims that 'democratic capitalism has at one and the same time
destroyed the foundation for the continued existence of the upper class way of life,
and also dramatically widened its vistas of power and influence' (p. 38). It is worth
noting that Finland Swedes are not by any means all of the upper class.

197 **Swedish Finland.**
Wilhelm Schalin. Helsingfors: Swedish Assembly of Finland, 1994.
12p. map.
The Swedish Assembly of Finland (Svenska Finlands Folkting), founded in 1919, is a
semi-official representative body of Finland's Swedish-speaking population. It has
published this pamphlet to summarize the position of the Swedish speakers in Finland
as far as their language, culture, education, media, politics and religion are concerned.
Gives statistics of the Swedish-speaking population by administrative district as at the
end of 1992.

Cultural minorities in Finland: an overview towards cultural policy.
See item no. 188.

Finnish onomastics. Namenkunde in Finnland.
See item no. 475.

Uppslagsverket Finland. (Finland encyclopaedia.)
See item no. 779.

Lapps

198 **The Sami culture in Finland.**
Samuli Aikio, Ulla Aikio-Puoskari, Johannes Helander, translations by
Ellen Valle, Merja Virtaranta.   Helsinki: Society for the Promotion of
Sami Culture, 1994. 160p. 7 maps. bibliog. (Lapin Sivistysseuran
julkaisuja [Publications of the Society for the Promotion of Sami
Culture], 49).

This book covers the history of the Lapps (Sami) throughout the northern region but
focuses on the Lapps in Finland. It offers a general and reliable introduction to
Lappish culture, the language, economic occupations, traditional crafts, chants and
music, literature, and to the 'Sami cause' (as an indigenous minority) and government
policy towards the Lapps.

199 **The Skolt Lapps: on their way of life and present-day living
conditions.**
Erkki Asp, Juhani Vakkamaa, Harri Aho.   Turku, Finland: Turun
yliopisto, 1982. [iv] + 62p. maps. bibliog. (University of Turku,
Department of Sociology and Political Research. Sociological Studies,
A, 6).

A summary of research about the Skolt Lapps, covering their history and way of life.
The Skolt Lapps were evacuated from the Petsamo region in 1939-40 and finally
resettled in Finnish Lapland near the Norwegian frontier.

200 **The Skolt Lapps today.**
Tim Ingold.   Cambridge: Cambridge University Press, 1976.
xi + 276p. maps. bibliog. (Changing Cultures).

An anthropologist's study of the condition of the Skolt Lapps. Good bibliography and
guide to further reading on the Lapps.

201 **Political and administrative responses to Sami self-determination:**
     a comparative study of public administrations in Fennoscandia on
     the issue of Sami land title as an aboriginal right.
     Lennard Sillanpää.   Helsinki: Finnish Society of Sciences and Letters,
     1994. xiii + 261p. map. bibliog. (Commentationes Scientiarum
     Socialium, 48).

Examines how the governments of Norway, Sweden and Finland have responded to
the issue of aboriginal self-determination recently advocated by the Lapp minorities
within their states.

202 **Greetings from Lappland: the Sami – Europe's forgotten people.**
     Nils-Aslak Valkeapää, translated by Beverley Wahl.   London: Zed
     Press, 1983. [vi] + ii + 128p. 5 maps.

Originally written in Finnish and published in 1971, this is a book of protest about the
position of the Lapps in Finland, and argues for 'a sort of autonomy' for them (p. 124).
Valkeapää was the first Lapp writer to establish a critical reputation.

Cultural minorities in Finland: an overview towards cultural policy.
See item no. 188.

Ethnicity and nation-building in the Nordic world.
See item no. 189.

Gypsies

203 **The gypsy identity and tradition in cultural interaction.**
     Tuula Kopsa-Schön.   *Arv: Scandinavian Yearbook of Folklore*,
     vol. 42 (1986), p. 175-94.

There is little in English on gypsies in Finland and this article looks, in a theoretical
framework, at gypsy identity in Finland and how gypsies react with Finns.

Cultural minorities in Finland: an overview towards cultural policy.
See item no. 188.

Jews

Finland and the holocaust: the rescue of Finland's Jews.
See item no. 158.

Cultural minorities in Finland: an overview towards cultural policy.
See item no. 188.

Emigration and Finns abroad

General

204 **Finnish diaspora. Papers from the Finn Forum conference, held in Toronto, Canada, November 1-3, 1979.**
Edited by Michael G. Karni.   Toronto: Multicultural History Society of Ontario, 1981. 2 vols. maps. bibliog.
A diverse but highly informative collection of papers on Finns in emigration: why they left, where they went, and the lives they made there. Volume I covers Finns in Canada, South America, Africa, Australia and Sweden, and volume II Finns in the United States.

Russia

205 **Migration from Finland to Russia during the nineteenth century.**
Max Engman.   *Scandinavian Journal of History*, vol. 3, no. 2 (1978), p. 155-77.
An authoritative survey of the main features of Finnish emigration to European Russia during the 19th century, noting especially the influence exerted on Finnish migration by the city of St Petersburg.

206 **The Finns in St Petersburg.**
Max Engman.   In: *Ethnic identity in urban Europe*.   Edited by Max Engman, Francis W. Carter, A. C. Hepburn, Colin G. Pooley. Aldershot, England: Dartmouth; New York: New York University Press, for the European Science Foundation, 1992, p. 99-130. 2 maps. bibliog. (Comparative Studies on Governments and Non-dominant Ethnic Groups in Europe, 1850-1940, vol. VIII).
On the migration of Finns to St Petersburg, their social structure, life there and language and ethnic identity in the period up to 1918.

207 **'Karelian fever': the Finnish immigrant community during Stalin's purges.**
Michael Gleb. *Europe-Asia Studies*, vol. 45, no. 6 (1993), p. 1,091-116.
Some 25,000 Finns from Canada, the United States and Finland emigrated to the Soviet Union in the 1920s and 1930s. About half may have stayed there, many in Eastern Karelia, until their leaders and many ordinary Finns were swept away in the terror of the 1930s, which this article describes. Eastern Karelia ceased at that time to be a Finnish communist promised land.

North America

208 **Migration from Finland to North America in the years between the United States Civil War and the First World War.**
Reino Kero. Turku, Finland: Turun yliopisto, 1974. [vii] + 260p. bibliog. (Annales Universitatis Turkuensis, B, 130).
This Turku University thesis describes the causes of Finnish emigration to North America and the mechanics of the operation. It distinguishes two long-term cycles in Finnish migration (1874-93 and 1894-1914), shows that almost all emigrants were from rural districts, and that most were men. The book, with the same title, was reprinted by the Institute of Migration, Turku, as 'Migration Studies, C 1'.

209 **Old friends – strong ties.**
Edited by Vilho Niitemaa, Jussi Saukkonen, Tauri Aaltio, Olavi Koivukangas. Turku, Finland: Institute for Migration, 1976. 349p.
Compiled in honour of the United States Bicentennial. The articles, by various authors, are gathered into three parts: A: Emigration from Finland to America; B: Finnish-American life; and C: Finland and the United States in 1917-76.

210 **Finnish identity in America.**
Edited by Auvo Kostiainen. Turku, Finland: Institute of History, General History, 1990. [v] + 125p. (Institute of History, General History, University of Turku. Publication, 11).
Contains four papers relating to Finns in the New Sweden Delaware colony. These originated in a conference held in 1988 to mark the 350th anniversary of the colony's foundation. Also four papers on various aspects of the social history of Finns in America and on immigrant generations there.

211 **The Finns in Canada.**
Varpu Lindstrom-Best. Ottawa: Canadian Historical Association, 1985. 19p. bibliog. (Canada's Ethnic Groups, 8).
Brief but excellent account, by a specialist in the subject, of Finnish immigration to Canada. Finns never comprised more than 0.5 per cent of the Canadian population although they were more visible than that figure would suggest because of geographical and occupational concentration and active participation in Canadian politics. Good suggestions for further reading.

Amerikansuomen sanakirja. A dictionary of American Finnish.
See item no. 493.

Australia

212 **Sea, gold and sugarcane: attraction versus distance. Finns in
Australia, 1851-1947.**
Olavi Koivukangas.   Turku, Finland: Institute of Migration, 1986.
[ii] + 400p. 9 maps. bibliog. (Migration Studies, C8).
Investigates the migration to Australia of Finns from the mid-19th century to the end
of the Second World War, considering migration in its international context and that
of economic and social developments in Finland, and studying the adaptation of Finns
to their new Australian environment.

Religion

General

213 **An introduction to Finnish religious life.**
Jan Edström. *Finnish Institute Yearbook*, 1995, p. 34-43.
Describes the 'religious geography' of Finland and notes particularly the growth of syncretist and non-Christian religious communities.

214 **The history of Finnish theology 1828-1918.**
Eino Murtorinne. Helsinki: Societas Scientiarum Fennica, 1988.
251p. bibliog. (The History of Learning and Science in Finland
1828-1918, 1).
Interprets the history of Finnish theology against the background of general theological and ideological trends, particularly those in Germany and Scandinavia.

Culture of the everyday: leisure and cultural participation in 1981 and 1991.
See item no. 734.

Lutheran Church

215 **The Evangelical Lutheran Church in Finnish society.**
Edited by Pirjo Työrinoja.   Helsinki: Church Council for Foreign
Affairs, Church Council, 1994. 91p. (Documents of the Evangelical
Lutheran Church of Finland, 6).
Nine papers on the development of the Church of Finland towards the year 2000,
touching on the 'folk church', liturgical reform, how the church communicates,
church-state relations, the growing independence of the church from the state, the
position of the church on religious education and the church's ecumenical contacts.

216 **Church in Finland: the history, present state and outlook for the
future of the Evangelical Lutheran Church of Finland.**
Helsinki: Church Council for Foreign Affairs, Ecclesiastical Board,
1989. 58p. (Documents of the Evangelical Lutheran Church of Finland,
1).
At the time of publication 88.6 per cent of the population of Finland belonged to the
Evangelical Lutheran Church of Finland. The legal position of the Church is defined
in the constitution of the country. This booklet sets out the Church's historical
background, its ecumenical links, its administration and activities (with useful
statistics), and looks forward to the future direction of the work of the Church in
general and of its parishes in particular.

217 **The church of the Finns.**
Martti Paananen, English translation by Gregory Coogan.   Helsinki:
Department of Communications of the Evangelical Lutheran Church,
1992. 21p.
A short introductory booklet about the Lutheran Church of Finland, its history, present
condition and future plans.

218 **The Evangelical-Lutheran Church in Finland.**
Tapani Ruokanen, English translation by Gregory Coogan.   Helsinki:
Information Centre of the Evangelical-Lutheran Church of Finland,
1987. 2nd rev. ed. 48p.
Older, and with more illustrations than *The church of the Finns* (see item no. 217),
this is somewhat fuller in its descriptions of the work of the Lutheran Church of
Finland.

219 **No east nor west: the foreign relations and mission of the
Evangelical Lutheran Church of Finland.**
Maunu Sinnemäki, Raimo Harjula, translated by Paula Wathén.
Helsinki: Evangelical Lutheran Church of Finland Council for Foreign
Affairs, [1988]. 32p. map.
On the relations between the Lutheran Church of Finland and other churches and
ecumenical organizations and on its mission activity overseas.

Orthodox Church

220 **Orthodoxy in Finland past and present.**
Edited by Veikko Purmonen.   Kuopio, Finland: Orthodox Clergy
Association, 1984. 2nd rev. and enl. ed. 110p. map.

On various aspects of orthodoxy in Finland, ranging from theological education to art
and ecumenical contacts. Mentions the Russian Orthodox parishes in Finland as well
as the Finnish ones. Provides statistics of church membership by parish.

Treasures of the Orthodox Church Museum in Finland.
See item no. 756.

Society

Social conditions and social policy

General

221 **Austerity and prosperity: perspectives on Finnish society.**
Edited by Marjatta Rahikainen.   Lahti, Finland: University of
Helsinki, Lahti Research and Training Centre, 1993. 207p. map.
bibliog. (Profiles of Finland – a Study Program. Teaching Monographs,
19).

An extremely useful collection of articles by authoritative authors about the
development of Finnish society and its current characteristics and problems. The
volume includes the following articles: Marjatta Rahikainen, 'A country and its people
in the passage of time'; Heikki Ylikangas, 'The government and the nation'; Timo
Myllyntaus, 'From hilltop to office corner – restructuring the economy and changing
lifestyles'; Leo Granberg, 'The difficult role – the path of the small farmer'; Marjatta
Rahikainen, 'From the poor laws to the welfare state'; Osmo Kivinen, Risto Rinne,
'Sustainable faith in education'; Marjatta Rahikainen, 'Education for all'; J. P. Roos,
'Education as a life project for women'; Sirpa Karjalainen, 'From traditional to
modern celebrations'; Martti Grönfors, 'Minorities and the common culture'; Matti
Peltonen, 'The problem of being a Finn'; and Marjatta Rahikainen, 'The Finns in a
changing world'.

222 **Small states in comparative perspective: essays for Erik Allardt.**
Edited by Risto Alapuro, Matti Alestalo, Elina Haavio-Mannila, Raimo
Väyrynen.   [Oslo]: Norwegian University Press, 1985. 306p. bibliog.

These essays presented to the eminent Finnish sociologist Professor Erik Allardt in
honour of his sixtieth birthday include several studies of particular relevance to
Finland, for example: Veronica Stolle-Heiskanen, Ilkka Heiskanen, 'Intellectual styles
and paradigmatic changes in Finnish sociology and political science' (on the
development of those disciplines); Matti Alestalo, Peter Flora, Hannu Uusitalo,

'Structure and politics in the making of the welfare state: Finland in comparative perspective'; Pertti Pesonen, Onni Rantala, 'Outlines of the Finnish party system' (including party ideologies, apparatus, social background and influence); Tapani Valkonen, 'The mystery of the premature mortality of Finnish men' (caused by lung cancer and respiratory diseases, cardiovascular disease and the high incidence of deaths from accidents, suicide and other violence); and Paavo Seppänen, 'Social change in Finland: an empirical perspective'.

223 **Class and social organisation in Finland, Sweden and Norway.**
Edited by Göran Ahrne, Raimo Blom, Harri Melin, Jouko Nikula.
Uppsala, Sweden: [University of Uppsala]; Stockholm: Almqvist & Wiksell International (distributor), 1988. 154p. bibliog. (Acta Universitatis Upsaliensis. Studia Sociologica Upsaliensis, 28).
'The aim of the study is to offer an overall picture of the development of the nordic countries from the point of view of class analysis' (p. 9). Covers the period from the 1920s to 1980. Emphasizes the importance of the peasantry and notes the heterogeneity of the middle and working classes. Suggests that a common feature between these countries is the obvious class basis in social organization.

224 **State, culture and the bourgeoisie: aspects of the peculiarity of the Finnish [*sic*].**
Pekka Kosonen, Markku Kuisma, Matti Peltonen, Henrik Stenius.
Jyväskylä, Finland: University of Jyväskylä, Research Unit for Contemporary Culture, 1989. 82p. bibliog. (Publications of the Research Unit for Contemporary Culture, 13).
The bourgeoisie in Finnish history has not been much studied and the four papers here (originally presented at a seminar) do a little to redress the balance. They consider the new entrepreneurs and the old bourgeoisie in 18th-century Finland, the mentality of the Finnish aristocracy at the beginning of the period of autonomy, the 'independent public' during the autonomy period, and the political and social role of the bourgeoisie after the Second World War.

225 **Family formation and structure in Finland.**
Jarl Lindgren. *Yearbook of Population Research in Finland*, vol. 32 (1994-95), p. 5-18.
Provides an overview of the changes in family formation and structure in Finland from the 1950s to the early 1990s. There are more divorces and there is a trend towards more families without children.

226 **The anatomy of the Finnish power elite.**
Ilkka Ruostetsaari. *Scandinavian Political Studies*, vol. 16, no. 4 (1993), p. 305-37.
Concludes that there is a fairly cohesive and unanimous single power élite in Finland. Considers the élite's recruitment and its networks: political, administration, business, organization, mass media, science and culture.

227   **The social implications of agrarian ghange [*sic*] in northern and eastern Finland.**
Edited by Tim Ingold.   Helsinki: Finnish Anthropological Society, 1988. 156p. maps. bibliog. (Transactions of the Finnish Anthropolocigal [*sic*] Society, 21).
The proceedings of a symposium held at the University of Manchester in 1986, dealing with how rural communities respond to industrialization which has involved much migration from the countryside to the towns. The papers are mostly based on fieldwork undertaken in north and east Finland. Stimulating and authoritative despite distressing misprints.

The Finns and their society: a national survey of opinions and attitudes, 1995.
See item no. 9.

Trends in Finnish ethnology.
See item no. 76.

Finland: people, nation, state.
See item no. 96.

Upper class life over three generations: the case of the Swedish Finns.
See item no. 196.

A place of their own: family farming in eastern Finland.
See item no. 407.

Women

228   **Wage from work and gender: a study of differentials in Finland in 1985.**
Tuovi Allén, Seppo Laaksonen, Päivi Keinänen, Seija Ilmakunnas. Helsinki: Statistics Finland, 1992. 85p. bibliog. (Statistics Finland. Studies, 190).
Based on the 1985 census, this study shows the segregation of occupations, according to gender and wage differentials, between men and women.

229   **The lady with the bow: the story of Finnish women.**
Edited by Merje Manninen, Päivi Setälä, translated by Michael Wynne Ellis.   Helsinki: Otava, 1990. 167p. bibliog.
Ten essays of good academic standard about the life and work of Finnish women from early times to the present, about their role in art and literature and in the modern welfare state.

230   **Women at the top: a study on women as leaders in the private sector.**
Helsinki: Statistics Finland, 1994. 66p. bibliog. (Statistics Finland. Studies, 211).
An examination, in several articles, of Finnish women at various levels of corporate management. Based on an enquiry conducted in Finland's two hundred largest companies and on the 1990 census. There are few women managers in big Finnish companies.

Women and men in the Nordic countries: facts and figures 1994.
See item no. 423.

More equal than most. Essays on women in Finnish society and culture.
See item no. 530.

Young people

231   **Youth and change.**
Edited by Jaana Lähteenmaa, Lasse Siurala.   Helsinki: Statistics Finland, 1992. 129p. map. bibliog. (Statistics Finland. Studies, 192).
Comprises several articles discussing changes that have taken place in the living conditions of young people in the 1980s, including education, work, leisure, youth culture, sexuality, tobacco, alcohol and drugs.

232   **The world view of young people: a longitudinal study of Finnish youth living in a suburb of metropolitan Helsinki.**
Helena Helve.   Helsinki: Suomalainen Tiedeakatemia, 1993. 347p. bibliog. (Suomalaisen Tiedeakatemian toimituksia [Proceedings of the Finnish Academy of Sciences], B, 267).
A study of the world-view of a group of Finnish youngsters from childhood to adulthood. Although specialized, the book does provide information about how some Finnish young people consider the world, society and religion.

Sexual mores

233   **Sexual pleasures: enhancement of sex life in Finland, 1971-1992.**
Osmo Kontula, Elina Haavio-Mannila.   Aldershot, England; Brookfield, Vermont: Dartmouth, 1995. x + 287p. bibliog.
Based on a survey of 2,250 people aged 18-74 conducted in 1992. Compares data with those from a similar survey in 1971. The results show greater diversity and equality in sex life and increasing sexual pleasures. These are seen as connected with the liberalization of sexual attitudes and earlier 'sexual debut'. Apparently eighty-eight per cent of Finnish men and seventy-nine per cent of women regard sexual activeness as beneficial for health and well being.

Social services, health and welfare
General

234 Social welfare in Finland.
Ministry of Social Affairs and Health.   Helsinki: Ministry of Social
Affairs and Health, 1993. 32p. (Brochures, 12).
A summary of Finnish welfare services, such as child welfare, family care and the
farm relief service.

235 Social security in Finland 1993.
Ministry of Social Affairs and Health.   Helsinki: Ministry of Social
Affairs and Health, Finance and Planning Department, 1995.
[vii] + 100p. bibliog. (Social Security, 1995: 2eng).
A description of social security expenditure (which in 1993 represented 37.8 per cent
of GDP), together with some Nordic and EU comparisons. Gives the numbers
receiving particular benefits, their cost, and how the expenditure is funded.

236 Finland.
Matti Alestalo, Hannu Uusitalo.   In: *Growth to limits: the Western
welfare state since World War II.* Vol. 1. *Sweden, Norway, Finland,
Denmark.*   Edited by Peter Flora.   Berlin; New York: Walter de
Gruyter, 1987, p. 197-292. (European University Institute. Series C,
Political and Social Sciences, 6.1).
A detailed exposition and analysis of the welfare state in Finland, including the
history of its evolution and the problems facing it in the mid-1980s, supported by
statistics and an extensive bibliography, which are in vol. 4, p. 123-90 (Series C, 6.4).

237 Health for all policy in Finland.
Copenhagen: World Health Organization, Regional Office for Europe,
1991 [printed 1992]. [ii] + vi + 231p. bibliog.
The 'health for all' policy was put forward by the World Health Organization and
Finland has acted as a pioneer in trying it out. This is a review, by a group of
international experts, of Finland's progress in this area, which not only looks at
current health policy but also at future plans.

Austerity and prosperity: perspectives on Finnish society.
See item no. 221.

Small states in comparative perspective: essays for Erik Allardt.
See item no. 222.

Housing

238 **Housing finance in Finland.**
John Doling. *Urban Studies*, vol. 27, no. 6 (December 1990),
p. 951-69.
Sets out the broad context of housing policy in Finland, developments in the national
capital markets, public and private expenditure on housing, and the structure and
amount of housing subsidies.

Children and young people

239 **The rights of the child in Finland: first periodic report by Finland.**
Ministry for Foreign Affairs. Helsinki: Ministry for Foreign Affairs,
1994. [ii] + 193p.
On the implementation by Finland of the Convention of the Rights of the Child.
Provides information about such matters as family environment and alternative care,
basic health and welfare, and education, leisure and cultural activities. Contains some
intriguing statistics.

240 **The politics of caring and the welfare state: the impact of the
women's movement on child care policy in Canada and Finland,
1960-1990.**
Vappu Tyyskä. Helsinki: Suomalainen Tiedeakatemia, 1995. 255p.
bibliog. (Annales Academiae Scientiarum Fennicae, Ser. B, 277).
This comparative study is based on a University of Toronto doctoral thesis. Good
information about child care policy in Finland and about related pressure group
politics.

241 **Welfare for girls, justice for boys?: treatment of troublesome
youth in the Finnish residential child welfare system.**
Tarja Pösö. *Scandinavian Studies in Criminology*, vol. 12 (1991),
p. 98-120.
Shows how the residential child welfare of 'troublesome youth' in Finland is
structured differently for boys and girls, so that the practice of the boys' institution is
'social defence' while that of the girls' is 'closely regulated upbringing' (p. 118).

Crime

242 **A historical review of violent crime in Finland.**
Heikki Ylikangas. *Scandinavian Studies in Criminology*, vol. 11
(1990), p. 46-64.
Sees the cause of violent crime in Finland as Finnish isolationism, a consequence of
the settlement pattern, the cold climate and the 'anxiety-creating pattern of social
behaviour, based on these factors. The Finn accumulates inside him real and imagined
experiences of insults. [This] ... motivates a drinking pattern [which] ... opens the
dams of spiritual frustration which consequently leads to violent behaviour' (p. 61).

243 **Of vice and women: shades of prostitution.**
Margaretha Järvinen, translated by Karen Leander. Oslo:
Scandinavian University Press, 1993. 191p. bibliog. (Scandinavian
Studies in Criminology, 13).
A detailed study of prostitution in Helsinki over the period 1945-86, as known to the
authorities. Covers the control of prostitution, the environments of prostitution, and
'amateurs and professionals'. Compared with other parts of Europe, Finnish
prostitution is thought amateurish.

244 **Money counterfeiting in Finland.**
Pekka Somerkoski, Matti Virén. *Bank of Finland Bulletin*, vol. 70,
no. 5 (May 1996), p. 7-11.
Money counterfeiting has increased in Finland in the 1990s, with the Finnish markka
and the US dollar being the main objects.

**Welfare for girls, justice for boys?: treatment of troublesome youth in
the Finnish residential child welfare system.**
See item no. 241.

The criminal justice system of Finland: a general introduction.
See item no. 287.

Finland.
See item no. 288.

Alcohol and drugs policy

Drinking

245 **Finnish drinking habits: results from interview surveys held in 1968, 1976 and 1984.**
Edited by Jussi Simpura, translated by Andrew McCafferty. Helsinki: Finnish Foundation for Alcohol Studies, 1987. 272p. bibliog. (Finnish Foundation for Alcohol Studies, volume 35).
Shows, on the basis of extensive interviews over a sixteen-year period, the part that drinking played in Finnish life during that time and how habits and attitudes changed. There will have been further change since this book was published but it remains of considerable interest.

246 **The Finnish alcohol monopoly and the European integration: the impact of the European Economic Area Agreement and possible membership of the European Communities on ALKO Ltd.**
Elena Savia. Helsinki: Yliopistopaino, 1993. [ii] + xiv + 462p. bibliog. (Publications of the Helsinki University Institute of International Economic Law, 7).
Begins with a helpful description of the origin and operation of the Finnish alcohol monopoly. Goes on to examine at length how that monopoly would fare under European Community law and particularly the laws relating to competition. Expresses concern that EEC and EEA rules would hinder the achievement of the objectives of Finnish alcohol policy by depriving of their effectiveness socially valuable measures which restrict the consumption of alcohol.

247 **History of the Finnish temperance movement: temperance as a civic religion.**
Irma Sulkunen, translated by Martin Hall. Lewiston, New York; Lampeter, Wales: Edwin Mellen Press, 1990. xi + 297p. 9 maps. bibliog. (Interdisciplinary Studies in Alcohol and Drug Use and Abuse, 3).
The book's aim is 'to explain the part played by the temperance movement in the change which occurred throughout the community during the first decades of the Finnish nation and society' (p. x). This is not, therefore, a history of the Finnish temperance movement but deals only with the period from the 1870s to about 1910. It considers particularly the organization of the movement and its role in social organization in Finland. Argues that temperance ideology acted as a 'civic religion' for the Finnish working class.

248 **The prohibition experiment in Finland.**
John H. Wuorinen. New York: Columbia University Press, 1931. x + 251p. bibliog.
Finland had prohibition from 1919 until the beginning of 1932. This book surveys the background to the law – the temperance movement in Finland – and the consequences

Society.

of prohibition: the problems of drunkenness; crime; alcoholism; and the cost of prohibition enforcement. The law was repealed following a referendum; the book makes reference to its proponents and opponents in the final sections.

Drugs

249 **Finnish drug control policy: change and accommodation.**
Ahti Laitinen. In: *Drugs, law and the state.* Edited by Harold H. Traver, Mark S. Gaylord. Hong Kong: Hong Kong University Press, 1992, p. 65-78.

Analyses drug legislation in Finland and other Nordic countries, the scope of drug use there, the organization of the drug trade within the region and Nordic drug policy. 'Compared to other European countries, the use of illegal drugs in Finland and the other Nordic countries is slight, and to a large degree limited to cannabis' (p. 75).

250 **Women and drug abuse with special reference to Finland: needing the 'courage to see'.**
Elizabeth Ettorre. *Women's Studies International Forum*, vol. 17, no. 1 (January-February 1994), p. 83-94.

The author claims that Finnish women drug abusers are not acknowledged as an important social issue in Finland, a matter on which she delivers her 'feminist fury' (p. 83).

251 **Special features of narcotics control and the narcotics situation in Finland.**
Osmo Kontula. *Scandinavian Studies in Criminology*, vol. 8 (1987), p. 53-66.

This article concludes that the narcotics situation in Finland was exceptionally good measured against international comparisons.

Politics and Government

Constitution and parliament

252 **Constitutional laws of Finland. Procedure of Parliament.**
Helsinki: Parliament of Finland; Ministry for Foreign Affairs; Ministry
of Justice, 1992. 62p.
English translations of the Constitution Act (1919), the Parliament Act (1928), the
Procedure of Parliament, the Ministerial Responsibility Act (1922) and the Act on the
High Court of Impeachment (1922), all as amended to the time of publication.
Together these laws and procedures form the constitution of Finland.

253 **The basic principles of the Finnish government decision-making
structure and procedure.**
Helsinki: Valtion painatuskeskus, 1988. 26p.
Brief but useful summary of the constitutional position and work of the government.
The pamphlet was produced by the Prime Minister's Office.

254 **The Finnish parliament: its background, operations and building.**
Edited by Liisa-Maria Hakala, Pekka Suhonen.   [Helsinki]:
Eduskunta, 1990. 157p. bibliog.
Rather more than a glossy picture-book as it contains good articles on the history of
parliament, how it functions, its role in international relations, and on its building, the
extension to the building, renovation, and interiors and works of art. Replaces a
similar but smaller volume: *The Finnish parliament* ([Jyväskylä, Finland]: Gummerus,
1979. 95p. bibliog.).

255 **The Nordic parliaments: a comparative analysis.**
David Arter.   London: Hurst, 1984. x + 421p.
Shows how the Nordic parliaments participate in the policy process. Contains much
useful information.

256   **The parliamentary ombudsman in Finland: position and functions.**
Helsinki: [Parliamentary Ombudsman], 1984. [3rd rev. ed.] 39p.
bibliog.
Describes the office, duties and procedure of the Ombudsman. Tables summarize the
work of the Ombudsman's office, and extracts are given of the relevant laws.

257   **The Finnish constitution in transition.**
Edited by Maija Sakslin.   Helsinki: Finnish Society of Constitutional
Law, 1991. 132p. bibliog.
Ten papers comprising Finnish contributions to the Third World Congress of the
International Association of Constitutional Law, Warsaw, September 1991. Topics
include the constitutionality of legislation, freedom of speech, the absence of regional
self-government in Finland, and constitutional aspects of local autonomy.

Political system

General

258   **The Finnish voter.**
Edited by Sami Borg, Risto Sänkiaho.   Helsinki: Finnish Political
Science Association, 1995. 259p. bibliog. (Books from the Finnish
Political Science Association, 17).
Eleven essays which look at the development of party divisions and the social
structure, the structure of party organizations and electoral systems, candidates and campaigns, the selection of candidates, participation in elections and the choice of parties
from the viewpoint of the elector, Finnish voters and the personification of Finnish
politics, and the development of the Finnish left. Useful 'Bibliography of Finnish
electoral research' (including works in English) by Matti Wiberg.

259   **Politics and policy-making in Finland.**
David Arter.   Brighton, England: Wheatsheaf Books; New York: St
Martin's Press, 1987. xii + 255p. bibliog.
A British political scientist's view of Finnish politics up to the elections of 1987.
Considers the development of politics in Finland since 1809, the way in which the
constitution works, the positions of the president and the cabinet and the way in which
policy, both foreign and economic, is made. Crucial political developments have
occurred since 1987 but the book remains of value.

260 **The consensual democracies? The government and politics of the Scandinavian states.**
Neil Elder, Alastair H. Thomas, David Arter. Oxford: Blackwell, 1988. rev. ed. xii + 248p. bibliog.
Considers what the Scandinavian democracies have in common and how Finland and the other countries fit into a possible pattern.

261 **Finnish democracy.**
Edited by Jan Sundberg, Sten Berglund. Helsinki: Finnish Political Science Association, 1990. 179p. bibliog. (Books from the Finnish Political Science Association, 9).
A collection of articles which identify the peculiarities that distinguish the Finnish parliamentary multi-party system from the democratic systems of other Western countries. One of the peculiarities identified, the strength of the Communist Party, no longer applies, and there have been some constitutional changes since 1990 but part of the theoretical background in the book remains of interest.

262 **Gender and politics in Finland.**
Edited by Marja Keränen. Aldershot, England; Brookfield, Vermont: Avebury, 1992. 128p. bibliog.
Articles by five Finnish women political scientists on Finnish women in top-level politics, Finnish women in state administration, the politics of an equality movement association, concepts of gender equality, and 'Modernity, modernism, women'.

263 **Consultation and political culture: essays on the case of Finland.**
Voitto Helander, Dag Anckar. Helsinki: Finnish Society of Sciences and Letters, 1983. 198p. bibliog. (Commentationes Scientiarum Socialium, 19).
Eight chapters on various aspects of political consultation and decision making in Finland.

264 **The North European exception: political advertising on TV in Finland.**
Tom Moring. In: *Political advertising in Western democracies: parties and candidates on television.* Edited by Lynda Lee Kaid, Christina Holtz-Bacha. Thousand Oaks, California; London: Sage, 1994, p. 161-85.
Unlike most northern European countries, Finland permitted political advertising in 1990. Explains the rules for political advertising and discusses the TV campaigns in the 1992 local elections.

265 **Political elite action: strategy and outcomes.**
Tom Moring. Helsinki: Finnish Society of Sciences and Letters, 1989. 179p. bibliog. (Commentationes Scientiarum Socialium, 41).
Part of a political science thesis which examines élite-level political action by means of three case-studies: on the survival of Finnish independence after the Second World War; on the 1940s-80s; and on the political culture of the late 1980s. The author notes the authoritarian tradition in Finnish political life.

266 **Nordic democracy: ideas, issues and institutions in politics, economy, education, social and cultural affairs of Denmark, Finland, Iceland, Norway, and Sweden.**
Editorial Board: Erik Allardt [and others]. Copenhagen: Det Danske Selskab, 1981. [viii] + 780p. bibliog.
Provides sections on: political democracy in the Nordic countries; governmental structure and functions; the economy and social affairs; groups and organizations; and inter-Nordic and international relations. Remains of interest because of the breadth of its coverage and comparative approach.

President Mauno Koivisto on the Finnish political scene.
See item no. 178.

Pitkä linja. Mauno Koivisto: valtiomies ja vaikuttaja. The long perspective. Mauno Koivisto: statesman.
See item no. 179.

A select list of books and articles in English, French and German on Finnish politics in the 19th and 20th century.
See item no. 795.

A select list of books and articles in English, French and German on Finnish politics in the 19th and 20th century. Volume II: Publications 1968-89.
See item no. 796.

Elections

267 **The March 1995 Finnish election: the Social Democrats storm back.**
David Arter. *West European Politics*, vol. 18, no. 4 (October 1995), p. 194-204.
An expert analysis of the background and result of the general election, which was a victory for the two left-wing opposition parties, and led to a broad 'rainbow' coalition government headed by Paavo Lipponen, leader of the Social Democrats. Useful information about party support.

268 **The 1994 Finnish presidential election: honesty was not the best policy!**
David Arter. *West European Politics*, vol. 17, no. 4 (October 1994), p. 190-192.

On the first presidential election in which the voters voted directly for the candidates and not for electors to an electoral college. The social democrat Martti Ahtisaari defeated the Swedish People's Party candidate Elisabeth Rehn, whose defence of the government's austerity programme was characterized by Arter as honest but politically ingenuous.

269 **The first direct election of Finland's president.**
Pertti Pesonen. *Scandinavian Political Studies*, vol. 17, no. 3 (1994), p. 259-72.

A more detailed account than Arter's (see item no. 268), and with more statistics.

270 **The Finnish election of 17 March 1991: a victory for opposition.**
David Arter. *West European Politics*, vol. 14, no. 4 (October 1991), p. 174-80.

Analyses the background to the general election, the campaign ('at once parochial and soporific' [p. 174]) and the results, including the formation of a four-party non-socialist coalition led by the chairman of the Centre Party, Esko Aho.

271 **The Finnish Leftist Alliance: 'a defensive victory'?**
David Arter. *Journal of Communist Studies*, vol. 7, no. 3 (September 1991), p. 398-404.

Analyses the Finnish extreme left and their performance in the 1991 parliamentary elections.

272 **Social structure and campaign style: Finland 1954-1987.**
Lauri Karvonen, Axel Rappe. *Scandinavian Political Studies*, vol. 14, no. 3 (1991), p. 241-59.

About Finnish election campaigns, analysing the editorials of the leading newspapers of the four largest political parties in the elections of 1954, 1966, 1975 and 1987. Concludes that campaign styles have become less ideological.

Political parties

273 Finland.
Jan Sundberg, Christel Gylling. In: *Party organizations: a data handbook on party organizations in Western democracies, 1960-90.* Edited by Richard S. Katz, Peter Mair. London; Newbury Park, California: Sage, 1992, p. 273-316.

The information is presented mostly in tabular form, showing, for example, election results (1962-91), the party composition of national governments, party membership, party structures and finance (including state subsidies). There is also a concise introduction on the political system.

274 Finland: nationalized parties, professionalized organizations.
Jan Sundberg. In: *How parties organize: change and adaptation in party organizations in Western democracies.* Edited by Richard S. Katz, Peter Mair. London; Thousand Oaks, California: Sage, 1994, p. 158-84.

On the membership and organization of the five main political parties active from the 1960s: the Communist Party; the Social Democratic Party; the Swedish People's Party; the Centre Party; and the National Coalition (conservatives).

275 Political parties in Finland: essays in history and politics.
Edited by Juhani Mylly, R. Michael Berry. Turku, Finland: Department of Political History, University of Turku, 1984. 191p. (University of Turku. Political History, C:21).

Eight essays on the history and development of the Finnish party system and Finnish political parties. With their emphasis on 'those aspects of Finland's historical evolution which explain the unusual development and nature of Finnish political parties and their role in Finnish society' (p. 5), these essays remain of interest.

276 Party behaviour in the Finnish parliament.
Guy-Erik Isaksson. *Scandinavian Political Studies*, vol. 17, no. 2 (1994), p. 91-107.

Looks at how the behaviour of Finnish political parties changes between government and opposition.

277 The emergence of the Finnish multi-party system: a comparison with developments in Scandinavia, 1870-1920.
Juhani J. Mylly. *Scandinavian Journal of History*, vol. 5, no. 4 (1980), p. 277-93.

Shows how party formation was governed first by the language question (Finnish and Swedish) and then by relations with Russia before finally differences of social outlook and class-consciousness became more important.

278 **The Finnish Communist Party in the Finnish political system,
1963-1982.**
Jukka Paastela.   Tampere, Finland: University of Tampere,
Department of Political Science and International Relations, 1991.
vii + 265p. bibliog. (University of Tampere, Department of Political
Science and International Relations. Research Reports, 111).

The Finnish Communist Party was of considerable importance in postwar Finland up
to 1983, often pursuing a very pragmatist line and participating in left-centre coalition
governments. The author concludes that representatives of the Party had a positive
influence on Finno-Soviet relations, including trade relations. Although the detailed
study of the Party ends in 1982, an epilogue describes its subsequent split and the
groupings that emerged in consequence.

Small states in comparative perspective: essays for Erik Allardt.
See item no. 222.

The Finnish voter.
See item no. 258.

Administration and local government

279 **Public administration in Finland. L'administration publique de la
Finlande.**
Edited by Tore Modeen.   Helsinki: Finnish Branch of the
International Institute of Administrative Sciences; Ministry of Finance;
Administrative Development Agency, 1994. 96p. bibliog.

Seven articles which together form a broad outline of the administrative system in
Finland. Includes an historical overview, and covers the following topics:
developments in Finnish public management in the 1990s; local government in
Finland; public economy in Finland; public sector personnel; indirect public
administration in Finland (on various statutory bodies); and the principle of
administrative legality. Summaries in French.

280 **An introduction to local government activities, administration and finance in Finland.**
Simo Hakamäki, Risto Harisalo, Paavo Hoikka. Tampere, Finland: Tampereen yliopisto, Kunnallistieteiden laitos, 1988. [iv] + 105 leaves. bibliog. (Tampereen yliopisto. Kunnallistieteiden laitos. Julkaisusarja [University of Tampere. Institute of Local Government Studies. Publications Series], 1/1988).
There is not much in English on local government in Finland and this account of its history, development, democratic participation, functions and finances, still has some value.

281 **Finnish local government in the postwar period: the development of the state-local relationship and the free-commune experiment.**
Krister Ståhlberg. Åbo, Finland: Åbo Academy, 1990. [ii] + 62p. bibliog. (Meddelanden från Ekonomisk-statsvetenskapliga fakulteten vid Åbo Akademi. Institutionen för offentlig förvaltning [Publications of the Åbo Academy Faculty of Economics and Political Science, Department of Public Administration], A:310. Fricommunprojektet, Rapport [Free Commune Project, Report], 2).
Looks at the relationship between the state and local government. The 'free-commune experiment' refers to legislation to give greater powers to local authorities.

282 **Aluluokitukset – kunnat. Regionala indelningar – kommunerna.** (Regional divisions – communes.) **1995.**
Helsinki: Tilastokeskus, 1995. [ii] + 57p. (Käsikirjoja [Handbooks], 28).
Annually-published list of the administrative communes in Finland, showing the regions and provinces to which they belong, their type (urban, densely populated and rural) and their linguistic status (Finnish-speaking, bilingual with a Finnish majority, Swedish-speaking, and bilingual with a Swedish majority).

Valtioneuvostosanasto. Statsrådsordlistan. Glossary on the Council of State in Finland. Staatsratsglossar. Vocabulaire du Conseil des ministres. Gosudarstvennyi sovet finliandii – slovar'-spravochnik. Vocabulario del Consejo de Ministros.
See item no. 494.

Suomen valtiokalenteri. Finlands statskalender. Julkaissut Helsingin yliopisto. Utgiven av Helsingfors universitet. (The Official Yearbook of Finland. Published by Helsinki University.)
See item no. 782.

Valtion virallisjulkaisut. Statens officiella publikationer. Government Publications in Finland. 1961- .
See item no. 798.

Finland.
See item no. 799.

Law and the legal system

Legal system

283 **An introduction to Finnish law.**
Edited by Juha Pöyhönen. Helsinki: Finnish Lawyers' Publishing, 1993. xvii + 412p. bibliog.
Not intended as a comprehensive book on Finnish law, this nevertheless provides a general introduction together with descriptions of the law in the following areas: constitutional law and human rights; contracts and torts; company law; labour law and non-discrimination law; property law; family law and inheritance law; legal procedure; administrative law; environmental law; and tax law.

284 **The Finnish legal system.**
Edited by Jaakko Uotila, translated by Leena Lehto. Helsinki: Finnish Lawyers Publishing Company, 1985. 2nd, completely rev. ed. 254p. bibliog.
Intended for foreign readers, this is an invaluable and comprehensive introduction to the Finnish legal system. There are chapters on Finland itself, the historical background to the legal system, the constitution, human rights, administration, language legislation, courts and their procedure, trade and business law, the law of obligations, contracts, land, family law, labour law, social security, environmental law, taxation, criminal justice and Finland's international agreements.

285 **Finnish national reports to the Fourteenth Congress of the International Academy of Comparative Law, Athens, 1994.**
Edited by Antti Suviranta. Helsinki: Finnish Lawyers' Publishing, 1994. xiv + 221p. (Studia Iuridica Helsingiensia, 15).
Eleven reports on various aspects of the law and legal practice in Finland. The topics are diverse, e.g. property and alimony in no-fault divorce, agriculture and the environment, corporate takeovers, the criminal liability of enterprises, and alternative penal sanctions.

286 **Finnish law: how does the Finnish legal system fit with EU membership?**
Kirsti Rissanen. *Finnish Institute Yearbook*, 1995, p. 100-07.
Identifies some of the tensions between the different approaches of European Union lawmaking and the Finnish legal system.

The right to private school education: on the interpretation of secs. 79 and 82 of the Finnish Form of Government Act.
See item no. 443.

Cultural policy in Finland: national report.
See item no. 639.

Finland.
See item no. 746.

Finnish press laws.
See item no. 765.

Criminal law and criminal justice

287 **The criminal justice system of Finland: a general introduction.**
Matti Joutsen. Helsinki: Ministry of Justice, 1995. [v] + 37p. bibliog.
(European Institute for Crime Prevention and Control. Criminal Justice
Systems in Europe).
Designed to foster international cooperation by setting out the principles behind the
Finnish criminal justice system. Covers, *inter alia*, the police, the courts, sentencing
and prisons. Also some information about the extent of crime.

288 **Finland.**
In: *Profiles of criminal justice systems in Europe and North America.*
Edited by Kristiina Kangaspunta. Helsinki: European Institute for
Crime Prevention and Control, 1995, p. 68-74.
A brief account of the background to the Finnish legal system, offences, sanctions,
and selected issues.

289 **The penal code of Finland and related laws.**
Translated by Matti Joutsen, with an introduction by Inkeri Anttila.
Littleton, Colorado: Fred B. Rothman; London: Sweet & Maxwell,
1987. xvii + 179p. (The American Series of Foreign Penal Codes, 27).
Gives the text of the Penal Code of 1889, as amended by 1986. An introduction
explains the structure of the Code and comments on such topics as types of offences,
responsibility, guilt, punishment, damages and recent trends. At the time of the book's
publication a review of the Penal Code was in progress.

Labour law

290 **Labour law and industrial relations in Finland.**
A. J. Suviranta.   Helsinki: Finnish Lawyers Publishing Company;
Deventer, Netherlands: Kluwer Law and Taxation Publishers, 1987.
187p. bibliog.
Comprehensive, both on the law itself and on the individual employment relationship
and collective labour relations, including collective bargaining and industrial action.
The bibliography includes some material, particularly articles, in English.

Commercial and consumer protection law

291 **Arbitration in Finland.**
Matti S. Kurkela, Petteri Uoti.   Helsinki: Lakimiesliiton Kustannus,
1994. ix + 272p. bibliog.
Describes how arbitration in commercial disputes works in Finland under the
Arbitration Act of 1992.

292 **Market control in Finland.**
Carl-Henrik Wallin.   Helsinki: Yliopistopaino, 1992. [ii] + vi + 144 +
[17]p. bibliog. (Publications of the Helsinki University Institute of
International Economic Law, 2).
Discusses product control in Finland, i.e. legal controls on consumer goods,
foodstuffs, labour protection and safety at work, and how those controls could be
harmonized with European Community requirements.

Human rights

293 **Finland and the international norms of human rights.**
K. Törnudd.   Dordrecht, Netherlands: Nijhoff, 1986. vii + 365p.
bibliog. (International Studies in Human Rights).
'This study is not merely an attempt to describe the realization of human rights in
Finland. It represents at the same time an approach which emphasizes policies and
processes in the continuous work to put human rights norms into practice' (p. vii).
Deals with life and liberty, rights of domicile, rights with regard to marriage and
property, belief, communication and assembly, participatory rights in government,
education and culture, security and equality.

294 **International human rights norms in domestic law: Finnish and Polish perspectives.**
Edited by Allan Rosas. Helsinki: Finnish Lawyers' Publishing Company, 1990. [ii] + iv + 299p. bibliog.

The book originated in a Finnish-Polish human rights seminar in 1989. Chapters on Finland are: 'The status of human rights conventions in Finnish domestic law'; 'The implementation of the European Convention on Human Rights in Finland'; 'International human rights and domestic legality: experiences of the Finnish parliamentary ombudsman'; 'The prohibition of discrimination in international and Finnish law'; 'Economic, social and cultural rights in Finland'; and 'The implementation of international humanitarian law in Finland' (which also covers related aspects of military and national defence law).

295 **Implementing humanitarian law applicable in armed conflicts: the case of Finland.**
Lauri Hannikainen, Raija Hanski, Allan Rosas. Dordrecht, Netherlands; Boston, Massachusetts: Nijhoff, 1992. ix + 179p. bibliog.

The law in question relates to such matters as the treatment of prisoners of war and of civilians in occupied territories. The book deals with the Civil War of 1918, the Second World War, the status of humanitarian law conventions in Finland, the dissemination of international humanitarian law there and its status in Finnish law.

296 **Expulsion in international law: a study in international aliens law and human rights with special reference to Finland.**
Matti Pellonpää. Helsinki: Suomalainen Tiedeakatemia, 1984. [ii] + xiii + 508p. bibliog. (Annales Academiae Scientiarum Fennicae. Dissertationes Humanarum Litterarum, 39).

A detailed university thesis which describes the law in Finland on the expulsion of aliens and looks at the practice of some other countries as well as at the background of international law. Covers the law as it was at 1 October 1983.

Legal history

297 **The legalists: Finnish legal science in the period of autonomy 1809-1917.**
Hannu Tapani Klami. Helsinki: Societas Scientiarum Fennica, 1981. 153p. bibliog. (The History of Learning and Science in Finland 1828-1918, 2).

Develops two main themes: the interaction between legal and political argument; and the influence of foreign doctrines on Finnish legal science.

Laws

298 **Suomen laki.** (The law of Finland.)
Helsinki: Suomen Lakimiesliitto, 1995. 2 vols.
The Union of Finnish Lawyers first published this systematic collection of laws in 1955. It is a comprehensive collection of the most important statutes in force. A new revised edition is published every two years. Volume I deals with civil rights and civil law, commercial and financial law and the law relating to transport and employment, criminal law and legal procedure; volume II covers administrative law, and the law relating to international relations and aliens, public order, education, the environment, rural occupations, social welfare and health, pensions and accidents. A Swedish-language collection, on the same lines, has been published since 1963: *Finlands lag* (The law of Finland) (Helsingfors: Finlands Juristförbund, 1995. 2 vols.).

299 **Suomen säädöskokoelma.** (The collected laws of Finland.)
Helsinki: Edita, 1860- .
Also published in Swedish: *Finlands författningssamling* (Helsingfors: Edita, 1860-). The titles (and publishers) vary. The Finnish edition was entitled *Suomen asetuskokoelma*, 1860-1980. The collection is published throughout the year and has an annual chronological index and an annual subject index. Cumulated indexes cover 1860-89, 1890-1909, 1910-19, 1920-31, 1932-37, 1938-50 (Swedish), 1938-44, 1945-50 (Finnish), 1951-60, 1961-70, 1971-80, 1981-85 and 1986-90. The series was preceded by *Samling af placater, förordningar, manifester och påbud* (Collection of edicts, decrees, manifestos and ordinances) (Åbo, Finland; Helsingfors, 1821-62. 17 vols.) covering 1808-59, and *Samling af de till efterlefnad gällande bref, förklaringar och föreskrifter* (Collection of letters, declarations and instructions currently in force) (Helsingfors, 1836-52. 7 vols.) covering 1809-59. There is an index to these: *Sakregister till Finlands författningssamling: hänförande sig till Författnings- och Brefsamlingarne från år 1808 till år 1860* (Subject index to the collected laws of Finland, referring to the collections of laws and letters from 1808 to 1860) (Helsingfors, 1876). Treaties are published in a separate series: *Suomen säädöskokoelman sopimussarja: ulkovaltain kanssa tehdyt sopimukset* (Swedish: *Finlands författningssamlings fördragsserie: överenskommelser med främmande makter*) (Treaty series of the collected laws of Finland: treaties concluded with foreign states). This is published throughout the year and has an annual index. The treaty series has covered treaties concluded since 1918 and has been published, with varying titles, since 1925. From 1994 there has been a separate series for treaties with the European Economic Area: *Suomen säädöskokoelman sopimussarja. Euroopan talousalue* (Swedish: *Finlands författningssamlings fördragsserie. Europeiska ekonomiska samarbetsområdet*) (Treaty series of the collected laws of Finland: European Economic Area). A separate series for the national budget was started in 1993: *Suomen säädöskokoelma. Talousarviosarja* (Swedish: *Finlands författningssamling. Budgetserien*) (The collected laws of Finland: national budget series).

Police

300 Police in Finland.
Ahti Laitinen. In: *Police practices: an international review.* Edited by Dilip K. Das. Metuchen, New Jersey; London: Scarecrow Press, 1994, p. 123-80.

An excellent account of the history, numbers, functions, personnel practices, leadership, standards, pay, morale and public relations of the Finnish police, together with an assessment of public confidence in them and present problems. Finnish police 'have a positive image' and police work in Finland is 'very attractive and charming' (p. 177).

301 Police: duties and organisation.
Ministry of the Interior. Helsinki: Ministry of the Interior, Police Department, 1992. 15p.

Basic information about the police in Finland, including an outline of their organization and some statistics of personnel, operations and equipment.

Defence forces

Defence forces and defence doctrine

302 Facts about the Finnish defence forces.
Helsinki: Information Section of the Defence Staff, 1995. 67p. maps.

A booklet about Finland's security policy and the role, organization and cost of the defence forces. Shows the command structure and indicates the peacetime deployment of units. Types of equipment, ships and aircraft are illustrated, as are the insignia of rank.

303 Cold will: the defence of Finland.
Tomas Ries. London: Brassey's, 1988. xiii + 394p. 10 maps. bibliog.

A highly effective analysis of Finland's defence policy combined with a military history of Finland since independence and a detailed description of the armed forces. Concludes that Finland's wars have left her with a legacy of deterrent credibility and that the Finnish armed forces prevent the development of a neutral military vacuum in the north.

304   Finland at peace and war, 1918-1993.

H. M. Tillotson.   Norwich, England: Michael Russell, 1993.
xiii + 354p. 19 maps. bibliog.

An account of the armed forces of independent Finland, written to mark their seventy-fifth anniversary. The chapters on operations in the Civil War of 1918 and the Winter War of 1939-40 are particularly good. Contains concise summaries of Finnish defence doctrine, the size and character of the armed forces in 1993, and of Finnish involvement in United Nations peacekeeping operations.

305   Evolution of the Finnish military doctrine, 1945-1985.

Pekka Visuri.   Helsinki: War College, 1990. 106p. 2 maps. (Finnish Defence Studies, 1).

Aims to show how Finnish military doctrine evolved and to explain the factors that determine it. Proceeds chronologically, starting with Finland's geostrategic position and the reconstruction of the defence forces after the Second World War. Considers neutrality policy and the doctrine of territorial defence, which has improved the credibility of Finland's defence since the 1970s. Concisely, the book covers strategic, operational and tactical doctrine. Appendices give the text of statements by senior Finnish officers at a seminar on military doctrine in 1990 about territorial defence, the posture and structure of the defence forces, military activities and training, and military budgeting and planning.

306   The development of military technology and its impact on the Finnish land warfare doctrine.

Markku Koli.   Helsinki: War College, 1992. 85p. bibliog. (Finnish Defence Studies, 4).

Examines the interaction between combat doctrine and military technology. Notes that the development of Finnish land warfare doctrine requires a heightened role for mobile anti-aircraft and long-range anti-armour weaponry as well as a modern communications system. Prints (p. 81-85) the text of the Agreement on the Foundations of Relations between the Republic of Finland and the Russian Federation of 20 January 1992 which replaced the Treaty of Friendship, Cooperation and Mutual Assistance of 1948 which had been a cornerstone of Finnish defence policy.

Finland's search for security through defence, 1944-89.
See item no. 162.

Englanti-suomi-englanti sotilassanasto ja lyhenteet. English-Finnish-English military vocabulary and abbreviations.
See item no. 500.

Air force

307 **Suomen ilmavoimien lentokoneet 1918-1993. The aircraft of the Finnish Air Force 1918-1993.**
Kalevi Keskinen, Kari Stenman.   Kangasala, Finland: AR Kustannus, 1992. 208p.

Rightly described as the most comprehensive pictorial book of the aircraft of the Finnish Air Force between 1918 and 1993, this provides superb black-and-white photographs of 149 different types of aircraft, together with colour photographs of those currently in use. Appendices cover technical details, lists of units and aircraft types. Text and captions in Finnish and English.

Military history

308 **Revue Internationale d'Histoire Militaire: Edition Finlandaise.**
(International Review of Military History: Finnish Edition.)
Helsinki: Comité International des Sciences Historiques, Commission d'Histoire Militaire Comparée, no. 23 (1961), p. 103-273. map. bibliog.

The entire issue is devoted to Finland and its articles – in French or English – deal with several important aspects of Finnish military history, including the War of 1808-09 and the wars of 1939-45. There is an extensive bibliographical essay by Yrjö Aav, p. 258-72.

309 **Revue Internationale d'Histoire Militaire.** (International Review of Military History.)
[Helsinki]: Commission Finlandaise d'Histoire Militaire, no. 62 (1985), 327p. 7 maps. bibliog.

Presents the results of recent research by Finnish historians in thirteen articles in English on Finnish security policy from 1917 to the present, with an emphasis on the diplomacy and operations of the Second World War period. Concludes with a useful bibliographical essay.

310 **The Finnish army 1881-1901: training the rifle battalions.**
J. E. O. Screen.   Helsinki: Finnish Historical Society, 1996. 315p. map. bibliog. (Studia Historica, 54).

Between 1881 and 1901 Finland raised a small army that was uniquely separate from the armed forces of the Russian Empire to which Finland then belonged. Although the focus of this book is on the training of the rifle battalions that made up the bulk of the Finnish army of 1881-1901, it ranges widely over the character and purpose of the army as a whole.

International human rights norms in domestic law: Finnish and Polish perspectives.
See item no. 294.

Arma Fennica. Suomalaiset aseet. Finnish firearms.
See item no. 663.

Suuri puukkokirja. Finnish knives and bayonets.
See item no. 665.

Harmoniemusik in Finland – on military music in eighteenth-century Savo.
See item no. 712.

Guide to the Military Archives of Finland.
See item no. 752.

Medals, money and posts

Orders

311 **Les ordres nationaux de la Finlande.** (The national orders of Finland.)
Klaus Castrén. Helsinki: Ministère des Affaires Etrangères, 1975.
70p.
Gives the regulations of the three Finnish orders of chivalry – the Cross of Freedom, the White Rose of Finland and the Lion of Finland – as well as illustrations of them, and the order of precedence of decorations in Finland. Short introduction on the history and design of these orders.

Money

312 **Suomen rahat.** (The money of Finland.)
Tuukka Talvio. Helsinki: Suomen Pankki, 1993. 2nd enl. ed. 199p.
bibliog.
A comprehensive work on Finnish money, both coins and banknotes, from Swedish times to the present. Although no translations from Finnish are provided, the extensive coloured illustrations are of value to the foreign user.

313 **Suomessa käytetyt rahat. Mynt och sedlar använda i Finland. Coins and banknotes used in Finland.**
Edited by Erkki Borg. Helsinki: Pohjoismainen Kirja, 1976. 2nd rev. ed. 656p. bibliog.

A large-format and large-scale work on Finnish coins and notes, with numerous illustrations, and appendices on Finnish medals and medallic art. Extensive bibliography. It is not fully academic in its character but is so large as to be almost comprehensive. A vocabulary is provided to help use the descriptions but the descriptive material appears in English as well as Finnish and Swedish. Regrettably there is no later edition and the prices in particular are out of date.

Postal services

314 **A history of the Finnish posts 1638-1988.**
Jukka-Pekka Pietiäinen, translated by Philip Binham. Helsinki: Government Printing Centre, 1988. 74p. maps.

A very brief summary of a massive two-volume work in Finnish. Concentrates on the conveyance of mail. A good choice of illustrations and some statistics.

315 **Suomen postitoimipaikat 1638-1985. Postoffices in Finland 1638-1985.**
[Helsinki]: Philatelic Federation of Finland, 1988. 298p. bibliog. (Publication Series of the Philatelic Federation of Finland, 9).

An alphabetical list of Finnish post offices and when they were in operation. There is an English summary about the postmarks used and a note of how to use the list itself.

Postage and other stamps

316 **Pikku Norma. Suomi luettelo. Finland katalog. Finland catalogue. 1856-1996.**
Helsinki: Suomen Postimerkkeily, 1996. 184p.

Short catalogue, with prices, of Finnish postage stamps, published more or less annually. A fuller version, *Norma. Suomi erikoisluettelo. Finland special catalogue. 1856-1995* (Helsinki: Suomen Postimerkkeily, 1994. 288p.), is published occasionally.

317 **Stamps of Sweden and Finland: the earlier issues.**
Ernest H. Wise. London: Heinemann, 1975. viii + 168p. bibliog. (Heinemann Philatelic Series, 6).

The section on Finland, p. 99-161, is divided into 'The "Primitive" stamps', 'The enlightened years 1875-1901' and 'The Russian designs'; it thus covers the autonomy period to 1917. Considerable detail is given of the different stamps in use, their printing, perforation and usage.

318   **Suomen postmerkkien käsikirja. III osa. Handbook of Finnish stamps. Vol. 3.**
Herbert Oesch, Heikki Reinikainen, Juhani Olamo, translated by Anneli Hovidonov, Michael Hovidonov.   Helsinki: Philatelic Federation of Finland, 1993. 2nd ed. 232p. (Publication Series of the Philatelic Federation of Finland, 14).
Only two volumes of the admirable series of Handbooks of Finnish postage stamps have appeared in a bilingual edition (Finnish and English) – see also item no. 319. This volume covers the stamps issued in 1875 and 1885.

319   **Suomen postimerkkien käsikirja. V osa. Handbook of Finnish stamps. Vol. 5.**
Helsinki: Philatelic Federation of Finland, 1986. 2nd ed. 204p. (Publication Series of the Philatelic Federation of Finland, 8).
This volume (in Finnish and English) covers the stamps issued in 1917 and 1918.

320   **Info: New Stamps from Finland.**
Helsinki: Finland Post Philatelic Centre, 1991?- . number of issues per year varies.
This bulletin, issued by the Finnish post office, gives a preview of forthcoming issues of stamps and describes how to order them. Further information is obtainable from: Finland Post, Philatelic Centre, P.O. Box 2, FIN-00011 POSTI. The Åland islands issue their own stamps and *Ålandsposten: filateli* (Åland post: philately) is a separate but similar bulletin (in Swedish). The Åland Post Philatelic Service, P.O. Box 100, FIN-22101 Mariehamn, Åland, Finland, offers information in English.

321   **The letter- and parcel stamps of the Finnish shipping companies.**
G. W. Connell.   [Helsinki]: Finnish Philatelic Federation, 1993. 174p. bibliog. (The Private Ship Letter Stamps of the World, 4).
A detailed, beautifully illustrated, specialized list.

322   **Suomen rautatiepakettimerkit. The railway parcel stamps of Finland.**
Kaj Hellman, Björn-Eric Saarinen.   Espoo, Finland: Kaj Hellman, 1993. 112p. bibliog.
A catalogue, with prices, of railway parcel stamps. Introduction on the railway mail system and on the railway to St Petersburg.

Filatelian sanasto. (Glossary of philately.)
See item no. 501.

Foreign Relations

Foreign and security policy

323 **Finland's security in a changing Europe: a historical perspective.**
Risto E. J. Penttilä. Helsinki: National Defence College, 1995. 78p.
(Finnish Defence Studies, 7).

An incisive survey of Finnish security policy and the movement towards the European
Union over the years 1990-95 which marked a fundamental change in Finland's
foreign and security policy. Considers Finland's foreign and defence policy 'after
neutrality'.

324 **Finland's security policy '95: consolidation and main discussions.**
Arto Nokkala. *Yearbook of Finnish Foreign Policy*, vol. 22 (1995),
p. 6-15.

A survey of the debate on security policy, with an emphasis on the government's
report on *Finland's security in a changing world*, presented to parliament in June
1995 (see item no. 326).

325 **Challenges for Finland's security policy.**
Pertti E. Nykänen. *RUSI Journal*, vol. 141, no. 2 (April 1996), p. 1-4.

An official Finnish view of the effects on Finland's security policy of the changed
international situation after the collapse of the Soviet Union.

326 **Security in a changing world: guidelines for Finland's security policy. Report by the Council of State to the Parliament, 6 June 1995.**
Ministry for Foreign Affairs. Helsinki: Ministry for Foreign Affairs, 1995. 79p. 2 maps. (Publication of [the] Ministry for Foreign Affairs, 8/1995).

The official statement of Finland's security policy. 'Finland can best further stability in northern Europe by remaining outside military alliances and by maintaining a credible independent defence' (p. 6).

327 **Åland islands: a strategic survey.**
Anders Gardberg, translated from the Swedish by Kate Törnroos. Helsinki: National Defence College, 1995. 97p. 4 maps. bibliog. (Finnish Defence Studies, 8).

An account of the strategic significance of the Åland islands from 1809 to the present together with an extensive discussion of their importance in the event of various military operations – against Finland, Sweden and Russia. Reprints the texts of various treaties concerning the islands' demilitarization and neutralization. 'From Finland's point of view it is ... important that we are able to prove to the world that we can defend Åland ourselves' (p. 70).

328 **The Finnish dilemma: neutrality in the shadow of power.**
George Maude. London: Oxford University Press for the Royal Institute of International Affairs, 1976. vi + 153p. bibliog.

This concise, informative and reliable study of Finnish foreign policy, with particular emphasis on Finnish-Soviet relations and on Finnish neutrality, remains valuable background reading.

329 **Finnish neutrality.**
Jukka Nevakivi. In: *Neutrality in history: proceedings of the Conference on the History of Neutrality organized in Helsinki 9-12 September 1992 under the auspices of the Commission of History of International Relations.* Edited by Jukka Nevakivi. Helsinki: Finnish Historical Society, 1993, p. 33-44.

Traces Finnish aspirations to neutrality from the 1780s to the present with an emphasis on the Second World War and postwar periods. Argues that 'Finnish neutrality has its roots deep not only in the past lessons but also in the present philosophy of the nation' (p. 43), seeking to avoid controversies and to solve them when they break out.

330 **A president's view.**
Urho Kekkonen, translated by Gregory Coogan. London: Heinemann, 1982. 195p.

Remains of interest as a statement of President Kekkonen's views on a variety of foreign policy issues, including relations between Finland and the Soviet Union and Finnish neutrality.

331 **The change in foreign policy during the presidency of Mauno Koivisto 1982-1994.**
Tapani Vaahtoranta. *Yearbook of Finnish Foreign Policy*, vol. 21 (1994), p. 6-15.
Notes the changes in the way foreign policy decision making occurred and in how foreign policy was discussed, as well as the changes in direction that occurred from the turn of the 1980s-90s because the world around Finland changed.

332 **Landmarks: Finland in the world.**
Mauno Koivisto. Helsinki: Kirjayhtymä, 1985. 159p.
Various extracts from President Koivisto's speeches and writings from the period 1979-85 are brought together by theme, e.g. Finland and the Soviet Union, Nordic security, economic relations.

333 **Foreign policy standpoints 1982-92: Finland and Europe.**
Mauno Koivisto, translated by Pearl Lönnfors. Henley on Thames, England: Aidan Ellis, 1992. [xiii] + 235p.
A collection (chronologically arranged) of speeches and statements made by President Koivisto on a variety of foreign policy issues. The author's cautious approach to foreign policy matters is clearly evident.

334 **Finland and the United States: diplomatic relations through seventy years.**
Edited by Robert Rinehart. Washington, DC: Institute for the Study of Diplomacy, Georgetown University, 1993. xv + 141p. 2 maps. bibliog.
Provides in four chapters a survey and evaluation of the history of Finnish-United States diplomatic relations from Finland's independence to the end of the 1980s and a series of comments on the views expressed in those chapters. A postscript carries the subject on to 1992. There are American and Finnish contributors.

335 **Yearbook of Finnish Foreign Policy 1973- .**
Helsinki: Finnish Institute of International Affairs, 1974- . annual.
'Deals with domestic and international questions that have during the year been important from the point of view of Finland's foreign policy'. Contains articles, speeches and documents and incorporates a chronology of events. The contributors (usually Finns) include politicians, civil servants, diplomats and scholars. Originally, many of the articles had first been published in *Ulkopolitiikka* (Foreign Policy), the journal of the Finnish Institute of International Affairs, but since 1993 they have been written expressly for the *Yearbook*. Essential reading on its subject.

Finland: people, nation, state.
See item no. 96.

Urho Kekkonen: a statesman for peace.
See item no. 177.

Suomen säädöskokoelma. (The collected laws of Finland.)
See item no. 299.

Facts about the Finnish defence forces.
See item no. 302.

Cold will: the defence of Finland.
See item no. 303.

Finland at peace and war, 1918-1993.
See item no. 304.

Evolution of the Finnish military doctrine, 1945-1985.
See item no. 305.

Development aid

336 **Finland's development co-operation in the 1990s: strategic goals and means.**
Ministry for Foreign Affairs. Helsinki: Ministry for Foreign Affairs, 1993. 34p.
Finland spends some 3 billion marks per annum on development aid and this official booklet sets out the aims and action plan relating to this expenditure.

Relations with the European Union

337 **Finland's political relations with the European Union.**
Clive Archer. *Finnish Institute Yearbook*, 1995, p. 6-13.
On how Finland can influence the European Union and what its approach may be at the 1996 Inter-Governmental Conference and towards the Common Foreign and Security Policy.

338 **The EU referendum in Finland on 16 October 1994: a vote for the West, not for Maastricht.**
David Arter. *Journal of Common Market Studies*, vol. 33, no. 3 (September 1995), p. 361-87.
Analyses the background to Finland's vote to join the European Union, including the negotiations and the EU debate. Argues that for many Finns the vote was to tie

Finland to a block of West European democracies to which it had in effect belonged through its political and economic systems since independence. More detailed than Arter's article in *Finland Institute Yearbook* (see item no. 339).

339   The Finnish referendum on EU.
David Arter.   *Finnish Institute Yearbook*, 1994, p. 60-67.
Analyses both the debate leading up to the referendum on Finland joining the European Union and the ensuing affirmative result.

340   The European Union 1996 and Finland.
Helsinki: Centre for Finnish Business and Policy Studies, 1995. 48p.
A contribution to the debate on Finland's role in the European Union and in particular its attitude to the issues relating to the Intergovernmental Conference on the Union's future. The Centre for Finnish Business and Policy Studies represents various economic interests.

341   Finnish EU-opinion, autumn 1995.
Helsinki: Centre for Finnish Business and Policy Studies, 1996. 46p.
The results of an extensive opinion poll on Finnish attitudes to the European Union. Support for Finnish membership of the EU was found to be at a similar level to that attained at the time of the referendum on membership.

342   The Finns are pleased with their membership in the EU: respect for leaders or critical evaluation?
Teija Tiilikainen.   *Yearbook of Finnish Foreign Policy*, vol. 22 (1995), p. 16-22.
Argues that Finnish opinion about membership of the EU has remained unchanged during the first year of membership. The view that Finns are, on balance, pleased with membership is based on the results of a survey.

343   Finland on the way to the European Community.
Raimo Väyrynen.   In: *The Nordic countries and the EC*.   Edited by Teija Tiilikainen, Ib Damgaard Petersen.   Copenhagen: Copenhagen Political Studies Press, 1993, p. 64-78, 190-91.
On the history of Finnish integration policy, how Finland has been moving from the semi-periphery of the international economy to its core, and also about the interaction of integration and domestic politics. Concludes that the EC issues bring 'a certain conflict between tradition and modernity to the surface of Finnish politics' (p. 78).

Suomen säädöskokoelma. (The collected laws of Finland.)
See item no. 299.

Integrating Finland's economy into the EU.
See item no. 352.

Finland: economics and politics of EU accession.
See item no. 353.

Relations with Russia

344   **Finland's position in the changing Europe: the Eastern dimension.**
Roy Allison.   *Finnish Institute Yearbook*, 1993, p. 20-31.
Considers how the changes in Europe since the collapse of communism have ended
Finland's traditional type of neutrality and modified its relationship with the former
Soviet Union. The article also analyses how changes in the European political order
and strategic balance in the early 1990s have been reflected in Finland's regional
foreign policy towards Russia, the Baltic states, the Karelian Autonomous Republic
and the Kola Peninsula.

345   **Finland's relations with the Soviet Union, 1944-84.**
Roy Allison.   London: Macmillan, 1985. ix + 211p. map. bibliog.
(St Antony's/Macmillan Series).
Describes and analyses Finnish-Soviet relations, concluding that both countries were
well served by a pragmatic policy of coexistence based on the unique security policy
entente which they established through the peace treaty of 1947 and the Treaty of
Friendship, Cooperation and Mutual Assistance of 1948.

346   **Soviet policies towards the Nordic countries.**
Örjan Berner.   Lanham, Maryland; London: University Press of
America, 1986. xiii + 192p. map. bibliog.
Traces the changing Soviet relationship with the Scandinavian countries from the late
1930s and includes much on Finland, which eventually served as an illustration for the
Soviet Union of how a special relationship with the USSR could be combined with
neutrality. A useful historical survey, by a Swedish diplomat.

**Territories, boundaries and consciousness: the changing geographies of
the Finnish-Russian border.**
See item no. 23.

The East-West interface in the European North.
See item no. 24.

Recent trends in crossborder interaction between Finland and Russia.
See item no. 384.

Economy, Finance and Banking

Economy

347 Economic Survey: Finland.
Helsinki: Economics Department, Ministry of Finance, 1949- . annual.
An important survey of the economic situation, public finance, trade, production, consumption, etc., including forecasts concerning developments over the following year. Appendices provide a diary of economic policy measures during the previous eighteen months and also statistical tables. The survey is an abridged version of an appendix to the budget proposal for the following year.

348 Country profile: Finland, 1995-96.
London: Economist Intelligence Unit, 1995. [ii] + 34p. map. bibliog.
A valuable annually-published general 'portrait' of Finland, with the emphasis on the economy, and giving clear statistics. It is supplemented by the Economist Intelligence Units's quarterly *Country Report: Finland* and *Country Forecast: Finland* which look at political and economic developments and trends.

349 OECD economic surveys 1995-1996: Finland.
Paris: Organisation for Economic Co-operation and Development, 1996. viii + 163p.
Examines the main features of Finland's export-led economic recovery and the short-term economic outlook as well as providing a review of economic policies. Also considers labour market developments and the Finnish education and training system. Includes a 'Chronology of the main economic events and policy measures', January 1994-March 1996, and a statistical appendix.

350 **Bank of Finland Bulletin.**
Helsinki: Bank of Finland, 1921- . monthly.

Publishes regular statistics, surveys of economic developments, inflation and monetary policy, authoritative specialized articles and news items. Formerly *Bank of Finland Monthly Bulletin*. A cumulative index has been published: *Articles published in the Bank of Finland Monthly Bulletin 1921-1977* (Helsinki: Bank of Finland, 1978. 51p.). This comprises a classified index (by UDC) and subject and author indexes.

351 **The Finnish Economy.**
Helsinki: Research Institute of the Finnish Economy, 1989- .
quarterly.

A useful periodical which contains short-term economic forecasts, the medium-term economic outlook, and studies of topical interest.

352 **Integrating Finland's economy into the EU.**
Jukka Ahonen, Ilmo Pyyhtiä. *Bank of Finland Bulletin*, vol. 70, no. 5 (May 1996), p. 3-6.

Examines the degree of economic convergence, looking particularly at foreign trade and manufacturing.

353 **Finland: economics and politics of EU accession.**
Kari Alho, Mika Widgrén. *The World Economy*, vol. 17, no. 5 (September 1994), p. 701-09.

Concludes that Finland's economic and political interests would be served by joining the European Union as opposed to participating in the European Economic Area. Looks particularly at the position of agriculture where, it is claimed, rationalization of the production pattern would bring about a gain for the economy. Argues for membership on political grounds as necessary for Finland's influence on decision making. The paper is followed by two comments, by Robert E. Baldwin (p. 711-14) and Lars Lundberg (p. 715-18), which sound a more cautious note.

354 **Finnish companies strengthen their balance sheets.**
Juhani Huttunen, Jukka Vesala. *Bank of Finland Bulletin*, vol. 69, no. 11 (November 1995), p. 7-12.

Describes how the capital structure of Finnish companies has been strengthened as economic conditions have improved since 1993.

355 **National Budget: Finland.**
Helsinki: Economics Department, Ministry of Finance, 1960- . annual.

An important annual forecasting economic developments in the year indicated. Previously entitled *National Budget for Finland*.

356 **Opening Finland: challenges for the future.**
Edited by Antti Rompponen, Seppo Leppänen. Helsinki: Government
Institute for Economic Research, 1994. 186p. bibliog. (VATT
Publications, 13).
Examines various economic scenarios to the year 2005 looking at how Finland's
economic environment may change. It predicts that unemployment may decline to half
its 1994 level by 2005 if the economy adapts successfully to the new competitive
environment.

357 **The Finnish economy 1860-1985: growth and structural change.**
Riitta Hjerppe. Helsinki: Bank of Finland; Government Printing
Centre, 1989. 295p. bibliog. (Bank of Finland Publications. Studies on
Finland's Economic Growth, 13).
A major study of the structural development and growth of the Finnish economy, with
the aid of prepared time series, which are set out in an appendix of tables.

358 **The economy of Finland in the twentieth century.**
Fred Singleton. Bradford, England: University of Bradford, 1986.
xi + 177p. 2 maps. bibliog.
A useful overview of the development of the Finnish economy, charting the
transformation of agrarian Finland into a prosperous country with a wide range of
manufacturing industries.

Austerity and prosperity: perspectives on Finnish society.
See item no. 221.

Unitas: Merita Group Economic Review.
See item no. 371.

Regional policy

OECD reviews of rural policy: Finland.
See item no. 429.

Rural policy in Finland.
See item no. 430.

**Regional and local responses to restructuring in peripheral rural areas
in Finland.**
See item no. 432.

Finance, banking and insurance

Financial policy

359 **Monetary policy in Finland.**
Ari Aaltonen, Esko Aurikko, Jarmo Kontulainen.   Helsinki: Bank of
Finland, 1994. 102p. (Publications of the Bank of Finland, A:92).
Describes how the Bank of Finland operates as well as the objectives and conduct of
monetary policy.

360 **The Finnish money market from the mid-1980s to the present day.**
Harri Lahdenperä.   *Bank of Finland Bulletin*, vol. 69, no. 2 (February
1995), p. 3-8.
Discusses the market for short-term funds.

361 **Payment and settlement systems in Finland.**
Helsinki: Suomen Pankki, 1993. 249p. bibliog. (Publications of the
Bank of Finland, A:88).
Aims to provide an overall picture of Finland's payment and settlement systems as
they were at the end of 1993.

362 **A framework for assessing the equilibrium exchange rate for the
Finnish markka.**
Tuomas Saarenheimo.   *Bank of Finland Bulletin*, vol. 70, no. 2
(February 1996), p. 7-10.
An analysis of Finland's exchange rate according to different models. Shows that
'Finland's current exchange rate is well in harmony with low inflation and sustained
current account surplus' (p. 10).

363 **Money and economic activity in Finland, 1866-1985.**
Tauno Haavisto.   Lund, Sweden: University of Lund, Department of
Economics, 1992. viii + 214p. bibliog. (Lund Economic Studies, 48).
An analytical study of the money stock, money supply and economic activity, based
on extensive data on 'Finnish monetary aggregates' (p. 201).

Money counterfeiting in Finland.
See item no. 244.

Suomen säädöskokoelma. (The collected laws of Finland.)
See item no. 299.

Investment

364 **OECD reviews of foreign direct investment: Finland.**
Paris: Organisation for Economic Co-operation and Development, 1995. 75p.
An examination of Finland's foreign direct investment policies, noting the country's greater openness to foreign investors.

Banks and banking

365 **The Finnish banking system.**
Helsinki: The Finnish Bankers' Association, 1993. 11th rev. ed. 54p.
Although banks have changed (and continue to change) since this pamphlet was published, it provides useful information about the financial markets, financial intermediaries (including credit institutions, investment activities and insurance), legislation, supervision and public finances. Contains statistics and addresses of banks and other institutions and firms in this sector.

366 **The Finnish banking sector: performance and future prospects.**
Heikki Koskenkylä, Jukka Vesala. *Bank of Finland Bulletin*, vol. 70, no. 6-7 (June-July 1996), p. 8-12.
Describes the performance of the deposit banks in 1995 when their operating losses were reduced but cost efficiency was weaker than in the banks in other Nordic countries.

367 **The Finnish banking crisis and its handling.**
Peter Nyberg, Vesa Vihriälä. Helsinki: Bank of Finland, 1993. 43p.
bibliog. (Bank of Finland Discussion Papers, 8/93).
Gives a brief description of the evolution and handling of the Finnish banking crisis in the early 1990s when borrowers, hit by recession, became insolvent, dragging down with them the banks, whose bad banking and bad policies in the 1980s had led to over-lending. Bust was followed by government rescue.

368 **Changing role of the Bank of Finland.**
Antti Suvanto. In: *Economic policy issues in financial integration. Proceedings of Nordic Seminar on European Financial Integration, University of Helsinki, Finland, September 20-21, 1993.* Edited by Seppo Honkapohja. Helsinki: Hakapaino, 1993, p. 73-96.
Looks particularly at the role of the Bank of Finland in relation to price stability.

369 **Do banks have market power? Behavioral evidence from Finland.**
Jukka Vesala. In: *Economic policy issues in financial integration.*
Proceedings of Nordic Seminar on European Financial Integration,
University of Helsinki, Finland, September 20-21, 1993. Edited by
Seppo Honkapohja. Helsinki: Hakapaino, 1993, p. 169-240.
On deregulation and competition. Includes an appendix giving the timetable of
banking deregulation in Finland between June 1982 and August 1993. The banking
situation in Finland has changed considerably since 1993 as the consequences of the
banking crisis, mentioned elsewhere in this chapter, continue.

370 **Bank of Finland Year Book.**
Helsinki: Bank of Finland, 1921- . annual.
Contains the Governor's review of the year and sections on economic developments,
monetary policy, payment systems and maintenance of the currency supply, and other
activities of the Bank. Gives numerous statistics as well as the Bank's accounts.

371 **Unitas: Merita Group Economic Review.**
Helsinki: Merita Bank, 1929- . quarterly.
Now published by the recently-amalgamated Merita Bank, *Unitas* contains articles on
various aspects of the Finnish economy (such as capital movements and general
economic surveys) and on related topics, including economic surveys of neighbouring
countries.

Insurance

372 **Insurance in Finnish society.**
Helsinki: Federation of Finnish Insurance Companies, 1991. 31p.
Provides general information about the insurance market and insurance companies in
Finland.

373 **Insurance companies in the Finnish capital markets.**
Tapani Myllymäki. *Bank of Finland Bulletin*, vol. 69, no. 8 (August
1995), p. 16-20.
Summarizes legislation relating to the investment activity of insurance companies in
Finland and describes the nature of, and outlook for, those companies' investments.

Taxation

374   **Taxation in Finland.**
Ministry of Finance.   Helsinki: Ministry of Finance; Painatuskeskus, 1995. 138p.

A useful guide to the principles of the taxation system and to how the various taxes work. Gives the rates of income tax, wealth tax, inheritance tax and gift tax and details of allowances. There is an index.

Wages, taxation and employment in Finland.
See item no. 415.

Trade, Industry and Transport

Foreign trade

General

375 **Country profile: Finland.**
Great Britain. Foreign and Commonwealth Office & Department of
Trade and Industry.   London: Foreign and Commonwealth Office;
Department of Trade and Industry, 1995. 70p. map. bibliog.
Valuable background information on the Finnish market, including descriptions of
particular sectors, methods of doing business, export procedures and the business
environment and regulations. The advice that contacts in Finland can be very hard to
reach between late June and mid-August applies to all walks of life and not simply to
business.

376 **Contact Finland 1996: a guide to Finnish business services,
organizations and authorities.**
Editor-in-chief Jukka Manner.   Helsinki: Mergin Publications, 1996.
128p. map.
A useful, annual guide containing general information about the country, lists of
business services and authorities and organizations, including government and public
departments, trade associations and universities.

377 **Directory of Finnish exporters 1995.**
Helsinki: Finnish Foreign Trade Association, 1995. 224p.
Designed to promote Finnish exports, this directory contains an alphabetical index of
goods. and services, giving the reference numbers under which the list of those goods
and services is arranged. This is followed by a list of firms, giving brief details about
them and their products. There is a list of trademarks.

378 **Foreign trade in the Finnish balance of payments in 1995.**
Jorma Hilpinen. *Bank of Finland Bulletin*, vol. 70, no. 2 (February 1996), p. 3-6.

Describes changes in the collection of data on Finnish foreign trade. Finland's external balance of trade was very favourable in 1995.

379 **Finland's foreign trade and trade policy in the 20th century.**
Riitta Hjerppe. *Scandinavian Journal of History*, vol. 18, no. 1 (1993), p. 57-76.

Shows the pattern and structure of foreign trade. Concludes that Finland's foreign trade policy followed West European trends although foreign policy and foreign trade matters were often considered superior to domestic policy.

380 **Finland and the new international division of labour.**
Kimmo Kiljunen. Basingstoke, England; London: Macmillan, 1992. xvii + 240p. bibliog.

Considers Finland as a case-study of trade and economic relations between a semi-peripheral economy and the developing countries. There are chapters on, for example, the 'International specialisation of Finland', and on competition from the less-developed countries over imports into Finland and in export markets. Derived from a University of Sussex thesis.

381 **Finn Niche.**
London: Finn-Niche, 1989- . quarterly.

'The magazine for promoting economic relations between Great Britain and Finland'. Contains brief articles and news items (mostly on commerce and industry but some on culture) and useful lists of relevant organizations and forthcoming events.

382 **Finnfax: Economic and Industrial News about Finland.**
Helsinki: Finnfacts on behalf of the Finland Promotion Board, 1992- . irregular.

Brief items on trade and business, with some economic indicators. Succeeded the similar *Finnfacts* (196?-91).

383 **Finnish Business Report.**
Helsinki: Edita, 1982- . 10 issues per year.

Contains news items and articles on Finnish business, economic and political life and related matters, with a little on current events, sport and culture in Finland.

Trade with Russia

384 **Recent trends in crossborder interaction between Finland and Russia.**
Daniel Austin.   *Idäntutkimus. Östeuropaforskning. The Finnish Review of East European Studies*, vol. 2, no. 4 (1995), p. 65-70.
Explains that the fulfilment of the idea of Finland as a 'gateway' between East and West would require considerable regional integration which in turn would depend on the political willingness of both sides to make the border between Finland and Russia more permeable.

385 **Making connections: Finland – gateway to Northern Europe.**
Helsinki: Finnish Foreign Trade Association, 1994. 33p. 5 maps.
Finland has high hopes of developing as a gateway for trade with Northern Europe, including Arctic Russia, by acting as a centre for transport, communications and business. This booklet promotes the gateway concept.

386 **Finnish-Soviet clearing trade and payment system: history and lessons.**
Juhani Laurila.   Helsinki: Bank of Finland, 1995. 144p. bibliog. (Bank of Finland Studies, A:94).
Deals with the history, operational mechanisms and procedures of clearing systems, with the emphasis on the Finnish-Soviet system, which was a political arrangement, based on the Soviet decision to make purchases from Finland in the context of its planning system.

387 **Finnish-Soviet economic relations.**
Edited by Kari Möttölä, O. N. Bykov, I. S. Korolev.   London: Macmillan in association with the Finnish Institute of International Affairs, 1983. xxi + 358p. map.
A joint Finnish-Soviet compilation, this book now forms an epitaph on the economic relationship between Finland and the Soviet Union. Topics considered include the principles for East-West cooperation, how bilateral and multilateral (CMEA) relations worked, industrial and scientific cooperation, credit relations and the significance of Finno-Soviet trade, which was considerable in its day. There are supplements giving the texts of trade agreements, trade statistics and information about joint projects.

Industry

388 **National industrial strategy for Finland.**
Ministry of Trade and Industry. Helsinki: Ministry of Trade and Industry in Finland, Industry Department, 1993. [ix] + 143 + 25 + [4]p. (Ministry of Trade and Industry Publications, 3/1993).
A policy statement arising out of the debate occasioned by the problems of the recession of the early 1990s. 'Technology and human capital are the main factors behind growth and transformation' (p. 143).

389 **HITEC Finland 96: the outlook for Finnish technology.**
Helsinki: Finnish Foreign Trade Association, 1995. 144p.
Promotional material for Finnish exporters, but giving an impression of the genuinely advanced state of Finnish technology in relation to industry. This issue provides information on automation, forest products and technology, energy, environment and food and beverages, in the form of articles on particular developments. Indexes of companies and products. Regularly published.

390 **Innovative companies from Finland 1995.**
Editor Kari Mettälä. Helsinki: Ministry of Trade and Industry, [1995]. 112p.
Brief details of companies active in the application of technology, ranging from biotechnology to materials production and processing.

391 **International competitive advantage of the Finnish chemical forest industry.**
Kaisa Ojainmaa. Helsinki: Research Institute of the Finnish Economy, 1994. [xii] + iv + 167p. bibliog. (Research Institute of the Finnish Economy. Series C 66).
Chemical forest industry products, particularly printing and writing papers, are among Finland's most successful export commodities. This study shows why the companies in this sector have an international competitive advantage and what factors are undermining it.

392 **Seeking efficiency by privatization.**
Matti Vuoria. *Unitas*, vol. 68, no. 2 (1996), p. 4-7.
On state-owned companies in Finland and how far the state is selling its controlling majority voting rights in some of them as part of a privatization process.

393 **A history of Outokumpu.**
Markku Kuisma. [Helsinki: Outokumpu], 1989. xiv + 240p.
Founded in 1914 to exploit the rich copper resources at Outokumpu in Northern Karelia, the Outokumpu Company has been and remains a technologically innovative firm which is at present one of the world's leading producers of base metals. This history in English is based on a more substantial work in Finnish.

394 **Electrifying Finland: the transfer of a new technology into a late industrialising economy.**
Timo Myllyntaus. Basingstoke, England: Macmillan; Helsinki: ELTA, 1991. xvi + 407p. 3 maps. bibliog. (ELTA – the Research Institute of the Finnish Economy Series, A 15).
Gives the history of electrification in Finland and evaluates the process of developing an electricity supply in Finland, describes the demand for and use of electricity, and analyses the interactive effects of electrification on the Finnish economy during the period 1877-1977. Finland developed its electrical supply industry by the transfer of technology without a great deal of foreign involvement thanks to a receptiveness to innovative entrepreneurship and innovations.

395 **Finnish industry in transition 1885-1920: responding to technological challenges.**
Timo Myllyntaus. Helsinki: Museum of Technology, 1989. 86p. bibliog. (Tekniikan museon julkaisuja [Publications of the Museum of Technology], IV).
Concentrates on the sawmill, paper and metallurgical and engineering industries, showing how technological change speeded up decisively as industry tried to improve its productivity, competitiveness and profits. 'The industrialisation of Finland was mainly a homespun product' (p. 72), with only a minor role played by foreign capital and multinational companies. Scholarly studies are rarely so pleasingly illustrated.

396 **Finnish Industry.**
Helsinki: Confederation of Finnish Industry and Employers, 1994- . three issues per year.
Descriptive and analytical articles about the performance of particular industrial sectors and companies and also about the economy and economic policy.

397 **Sininen kirja 28. Talouselämän suurhakemisto. Finlands affärskalender. Business directory of Finland.**
Helsinki: Helsinki Media, 1996. 2 vols.
The major Finnish business directory, giving information about some 100,000 companies and public administration facilities. Volume 1 arranges companies by branch of activity and provides a list of companies by municipal area. Volume 2 gives companies and organizations in alphabetical order. Some information about how to use the directory is given in English.

Women at the top: a study on women as leaders in the private sector.
See item no. 230.

Advanced environmental technology from Finland 1993.
See item no. 427.

Transport

General

398 **Suomen kulkuneuvot. Finlands kommunikationer.** (Finnish Transport.)
Helsinki: Suomen matkailuliitto, 1930- . two issues per year.
Published by the Finnish Travel Association, this is the complete timetable of public transport in Finland: trains, buses (except local city transport), air, sea, and lake vessels. Known popularly by the name of its precursor, *Turisti* (1891-1930), the timetable includes directions for use and notes in English, German, French and Russian as well as Finnish and Swedish.

Shipping

399 **Sea Finland: Finnish seafaring in pictures.**
Compiled by Henry Forssell. Helsinki: National Board of Antiquities, 1985. [111]p. maps.
From early log and sewn boats to modern icebreakers, from fishing to trading, from naval fleets to the evidence of wrecks, this extremely attractive book sets out, with excellent illustrations, Finland's many links with the sea throughout the ages.

400 **A history of Finnish shipping.**
Yrjö Kaukiainen. London; New York: Routledge, 1993. [xvi] + 231p. 2 maps. bibliog. (Maritime History).
A detailed history of Finnish shipping from the middle ages to the present day which shows the influence of maritime transport on Finland's international economic relations. Finnish shipping developed strongly from the late 18th century to the 1870s when the transport revolution represented by steam-powered ships reduced the profitability of the Finnish sail-driven merchant fleet and hence the possibilities for its modernization. Finland now has a very modern merchant fleet, with much of its gross freight originating in trade between Finland and Sweden.

401 **The last tall ships: Gustaf Erikson and the Åland sailing fleets 1872-1947.**
Georg Kåhre, edited and with an introductory chapter by Basil Greenhill. Greenwich, England: Conway Maritime Press, 1978. 208p. map. bibliog.
This book, translated from the Swedish original edition of 1948 by Louis Mackay and with a few editorial changes, chronicles the life and times of Gustaf Erikson, the famous Mariehamn shipowner, and the sailing fleets of the Åland islands in the period 1872-1947. The magnificent illustrations were selected by the editor, who was then Director of the National Maritime Museum at Greenwich. Appendix I lists the sailing vessels in Erikson's fleet and appendix II is a list of books for further reading.

The letter- and parcel stamps of the Finnish shipping companies.
See item no. 321.

Railways

402 **Railway network 2000.**
Helsinki: Finnish State Railways, 1995. 32p. maps.
On the railways and plans to improve them, particularly as far as track and electrification are concerned. The State Railways also publish an English version of their *Annual Report* summarizing their operations and giving statistics.

Suomen rautatiepakettimerkit. The railway parcel stamps of Finland.
See item no. 322.

Roads

403 **Auto ja tie 1995. Automobiles and highways in Finland 1995.**
Helsinki: Finnish Road Association, 1995. 116p. map.
A bilingual publication, mostly made up of statistics but with some comment, about the number and distribution of vehicles, the road network and road traffic (including accidents and road traffic taxation and expenditure), and the consumption of energy in transport.

Air travel

404 **Finnair: the art of flying since 1923.**
John Wegg.   [Helsinki: Finnair], 1983. 297p. map.
A history of Finnair, the Finnish national airline, from its foundation in 1923 to 1983, with good illustrations and careful attention to the types of aircraft used. Finnair publishes an *Annual Report* in English.

Agriculture and Forestry

Agriculture

405 **Finnish agriculture in 1994.**
Lauri Kettunen. Helsinki: Agricultural Economics Research Institute, 1995. 63p. (Agricultural Economics Research Institute, Research Publications, 76a).
A regularly-published survey of the agricultural year, its favourability (or otherwise) for farmers, giving information on production, incomes, etc., and with a look at agricultural policy, particularly as regards the European Union.

406 **National policies and agricultural trade. Country study: Finland.**
Paris: Organisation for Economic Co-operation and Development, 1989. 169p. bibliog.
Provides an overview of Finnish agriculture and agricultural policy in the period 1979-86, giving numerous statistics.

407 **A place of their own: family farming in eastern Finland.**
Ray Abrahams. Cambridge; New York: Cambridge University Press, 1991. xi + 210p. map. bibliog. (Cambridge Studies in Social and Cultural Anthropology, 81).
A study by an anthropologist, based on fieldwork conducted in 1980-82, of the connections between farm and family and the pressures the farming families are under in trying to maintain their farms and communities as viable units.

408 **Farming in Finland.**
W. R. Mead. London: Athlone Press, 1953. [xv] + 248p. maps.
'A descriptive study of the geography of Finnish farming'. Shows how land has been won for cultivation, describes the exploitation of the forest, grassland and crop husbandry, and

looks at the land ownership pattern. The problems involved in the resettlement of refugees after the wars of 1939-40 and 1941-44 are carefully described. This book has not been displaced as an account of Finnish farming of the 1940s and early 1950s.

409   Finnish farming: typology and economics.
Uno Varjo.   Budapest: Akadémiai Kiadó, 1977. 146p. maps. bibliog. (Geography of World Agriculture, 6).

This important study of farming in Finland, dealing with the natural conditions, settlement, mechanization, land ownership and utilization, arable farming, animal husbandry, forestry on the farm, and the basic farm production types and farming regions, remains of interest.

Austerity and prosperity: perspectives on Finnish society.
See item no. 221.

The social implications of agrarian ghange [*sic*] in northern and eastern Finland.
See item no. 227.

Finland: economics and politics of EU accession.
See item no. 353.

Forestry

410   Finland the country of evergreen forest.
Simo Hannelius, Kullervo Kuusela.   [Forssa, Finland]: Forssan Kirjapaino, 1995. 192p. maps. bibliog.

Attractively illustrated but with a good text, this book presents 'an overview of Finland's forests and their importance for the country's economy, and the principles of silviculture based on the ecology of the boreal coniferous forests' (p. 7).

411   The effects of air pollution on forests in Finland, 1900-2040.
Pertti Hari, Taisto Raunemaa, Maria Holmberg, Markku Kulmala, Pia Anttila, Jaakko Kukkonen, Erik Spring.   Helsinki: Ministry of the Environment, Environmental Protection and Nature Conservation Department, 1987. 61p. bibliog. (Ympäristöministeriön ympäristön- ja luonnonsuojeluosaston julkaisut [Publications of the Environmental Protection and Nature Conservation Department of the Ministry of the Environment], A, 58).

A scientific analysis of forest growth in Finland, 1900-2040, based on nutrients and toxic compounds in the atmosphere and in forest soil, which shows an increase in forest productivity since the beginning of the century but expects a decline in forest growth during the coming decades.

412　**Death by a thousand cuts.**
Martin Wright.　*New Scientist*, vol. 145, no. 1964 (11 Feb. 1995),
p. 36-40.
Controversial article suggesting that timber from Finland does not necessarily come
from sustainably managed forests.

413　**The Finnish Timber and Paper Directory 1994-95.**
Edited by Irmeli Hannula.　Helsinki: Finnish Paper and Timber
Journal Publishing Company, 1994. 27th ed. 278p.
A regularly-published English-language directory of the Finnish forestry industry,
including information about forestry in general, research on forestry and forest
products, and details of the firms involved in particular sectors, such as sawmills,
prefabricated timber houses, wood-based panels, and pulp, paper and board.

**International competitive advantage of the Finnish chemical forest
industry.**
See item no. 391.

**The history of botany in Finland 1828-1918. With an appendix on forest
science.**
See item no. 455.

Employment and Labour

Employment

414 **From full employment to mass unemployment: new government aims at halving unemployment.**
Pertti Sorsa. *Bank of Finland Bulletin*, vol. 70, no. 4 (April 1996), p. 8-12.
Describes measures to reduce unemployment, which became a serious problem from 1990 onwards. Economic growth had slowed in 1995, causing the fall in unemployment to drop below the official target.

415 **Wages, taxes and employment in Finland.**
Timo Tyrväinen. *Bank of Finland Bulletin*, vol. 69, no. 12 (December 1995), p. 9-12.
Discusses the determination of wages and employment, especially the impact of taxes on equilibrium in the labour market.

Wage from work and gender: a study on differentials in Finland in 1995.
See item no. 228.

Women at the top: a study on women as leaders in the private sector.
See item no. 230.

Labour law and industrial relations in Finland.
See item no. 290.

Trade unions

416 **Finland.**
Hannu Soikkanen. In: *European labor unions.* Edited by Joan
Campbell. General Consultant John P. Windmuller. Westport,
Connecticut; London: Greenwood Press, 1992, p. 101-18.

A short but authoritative survey (with a bibliography) of the history and state of the
trade union movement in Finland, together with a list of the confederations of Finnish
trade unions, giving their history, composition and membership.

Statistics

417   **Suomen virallinen tilasto.** (Official statistics of Finland.)
      Helsinki: 1866- .
This is the most important national statistical series, originally published in 1866-1904 with the title *Suomenmaan virallinen tilasto* (Official statistics of Finland). There are numerous sub-series, many produced by Statistics Finland (the Central Statistical Office) and some by other organizations. For a good list of the various series see Elemer Bako, *Finland and the Finns: a selective bibliography* (item no. 787), p. 14-18. Series published by Statistics Finland cover housing, living conditions, energy, prices, public economics, national accounts, trade, education, culture and mass media, transport, agriculture and forestry, justice, wages and salaries, services, construction, social welfare, industry, health, science and technology, incomes and consumption, labour market, foreign trade, elections, insurance, population, environment, enterprises, index of earnings, consumer price index, producer price indices, and building cost index. See also *Tilasto-opas* (item no. 421) and *Guide to Finnish statistics 1977* (item no. 422).

418   **Suomen tilastollinen vuosikirja. Statistisk årsbok för Finland. Statistical Yearbook of Finland.**
      Helsinki: Tilastokeskus, 1878- . annual.
The *Statistical Yearbook of Finland* contains a wide selection of the most important statistical data on the country, and in recent years also information about other countries for comparative purposes. The yearbook was entitled *Suomenmaan tilastollinen vuosikirja. Annuaire Statistique pour la Finlande* (Statistical Yearbook of Finland) from 1879-1902, vols. 1-23. A new series began in 1903 which still continues, although with the issue for 1953 English displaced French as the foreign language used and the English title (Statistical Yearbook of Finland) was added to the Finnish and Swedish (Statistisk årsbok för Finland) titles. The texts and tables are thus now in Finnish, Swedish and English.

Statistics

419 **Finland in Figures.**
Helsinki: Statistics Finland, 1977- . annual.
Small-format, extremely handy guide to basic statistics about Finland, covering population, industry, agriculture, trade, national accounts, wages and salaries, education, culture, etc.

420 **Tilastokatsauksia. Statistiska översikter. Bulletin of Statistics.**
Helsinki: Statistics Finland, 1924- . quarterly.
Provides important statistics on social and economic developments in Finland. Information on the population, industry, construction, financial markets, trade, national accounts, government finance, prices and wages, transport, working life, and justice. The contents and headings of tables appear in Finnish, Swedish and English.

421 **Tilasto-opas.** (Guide to statistics.)
Helsinki: Tilastokeskus, 1995. [xi] + 247p.
Published every other year and unfortunately not available in English, this little guide to Finnish statistics provides a general description of statistics available in Finland, arranged by category, e.g. energy, agriculture, health. Also gives the publisher, since not all are published by Statistics Finland (the central statistical office), and the name and telephone number of a contact for further information. The postal address of Tilastokeskus/Statistics Finland for orders and enquiries is: Julkaisumyynti (Sales), PL 3B, FIN-00022 TILASTOKESKUS, Finland.

422 **Guide to Finnish statistics 1977.**
Edited by Mauri Levomäki, Matti Kyrö. Helsinki: Tilastokeskus, 1977. [2] + 51p. (Käsikirjoja. Handböcker. Handbooks, 8).
Unfortunately never updated, this is the only guide in English to who compiles statistics in Finland and where they are published. It is still worth consulting, although based on *Tilasto-opas 1975* (Guide to statistics 1975), and inevitably much has changed. See also *Tilasto-opas* (Guide to statistics) (item no. 421).

423 **Women and men in the Nordic countries: facts and figures 1994.**
Copenhagen: Nordic Council of Ministers, 1994. 96p. map. (Nord, 1994:3).
A statistical overview of women and men in the Nordic countries, considering equal opportunities, with notes on each country and statistics presented so as to provide comparisons between the Nordic countries. Coverage includes health, education, income and employment.

Auto ja tie 1995. Automobiles and highways in Finland 1995.
See item no. 403.

Developments in education Finland: 1992-1994. International Conference on Education, Forty-fourth session, Geneva, 1994. National report from Finland.
See item no. 433.

Cultural policy in Finland.
See item no. 639.

Finnish mass media.
See item no. 760.

Finland and the Finns: a selective bibliography.
See item no. 787.

Environment and Rural Policy

Environment

424   **The state of the Finnish environment.**
Edited by Erik Wahlström, Eeva-Liisa Hallanaro, Tapio Reinikainen, translated by Greg Coogan.   Helsinki: National Board of Waters and the Environment, Environment Data Centre; Ministry of the Environment, 1993. 163p. maps.
An abridged version of a work in Finnish and Swedish, this is a good account of how the environment in Finland is faring. Plenty of factual information, accompanied by pleasing illustrations. Covers pollution from abroad, nature, energy, industry, agriculture, transport, wastes, air, acidification, forests, waters, food and health and the law on environmental protection.

425   **Environmental policies in Finland.**
Paris: Organisation for Economic Co-operation and Development, 1988. 230p. 14 maps.
A comprehensive, expert review of Finnish environmental policy, concluding that good progress had been made in improved water quality with respect to organic pollution, improved management of municipal waste and extended protection of outstanding natural areas. Problems remained as a consequence of economic growth. The review covers energy, agriculture, the forests, inland water management, nature and wildlife (the Saimaa seal is not forgotten), the marine environment, air, and waste management and the control of chemicals.

426   **Kansallispuistoissa. Exploring Finland's national parks.**
Hannu Hautala, Lassi Rautiainen, English translation by Tim Steffa. Helsinki: Otava, 1995. 158 + [1]p. map.
A volume in Finnish and English which describes the national parks one by one and provides fine illustrations of their landscape, fauna and flora.

427 **Advanced environmental technology from Finland 1993.**
Ministry for Foreign Affairs, Ministry of the Environment & Ministry of Trade and Industry.   Helsinki: Ministry for Foreign Affairs; Ministry of the Environment; Ministry of Trade and Industry, 1993. rev. and expanded ed. 382p.
Provides details of the government departments, associations, universities and research centres active in the environmental area, but deals principally with how particular problems can be tackled, from water and sludge technology to electrostatic precipitators for clearing forest industry flue gases. Gives details of the companies providing particular services.

428 **Are environmental attitudes and behaviour inconsistent? Findings from a Finnish study.**
Liisa Uusitalo.   *Scandinavian Political Studies*, vol. 13, no. 2 (1990), p. 211-26.
Gives the results of a survey taken to illustrate the conflict between individual utility and collective welfare which is an obstacle to environmental protection. Nevertheless, the willingness expressed to pay for good environmental quality was quite high.

The climate of Finland in relation to its hydrology, ecology and culture.
See item no. 27.

Rural policy

429 **OECD reviews of rural policy: Finland.**
Paris: Organisation for Economic Co-operation and Development, 1995. 133p. 10 maps. bibliog.
A thorough review of rural development policies in Finland, considering in particular territorial statistics and rural indicators, the promotion of rural employment, infrastructures and services, and the institutional aspects of tackling rural development.

430 **Rural policy in Finland.**
Ministry of the Interior; Ministry of Agriculture and Forestry. Helsinki: Rural Policy Committee, 1992. 100p.
Provides some information about the condition of rural areas as well as a programme for rural development.

431   **Finnish [*sic*] find renewal in village action.**
Lauri Hautamäki.   *Town and Country Planning*, vol. 62, no. 10
(October 1993), p. 283-85.

Describes how a programme to stimulate rural self help has revitalized the rural
communities taking part in it, often by providing new channels for public investment.

432   **Regional and local responses to restructuring in peripheral rural
areas in Finland.**
Jukka Oksa.   *Urban Studies*, vol. 29, no. 6 (August 1992),
p. 991-1,002.

Considers rural policy since the Second World War, focusing on the changes from a
settlement policy to an industrial welfare state and from that to a new rural policy
attempting to channel former agricultural policy funds into rural development work.

Education

General

433 **Developments in education Finland: 1992-1994. International Conference on Education, Forty-fourth session, Geneva, 1994. National report from Finland.**
Ministry of Education.   Helsinki: Ministry of Education, 1994. 98p. (Ministry of Education. Reference Publications, 17).
A helpful basic introduction to the education system in Finland at all levels, with statistics, and a list of development measures proposed for 1994-96.

434 **The education system of Finland 1994.**
National Board of Education.   Helsinki: National Board of Education, 1994. 39p.
A short, official description of the education system, covering administration, pre-school and school education, vocational education and training, higher education and adult education.

435 **Educational strategies in Finland in the 1990s.**
Edited by Osmo Kivinen, Risto Rinne.   Turku, Finland: University of Turku Research Unit for the Sociology of Education, 1992. 134p. bibliog. (University of Turku, Research Unit for the Sociology of Education. Research Reports, 8).
Considers the transition from secondary to higher education, aspects of adult education in relation to the labour market, the problems of state educational planning and the consequences of the expansion of education.

436 **The science of education in Finland 1828-1918.**
Taimo Iisalo. Helsinki: Societas Scientiarum Fennica, 1979. 110p.
bibliog. (The History of Learning and Science in Finland 1828-1918,
18).
A history of the aims and theories of education in Finland during the period 1828-1918.

Austerity and prosperity: perspectives on Finnish society.
See item no. 221.

Higher education

437 **Higher education policy in Finland.**
Ministry of Education. Helsinki: Ministry of Education, 1996. 118p.
bibliog.
Describes the state of Finnish higher education and, to a lesser extent, research.
Considerable details are given of the university sector, how universities are run, their
degree structures, student intake, adult education, research and resources. The
polytechnics are also considered and there is a look at the internationalization of
higher education. Also contains useful statistical appendices and the addresses of
relevant central institutions, the universities and polytechnics.

438 **Reviews of national policies for education: Finland. Higher
education.**
Paris: Organisation for Economic Co-operation and Development,
1995. 246p. bibliog.
A valuable report, providing a clear description of the education system as well as
more detailed consideration of higher education covering both the university and new
polytechnic sectors.

439 **Educational studies and teacher education in Finnish universities,
1994: a commentary by an international review team.**
Edited by Johanna Vähäsaari. Helsinki: Ministry of Education, 1994.
[iv] + 51p. bibliog. (Opetusministeriö. Koulutus- ja tiedepolitiikan
linjan julkaisusarja [Ministry of Education. Education and Research
Policy Series], 14).
A review of education facilities and of the quality of Finnish teacher education.

440 **Finnish polytechnics: an experimental reform.**
Ministry of Education. Helsinki: Ministry of Education, 1994. 16p.
Describes the 'experimental polytechnics' which have been set up to offer courses in
higher vocational education.

441 **Study in Finland: international programmes in Finnish higher education 1996-97. Part 1: University sector. Part 2: Non-university sector.**
Helsinki: Centre for International Mobility, 1996. 2 vols.
Two pamphlets, annually published, which form an extensive guide to a wide variety of courses at higher educational establishments.

442 **Living in Finland: a practical guide for international students and trainees.**
Helsinki: Centre for International Mobility, [1994?]. 40p. map.
Fulfils the promise of its sub-title and provides a helpful basic source of information. The Centre for International Mobility (CIMO) works under the Finnish Ministry of Education to provide international exchanges for students, trainees and researchers.

Yliopiston Helsinki. University architecture in Helsinki.
See item no. 704.

Aspects of musical life and music education in Finland.
See item no. 725.

The Helsinki University Library: an architectural jewel.
See item no. 748.

Schools

443 **The right to private school education: on the interpretation of secs. 79 and 82 of the Finnish Form of Government Act.**
Tore Modeen. *Scandinavian Studies in Law*, vol. 32 (1988), p. 211-42.
A convenient summary of Finnish legislation relating to schools of all types. Suggests that generous legislation with regard to private schools (which are very rare) would preserve the principle of freedom of education as required by the constitution.

444 **The development of co-education in Finland during the 19th century and some points of comparison in neighboring countries.**
Saara Hakaste. *Koulu ja menneisyys. Suomen Kouluhistoriallisen Seuran vuosikirja* (The School and the Past. Yearbook of the Finnish School History Society), vol. 31 (1993), p. 122-36.
A discussion of coeducation, which began in Finland in the 1880s at the higher secondary school level and led on to university.

445   **Education of the elementary-school teachers and images of citizenship in Finland during the 19th and 20th centuries.**
Osmo Kivinen, Risto Rinne.   *Scandinavian Journal of Educational Research*, vol. 39, no. 3 (September 1995), p. 237-56.
On the changing role of the teacher and the shift in the image of citizenship. Extroversion has replaced piety as one of the criteria for would-be teachers.

446   **Exploring the secret of Finnish reading literacy achievement.**
Pirjo Linnakylä.   *Scandinavian Journal of Educational Research*, vol. 37, no. 1 (1993), p. 63-74.
Finland has a high level of literacy, measured against international comparisons. Reasons given include society's high expectations in reading proficiency and easy access to books and papers.

Developments in education Finland: 1992-1994. International Conference on Education, Forty-fourth sessions, Geneva, 1994. National report from Finland.
See item no. 433.

The education system of Finland 1994.
See item no. 434.

Other education

447   **The changing role of vocational and technical education and training in Finland.**
Edited by Matti Kyrö.   Helsinki: National Board of Education, 1993. [vii] + 76 leaves. bibliog.
Describes the historical context of vocational and technical education and training in Finland, looks in detail at arrangements in the hotel and restaurant 'industry', the graphic arts and construction, and considers trends in the 1990s.

448   **Vocational education in Finland.**
Helsinki: National Board of Education, 1993. [8]p.
Very brief pamphlet setting out the principal features of the Finnish system of vocational education and training and how those from abroad may participate in study programmes in Finland.

449   **Lessons from the European periphery: some features of Finnish vocational education.**
Anja Heikkinen.   London: Post-16 Education Centre, Institute of Education, University of London, 1992. [i] + 42p. bibliog. (European Perspectives, 4).
Describes briefly the background, present situation and reform plans of the vocational education system.

450   **The Finnish model of special education: a mixture of integration and segregation.**
Joel Kivirauma.   *Scandinavian Journal of Educational Research*, vol. 35, no. 3 (1991), p. 193-200.
Examines the development of special education in the Finnish compulsory education system in the 1990s.

Learning, Science and Technology

Scholarship and the sciences

Learned societies and institutions

451 **Suomen tieteelliset seurat 1995. Finlands vetenskapliga samfund. Finnish learned societies.**
Compiled by Eeva-Liisa Aalto.   [Helsinki]: Federation of Finnish Scientific Societies, [1996?]. 130p.
Provides information, in a standardized format, about the scientific societies of Finland (covering all areas of scholarship). The key to the information is given in English as well as Finnish and Swedish. An index of societies is also provided.

452 **A forward look: the Academy of Finland.**
[Helsinki]: Academy of Finland, 1993. 37p.
On the objectives and strategies of the Academy of Finland, whose role is to fund research.

453 **Research in Finland: a brief guide to research institutions.**
Edited by Sirkka-Liisa Korppi-Tommola.   Munich; Helsinki: TEKES (Technology Development Centre Finland), 1995. 48p.
Aims 'to offer a glimpse into research in Finland and to serve as a first contact to Finnish research institutes'. Covers the Academy of Finland, the Technology Development Centre Finland, the universities and the state research institutes as well as such specialized points of contact as the Centre for International Mobility (which promotes international exchanges for researchers, students and trainees). Includes a brief characterization of each research centre, an indication of its size (staff/students/ scientists), subordinate departments or research areas, and points of contact, often giving e-mail addresses.

454   **Finnish Institute Yearbook.**
London: Finnish Institute in London, 1993- . annual.
The Finnish Institute in London provides information about opportunities for study,
training and research in Finland and supplies Finns with information about education
in the United Kingdom. The Institute also develops links between British and Finnish
arts and cultural organizations through an active programme of seminars, lectures and
exhibitions. The *Yearbook* publishes some of the lectures and seminar papers:
historical, cultural, artistic and political themes predominate.

History of science and learning

455   **The history of botany in Finland 1828-1918. With an appendix on
forest science by Yrjö Ilvessalo.**
Runar Collander.   Helsinki: Societas Scientiarum Fennica, 1965.
159p. bibliog. (The History of Learning and Science in Finland
1828-1918, 8).
One of the first volumes to be published in a distinguished series.

456   **The history of chemistry in Finland 1828-1918, with chapters on
the political, economic and industrial background.**
Terje Enkvist.   Helsinki: Societas Scientiarum Fennica, 1972. 161p.
map. bibliog. (The History of Learning and Science in Finland
1828-1918, 6).
Includes pharmaceutical chemistry and chemical technology.

457   **Classical studies in Finland 1828-1918.**
Pentti Aalto.   Helsinki: Societas Scientiarum Fennica, 1980. 210p.
bibliog. (The History of Learning and Science in Finland 1828-1918,
10a).
Looks at Latin and Greek philosophy, ancient history, Roman law, ancient philosophy,
fine arts, and New Testament philology and patristics. Has a final chapter on 'The
contribution of Finland to classical scholarship'.

458   **The history of geology and mineralogy in Finland 1828-1918.**
Hans Hausen.   Helsinki: Societas Scientiarum Fennica, 1968. 147p.
bibliog. (The History of Learning and Science in Finland 1828-1918,
7a).
Covers the history of geology and mineralogy, the work of the Geological
Commission and prospecting and mining enterprises.

Learning, Science and Technology. Scholarship and the sciences. History of science and learning

459 **The history of geophysics in Finland 1828-1918.**
Heikki Simojoki. Helsinki: Societas Scientiarum Fennica, 1978. 157p. bibliog. (The History of Learning and Science in Finland 1828-1918, 5b).

On geophysics, meteorology, oceanography, hydrography, geomagnetism and seismology.

460 **The history of mathematics in Finland 1828-1918.**
Gustav Elfving. Helsinki: Societas Scientiarum Fennica, 1981. 195p. bibliog. (The History of Learning and Science in Finland 1828-1918, 4a).

Focuses on individual mathematicians and their work.

461 **The history of medicine in Finland 1828-1918.**
Bertel von Bonsdorff. Helsinki: Societas Scientiarum Fennica, 1975. 309p. map. bibliog. (The History of Learning and Science in Finland 1828-1918, 3).

Includes brief sections on dentistry and veterinary medicine.

462 **Modern language studies in Finland 1828-1918.**
Pentti Aalto. Helsinki: Societas Scientiarum Fennica, 1987. 248p. bibliog. (The History of Learning and Science in Finland 1828-1918, 10c).

Covers Romance studies, Germanic studies, English studies, Slavonic and Baltic philology, the study of loanwords, Slavonic and Baltic folklore and phonetic studies.

463 **Oriental studies in Finland 1828-1918.**
Pentti Aalto. Helsinki: Societas Scientiarum Fennica, 1971. 174p. map. bibliog. (The History of Learning and Science in Finland 1828-1918, 10b).

A concise and informative account of its subject, including much on exploration by Finns as well as on linguistic, literary, archaeological, ethnographical and anthropological studies.

464 **The history of physics in Finland 1828-1918.**
Peter Holmberg. Helsinki: Societas Scientiarum Fennica, 1992. 267p. bibliog. (The History of Learning and Science in Finland 1828-1918, 5a).

Includes biographies of notable Finnish physicists and a useful chapter on weights and measures in Finland in the 19th century and the introduction of the metric system.

Small states in comparative perspective: essays for Erik Allardt.
See item no. 222.

Scientific and industrial policy

465 **Explaining technical change in a small country: the Finnish national innovation system.**
Edited by Synnöve Vuori, Pentti Vuorinen.   Heidelberg, Germany: Physica; Helsinki: ETLA; New York: Springer, 1994. xi + 215p. bibliog.

The proceedings of a seminar held in 1993, on how technical change has taken place in Finland, the social infrastructure of innovation, and technological policy, giving some international comparisons.

Languages

Finnish

General studies

Finnish as a Finno-Ugrian language

466 **Finno-Ugrian languages and peoples.**
Péter Hajdú, translated and adapted by G. F. Cushing.   London:
Deutsch, 1975. 254p. 5 maps. bibliog. (The Language Library).
Retains its value as a description of the Finno-Ugrian peoples and languages to
interested, but non-specialist, English-speaking readers. Sets the Finns and Finnish, as
well as the Lapps and Lapp, into their Finno-Ugrian context.

467 **Finno-Ugrian language studies in Finland 1828-1918.**
Mikko Korhonen.   Helsinki: Societas Scientiarum Fennica, 1986.
226p. 2 maps. bibliog. (The History of Learning and Science in Finland
1828-1918, 11).
Shows the influence of the Finnish national movement on Finno-Ugrian language
studies and the consequences for those studies of the rise of comparative linguistics
and the later domination of the neogrammarian school.

Studies on Finnish

468 **Case and other functional categories in Finnish syntax.**
Edited by Anders Holmberg, Urpo Nikanne. Berlin; New York:
Mouton de Gruyter, 1993. ix + 248p. bibliog. (Studies in Generative
Grammar, 39).

Contains ten articles which together form an overview of the different approaches
currently used in research on Finnish theoretical syntax. The introduction gives 'a
condensed overview of Finnish grammar with special attention ... to inflectional
morphology' (p. 1). This enhances the value of the book to linguists with no previous
knowledge of Finnish.

469 **On definiteness: a study with special reference to English and
Finnish.**
Andrew Chesterman. Cambridge; New York: Cambridge University
Press, 1991. xi + 221p. bibliog. (Cambridge Studies in Linguistics, 56).

Considers definiteness in English and Finnish, the former language having articles, the
latter not. For the theorist.

470 **Semantic structure and the Finnish lexicon: verbs of possibility
and sufficiency.**
Aili Flint. Helsinki: Suomalaisen Kirjallisuuden Seura, 1980.
[x] + 220p. bibliog. (Suomalaisen Kirjallisuuden Seuran toimituksia
[Publications of the Finnish Literature Society], 360).

A revised version of a Columbia University thesis. Studies the rich lexical network of
Finnish in the semantic area of verbs which have the common characteristic of
'gauging reserves ... against the demands of challenges' (p. 153).

471 **Buts about conjunctions: a syntactic study of conjunction
expressions in Finnish.**
Riitta Korhonen. Helsinki: Suomalaisen Kirjallisuuden Seura, 1993.
[x] + 199p. bibliog. (Studia Fennica. Linguistica, 4).

This thesis considers the different types of conjunctions in Finnish and the relations
between clauses and phrases linked by conjunctions.

472 **Free word order in Finnish: its syntax and discourse functions.**
Maria Vilkuna. Helsinki: Suomalaisen Kirjallisuuden Seura, 1989.
280p. bibliog. (Suomalaisen Kirjallisuuden Seuran toimituksia
[Publications of the Finnish Literature Society], 500).

This Helsinki University thesis is an 'in-depth study of word order variation' in
Finnish. For specialists in Finnish or linguistics.

More equal than most. Essays on women in Finnish society and culture.
See item no. 530.

Periodicals

473 **Sananjalka: Suomen kielen seuran vuosikirja.** (Yearbook of the
Finnish Language Society.)
Turku, Finland: Suomen kielen seura, 1959- . annual.
An annual on the Finnish language and the linguistic aspects of literature and
ethnography.

474 **Virittäjä: Kotikielen seuran aikakauslehti.** (Journal of the Society
for the Mother Tongue.)
Helsinki: Kotikielen Seura, 1883, 1886, 1897- . quarterly.
The most important periodical for the study of Finnish. Publishes articles, reviews and
a section on current information. The articles have abstracts in English or German.

Onomastics

475 **Finnish onomastics. Namenkunde in Finnland.**
Edited by Heikki Leskinen, Eero Kiviniemi, translated by David
Steadman, Marianne Reukauf, Ingrid Schellbach-Kopra, Eugene
Holman, Elizabeth Pitkänen. Helsinki: Suomalaisen Kirjallisuuden
Seura, 1990. 140p. maps. bibliog. (Studia Fennica. Review of Finnish
Linguistics and Ethnology, 34).
As the preface notes (p. 7), few results of Finnish onomastic research have been
published in foreign languages. The six essays in English and three in German
published here help redress the balance. The emphasis is on place-names (both Finnish
and Swedish) but there is also an essay by Marianne Blomqvist on Swedish family
names in Finland and a description by Eeva Maria Närhi of the Central Onomastic
Archives in Finland.

Dictionaries

Finnish

General

476 **Suomen kielen perussanakirja.** (A fundamental dictionary of the
Finnish language.)
Helsinki: Valtion painatuskeskus; Kotimaisten kielten tutkimuskeskus,
1990-94. 3 vols. (Kotimaisten kielten tutkimuskeskuksen julkaisuja
[Publications of the Research Centre for the Languages of Finland], 55).
The first major monolingual Finnish dictionary since *Nykysuomen sanakirja* (item no.
477), containing almost 100,000 entries, over one-fifth of which are not in

Nykysuomen sanakirja. Covers the vocabulary of contemporary standard Finnish, both written and spoken, but with few literary citations. Clearly presented entries. Information about inflections is included in vol. I. Essential for knowledge of the present-day language.

477 Nykysuomen sanakirja. Lyhentämätön kansanpainos. (Dictionary of modern Finnish. Unabridged popular edition.)
Porvoo, Finland; Helsinki: Werner Söderström, 1988-90. various printings. 8 vols.

Originally published in 1951-61, this standard dictionary of the Finnish language containing some 200,000 entries) remains valuable for its breadth of coverage of the vocabulary and for its literary citations. Volumes 1-3 comprise the dictionary proper, volume 4 is a dictionary of foreign words in Finnish (*vierasperäiset sanat*), volume 5 contains neologisms, slang, abbreviations and foreign place-names, volume 6 is an etymological dictionary, volume 7 a dictionary of synonyms, and volume 8 an etymological dictionary of foreign words.

478 Suomea suomeksi: suomen kielen sanakirja. (Finnish in Finnish: dictionary of the Finnish language.)
Timo Nurmi, Ilkka Rekiaro, Päivi Rekiaro.   Jyväskylä, Finland; Helsinki: Gummerus, 1993. 863p.

A non-specialized general Finnish dictionary with 45,000 entry words. Derived principally from *Nykysuomen sanakirja* (see item no. 477). Helpful for those who do not want or need one of the larger dictionaries. Very small print.

Dialect

479 Suomen murteiden sanakirja. (Dictionary of Finnish dialects.)
Chief editor: Tuomo Tuomi.   Helsinki: Kotimaisten kielten tutkimuskeskus; Valtion painatuskeskus, 1985- . Vol. 1- . maps.

A dictionary of Finnish dialects has been long in planning and preparation and what will eventually be a work of some twenty volumes is appearing at the rate of one volume approximately every three years. Volume 4 (huka-iätös) was published in 1994. The dialect words are entered under the corresponding standard Finnish headword. Numerous examples are provided and the parish of origin is indicated. There is a separately published introduction (1989).

Etymological

480 **Suomen sanojen alkuperä: etymologinen sanakirja.** (The origin of
Finnish words: an etymological dictionary.)
Helsinki: Suomalaisen Kirjallisuuden Seura; Kotimaisten Kielten
Tutkimuskeskus, 1992- . Vol. 1- . bibliog. (Suomalaisen
Kirjallisuuden Seuran toimituksia [Publications of the Finnish
Literature Society], 556. Kotimaisten Kielten Tutkimuskeskuksen
julkaisuja [Publications of the Research Centre for the Languages of
Finland], 62).
An etymological dictionary covering the spoken and literary language as well as some
vocabulary from the older literary language, dialects and folk poetry. Volume I covers
A-K; volume II (1995) L-R; volume III, covering S-Ö, is due for publication in 1999.

Idioms

481 **Naulan kantaan: nykysuomen idiomisanakirja.** (Hitting the nail on
the head: a dictionary of modern Finnish idioms.)
Erkki Kari. Helsinki: Otava, 1993. 232p.
Explanations of some 9,000 idioms in modern Finnish, ranging from formal usage to
slang. In Finnish.

Slang

482 **Nykyslangin sanakirja.** (Dictionary of modern slang.)
Kaarina Karttunen. Porvoo, Finland; Helsinki: Werner Söderström,
1979. 2nd ed. 333p.
A dictionary (in Finnish) of about 6,000 entry words of Finnish slang, from both oral
and literary sources, the latter taken from original Finnish and translated literature of
the 1960s-70s. Particularly useful, therefore, when reading modern Finnish literature.

Frequency

483 **Suomen kielen taajuussanasto. A frequency dictionary of Finnish.**
Pauli Saukkonen, Marjatta Haipus, Antero Niemikorpi, Helena Sulkala.
Porvoo, Finland: Werner Söderström, 1979. 536p.
This general frequency dictionary of Finnish was drawn from an analysis of over
400,000 word occurrences collected in the 1960s. The explanatory introduction is in
English as well as Finnish.

Reverse

484 Suomen kielen käänteissanakirja. Reverse dictionary of modern standard Finnish.
Tuomo Tuomi. Helsinki: Finnish Literature Society, 1980. 2nd ed.
xxx + 546p. (Suomalaisen Kirjallisuuden Seuran toimituksia
[Publications of the Finnish Literature Society], 274).

Invaluable for teachers of Finnish, this reverse dictionary prints out all the headwords in *Nykysuomen sanakirja* (item no. 477) and has its commentary in English and Finnish.

Finnish-English

485 Uusi suomi-englanti suursanakirja. Finnish-English general dictionary.
Raija Hurme, Riitta-Leena Malin, Olli Syväoja. Porvoo, Finland;
Helsinki: Werner Söderström, 1984. 5th ed. xxiv + 1,446p.

Extensive Finnish-English dictionary, with some 160,000 headwords and phrases. The Finnish vocabulary was taken from the then unpublished *Suomen kielen perussanakirja* (see item no. 476) as well as *Nykysuomen sanakirja* (item no. 477) and is therefore quite up-to-date. Intended for Finnish users although it makes a few concessions to the English-language user, for example by translating the abbreviations, but unfortunately not the directions for use. Clear text. Regularly reprinted. The older Finnish-English dictionary by Alanne (item no. 486) remains useful as it often has more examples of usage.

486 Suomalais-englantilainen suursanakirja. Finnish-English general dictionary.
V. S. Alanne. Porvoo, Finland; Helsinki: Werner Söderström, 1979.
3rd ed., reprinted. xxxv + 1,111p.

This older Finnish-English dictionary remains worth consulting because of its size, its many examples of usage and some colloquialisms. It includes a number of features of value to the English-speaking user, e.g. the citation alongside the infinitive of the present tense first-person singular where this is irregular.

487 Suomi-englanti-suomi sanakirja. (Finnish-English-Finnish dictionary.)
Ilkka Rekiaro, Douglas Robinson. Jyväskylä, Finland; Helsinki:
Gummerus, 1995. 2nd rev. and enl. ed., reprinted. 1,460p.

Contains some 60,000 words in all, of Finnish and American English. Intended for Finns, there are no directions for the non-Finnish user. Otherwise this is quite a handy, medium-sized, recent dictionary.

English-Finnish

488   **Englanti-suomi suursanakirja. English-Finnish general dictionary.**
Raija Hurme, Maritta Pesonen, Olli Syväoja.   Porvoo, Finland;
Helsinki: Werner Söderström, 1990. 3rd ed. xx + 1,525p.
A complete revision of a dictionary originally published in 1973. Extensive, wit
some 90,000 headwords. Intended for Finnish users and with the same characteristics
good and bad, as its companion Finnish-English volume (item no. 485). Regularl
reprinted.

489   **Englantilais-suomalainen sanakirja.** (English-Finnish dictionary.)
Aune Tuomikoski, Anna Slöör.   Helsinki: Suomalaisen Kirjallisuuder
Seura, 1973. 6th ed. xiii + 1,100p.
Although old, this dictionary continues to be valuable because of its broad scope an
good examples of usage.

490   **Englanti-suomi opiskelusanakirja.** (English-Finnish study
dictionary.)
Raija Hurme, Maritta Pesonen, Olli Syväoja.   Porvoo, Finland;
Helsinki: Werner Söderström, 1996. 2nd ed. 927p.
Contains some 55,000 entry words, distinguishing between British and America
English. Unusually for a dictionary published in Finland, it has directions for use i
English as well as Finnish.

491   **Englantilais-suomalais-englantilainen yleiskielen käyttösanakirja.
English-Finnish-English general dictionary.**
Heikki Särkkä.   Helsinki: Otava, 1995. 3rd ed. 812p.
Comprises some 20,000 words with an emphasis on contemporary English. Include
directions for English-language users.

American English and American Finnish

492   **Slangi: amerikanenglannin slangisanakirja.** (Slang: dictionary of
American English slang.)
Ilkka Rekiaro.   Porvoo, Finland; Helsinki: Werner Söderström, 1995.
676p.
Includes modern and older slang, comprising some 20,000 entry words. Perhaps
inevitably, some of the American terms appear to lose some of their effect in translation.

493   **Amerikansuomen sanakirja. A dictionary of American Finnish.**
Pertti Virtaranta.   Turku, Finland: Institute of Migration, 1992. 329p.
2 maps. bibliog.
Contains 4,556 different words, mostly from the spoken language recorded during
fieldwork, but with some from the written language, as used in the Finnish of Finns

who emigrated to North America before the 1930s. The summary of the preface and directions for use are in English. There is also an English index.

Specialized dictionaries and glossaries

Administration

494   **Valtioneuvostosanasto. Statsrådsordlistan. Glossary on the Council of State in Finland. Staatsratsglossar. Vocabulaire du Conseil des ministres. Gosudarstvennyi sovet finliandii - slovar'-spravochnik. Vocabulario del Consejo de Ministros.**
      Helsinki: Valtioneuvoston kanslia, 1992. 172p. (Kielipalvelun julkaisusarja ... Publication Series of the Terminology Service).
      This helpful work gives the foreign equivalents for various Finnish ministries and government offices (current and historical) and civil servants' titles, with an explanatory gloss. The languages used are Finnish, Swedish, English, German, French, Russian and Spanish. Provides indexes for each language. Includes a total of 102 terms.

Economics

495   **Taloussanasto: yritys- ja kansantaloutta suomeksi, ruotsiksi, englanniksi, saksaksi ja ranskaksi.** (Glossary of economics: business and the economy; Finnish, Swedish, English, German and French.)
      Helsinki: Taloustieto, 1995. 6th rev. ed. 571p.
      Contains some 3,000 concepts with the Finnish term first, then the equivalents in Swedish, English, German and French, followed by a definition in Finnish. The indexes appear in Swedish, English, German and French.

Electronics

496   **Suomalais-englantilainen elektroniikan sanakirja. Finnish-English dictionary of electronics.**
      Petri Hukki, Urpo Pakarinen.   Ikaalinen, Finland: Hukki & Pakarinen, 1995. 3rd rev. and exp. ed. 380p.
      Over 24,000 words on electronics, widely interpreted. Provides single equivalents, with no explanations.

497 **Englantilais-suomalainen elektroniikan sanakirja. English-Finnish dictionary of electronics.**
Petri Hukki, Urpo Pakarinen.   Ikaalinen, Finland: Hukki & Pakarinen, 1995. 3rd rev. and exp. ed. 584p.
Some 23,000 words, with some explanations in Finnish as well as direct equivalents.

Law

498 **Suomi-englanti-suomi. Lakikielen perussanakirja.** (Finnish-English-Finnish. Basic dictionary of law terminology.)
Jari Eriksson.   Helsinki: Lakimiesliiton kustannus, 1995. x + 412p.
Contains 12,500 entry words relating to law and administration, quite widely interpreted. There are no directions for possible English users but it would nevertheless be helpful to them. Notes differences between English and American usage.

499 **Lakikielen sanakirja. Suomi-englanti.** (Dictionary of legal terminology. Finnish-English.)
Matti Joutsen.   Porvoo, Finland; Helsinki: Werner Söderström, 1995. 2nd rev. and enl. ed. 622p.
Contains over 23,000 entry words, interpreting law widely. Has directions for the user in English as well as Finnish and the expansions of the abbreviations are also in both Finnish and English.

Military

500 **Englanti-suomi-englanti sotilassanasto ja lyhenteet. English-Finnish-English military vocabulary and abbreviations.**
Helsinki: Pääesikunnan koulutusosasto, 1992. 3rd rev. ed. 384p.
An officially-produced, useful up-to-date vocabulary. The abbreviations are only from English to Finnish. There is an appendix giving the English equivalents of the departments and sections of the Finnish Defence Staff and of the headquarters and formations of the defence forces.

Philately

501 **Filatelian sanasto.** (Glossary of philately.)
Helsinki: Suomen Filatelistiliitto, 1989. 2nd, rev. and enl. ed. 188p.
(Suomen Filatelistiliiton julkaisusarjan julkaisu [Publication Series of the Philatelic Federation of Finland], 12).
An excellent illustrated glossary, with German, English and French equivalents of the Finnish terms, and indexes in English, French, Swedish and German. Appendices

138

cover printing methods used for Finnish stamps, cancellations, and names used to describe the symbols used on Finnish stamps.

Social security

502 **Sosiaaliturvan sanasto.** (Social security glossary.)
Helsinki: Huoltaja-säätiö, 1992. 176p.
A structured vocabulary relating to social security, giving the Swedish, English and German equivalents of 162 terms, with an alphabetical section in Finnish (giving equivalents in all languages) and indexes in German, English and Swedish.

Sport

503 **Englanti-suomi-englanti yleisurheilusanasto.** (English-Finnish-English athletics glossary.)
Kari Wauhkonen. Helsinki: [Suomen urheiluliitto], 1993. 2nd ed. 84p.
About 1,200 words in English and 1,000 in Finnish in the field of athletics.

Technical and commercial

504 **Suomi-englanti. Tekniikan ja kaupan sanakirja.** (Finnish-English. Technical and commercial dictionary.)
Jyrki K. Talvitie, Ahti Hytönen. Porvoo, Finland; Helsinki: Werner Söderström, 1995. 4th rev. ed. 1,136p.
Useful because of its size (over 140,000 entry words) but contains no directions in English.

505 **Englanti-suomi. Tekniikan ja kaupan sanakirja.** (English-Finnish technical and commercial dictionary.)
Jyrki K. Talvitie, Ahti Hytönen, Tapani Palavuori, Yrjö Talvitie.
Porvoo, Finland; Helsinki: Werner Söderström, 1995. 11th ed. 956p.
Contains about 200,000 entry words. First published in 1951 and last revised in 1991, this is an important reference work for technical and commercial vocabulary.

Grammars and courses

Grammars

In English

506 Finnish grammar.
Fred Karlsson, translated by Andrew Chesterman.   Porvoo, Finland;
Helsinki: Werner Söderström, 1987. 2nd ed. 222p. bibliog.
'Primarily intended for foreigners wanting to learn the basics of the language. The
book covers the grammatical core; rare forms and constructions have not been
included' (p. 3). A thorough work, clear to follow, and with numerous examples. Also
includes a chapter on colloquial spoken Finnish.

507 Finnish.
Helena Sulkala, Merja Karjalainen.   London; New York: Routledge,
1992. xv + 426p. bibliog. (Descriptive Grammars).
Intended to be a description of Finnish for linguists. Arranged into sections on syntax,
morphology, phonology, ideophones and interjections, and with a lexicon of words
according to 'structured semantic fields' – e.g. kinship, parts of the body – followed
by a short general vocabulary.

In Finnish

508 Suomen kielioppi. (Finnish grammar.)
Aarni Penttilä.   Porvoo, Finland; Helsinki: Werner Söderström, 1963.
2nd rev. ed. 692 + 36p. bibliog.
Old, but still worth study and reference as a large and thorough Finnish grammar.

509 Kieliopas. (Guide to the language.)
Terho Itkonen.   Helsinki: Kirjayhtymä, 1991. 5th ed. 473p. bibliog.
A guide to Finnish usage (in Finnish) with an extensive list of foreign and Finnish
words whose use or spelling require special guidance. Includes examples of the
Finnish proof correction system.

510 Nykysuomen käsikirja. (Handbook of modern Finnish.)
Edited by Osmo Ikola.   Espoo, Finland: Weilin & Göös, 1992.
3rd rev. ed. 398p. bibliog.
Contains a grammar, a list of foreign words in Finnish, a list of place-names with a
guide to their spelling and declension, and an index of subjects and words. In Finnish.

Courses

511 **Mastering Finnish.**
Börje Vähämäki.   New York: Hippocrene Books, 1994. [xiv] + 386p.
2 cassettes. (Hippocrene Master Series).
Aims 'to enable students to acquire practical skills in everyday Finnish necessary to interact with native speakers of Finnish' (p. 3). Contains dialogues (reflecting everyday situations), information (e.g. Finnish has no equivalent of Ms), vocabulary and structural explanations including sound grammar. Also a grammatical appendix and exercises with answers. A useful introduction.

512 **Finnish for foreigners (1, 2 and 3).**
Maija-Hellikki Aaltio.   Helsinki: Otava, 1980-95. 3 vols. (in 5).
This Finnish course, the first versions of which appeared in the 1960s, is regularly reprinted. Volume 1 emphasizes the basics of the spoken language and volume 2 develops the ability to read. Each has a separate volume of exercises. Volume 3 is a reader which offers a good range of texts. Cassettes are sold separately to accompany volumes 1-2.

513 **Finnish: a complete course for beginners.**
Terttu Leney.   London: Hodder & Stoughton, 1993. [iii] + 348p.
cassette. (Teach Yourself Series).
Practical, lively and attractive language course, which also imparts a good deal of information about Finnish life. Contains sensible dialogues but the grammatical rules might be clearer. The work also provides a key to exercises and a Finnish-English vocabulary.

514 **Suomea suomeksi 1-2.** (Finnish in Finnish 1-2.)
Olli Nuutinen.   Helsinki: Suomalaisen Kirjallisuuden Seura, 1994.
2 vols. (Vol. 1: 10th printing; vol. 2: 7th printing). (Suomalaisen Kirjallisuuden Seuran toimituksia [Publications of the Finnish Literature Society], 338).
Designed as a one-year taught course in Finnish, which uses Finnish only. Vocabularies have been produced in numerous languages; see item no. 515 for the English ones. See also *Suomen harjoituksia 1-2* (item no. 516) for exercises designed to accompany the course. Obviously not for self instruction.

515 **Finnish in Finnish. Vocabulary Suomea suomeksi 1-2.**
Olli Nuutinen, vocabulary in English by Michael O'Dell.   Helsinki: Suomalaisen Kirjallisuuden Seura, 1978-90. 2 vols. (Vol. 1: 6th ed.).
Designed to accompany *Suomea suomeksi* (item no. 514). The vocabularies are arranged lesson by lesson, Finnish-English, with a single Finnish word list at the end of each book.

516   **Suomen harjoituksia 1-2.** (Finnish exercises 1-2.)
       Eila Hämäläinen.   Helsinki: Suomalaisen Kirjallisuuden Seura,
       1992-93. reprint. 2 vols. (Suomalaisen Kirjallisuuden Seuran
       toimituksia [Publications of the Finnish Literature Society], 344, 381).
       The exercises are designed to accompany *Suomea suomeksi* (item no.
       514) but can also be used independently. They take the user from phonetic drills through grammar drills and on to dialogues and comprehension passages. Instructions are given for the student in English, German and Swedish, and for the teacher in Finnish.

Study aids

517   **A student's glossary of Finnish: the literary language arranged by
       frequency and alphabet. English-French-German-Hungarian-
       Russian-Swedish.**
       Michael Branch, Antero Niemikorpi, Pauli Saukkonen.   Porvoo,
       Finland: Werner Söderström, 1980. 378p.
       This sturdily produced glossary contains 1,899 words, providing a vocabulary for a basic course in Finnish. The introductory sections discuss the applications of the glossary in the teaching of Finnish and give a brief report on the programming principles involved in the selection of the vocabulary. The glossary in order of frequency is followed by an alphabetical section which includes frequency codes, enabling teachers to assess the level of difficulty of a text. The work can serve as a textbook for teacher and student and as a reference book for the student. It is especially helpful for teaching students to read Finnish, the translations in six languages widening the opportunities of use. A set of paradigms is reproduced at the end of the book.

518   **Finnish into English: an introduction to translation.**
       Andrew Chesterman, Liisa Korpimies, Jackie Lento, Beryl Sandlund,
       Krista Varantola, Philip Binham, Aulis Rantanen.   Helsinki:
       Gaudeamus, 1979. 200p.
       Although intended for students of English in Finland, this book lists various translation difficulties which can affect English students of Finnish.

519   **Handbook of Finnish verbs: 231 Finnish verbs fully conjugated in
       all the tenses. Alphabetically arranged.**
       Eugene Holman.   Helsinki: Suomalaisen Kirjallisuuden Seura, 1984.
       [ii] + vi + 386p. bibliog. (Suomalaisen Kirjallisuuden Seuran
       toimituksia [Publications of the Finnish Literature Society], 408).
       Contains an introduction on the Finnish verb as well as the paradigms.

520 **Kerro Suomesta 5 kielellä. Englanti, ruotsi, saksa, ranska, venäjä.**
(Tell about Finland in five languages. English, Swedish, German,
French, Russian.)
Helsinki: Kansainvälisen Kaupan Koulutuskeskus FINTRA, 1996.
292p. (FINTRA-julkaisu [Finnish Institute for International Trade
Publication], 108).

Published by the Training Centre of the Finnish Institute for International Trade, this book is intended to enable Finns to give foreigners information about their country. It could also be used as a reader by foreigners with a little knowledge of Finnish who want factual information clearly expressed in short sentences together with some lists of vocabulary. Covers basic information, history, the Finns, society, foreign relations, economic life, education and culture, the church, leisure, holidays, cooking and daily questions. Each language section is separate, with English on p. 9-60. Users will have no excuse for not knowing that 'Postboxes are yellow and rectangular' or that 'It is allowed to pick berries and mushrooms in forests'.

Finnish for foreigners (1, 2 and 3).
See item no. 512.

Phrase book

521 **Berlitz Finnish phrase book.**
Oxford: Berlitz, 1993. reprint. 192p. map.

Gives phrases for particular contexts likely to be needed or encountered by the tourist.

Where to study Finnish

522 **Suomea. Finska. Finnish. Suomen kielen ja Suomen kulttuurin
kesäkurssit 1996. Suomen kielen ja kulttuurin opetusta antavat
ulkomaiset yliopistot. Suomen kielen oppikirjoja
ulkomaalaisopetukseen. Sommarkurser i finska språket och
Finlands kultur 1996. Utländska universitet med undervisning i
finska språket och Finlands kultur. Böcker on finska som
främmande språk. Summer courses in Finnish language and
culture 1996. Foreign universities offering instruction in Finnish
language and culture. Books about Finnish as a foreign language.**
Helsinki: Council for Instruction of Finnish for Foreigners, Ministry of
Education, 1995. 54p. bibliog.

This annual work provides details of courses in Finland for the beginner and the more advanced student. Also lists universities outside Finland where Finnish language and culture are taught and gives the names of teachers. Useful list of textbooks.

Swedish

523   **Ordbok över Finlands svenska folkmål.** (Dictionary of Swedish
       dialects in Finland.)
       Helsingfors: Forskningscentralen för de inhemska språken, 1982- .
       Vol. 1- . map. bibliog. (Forskningscentralen för de inhemska språken.
       Skrifter [Research Centre for the Languages of Finland. Publications],
       1).

This important dialect dictionary is being compiled from published and unpublished
source material dating principally from about 1860 onwards. Two of the five volumes
planned have so far appeared. Vol. 1, A-E (completed in 1982) and vol. 2, F-Hu
(completed in 1992), both by Olav Ahlbäck, the latter finished by Peter Slotte.

Lapp

524   **Lappische Grammatik mit Lesestücken.** (Lapp grammar with
       reading passages.)
       Knut Bergsland, translated from the Norwegian by Werner Dontenwill.
       Wiesbaden, Germany: Otto Harrasowitz, 1976. 117p.
       (Veröffentlichungen der Societas Uralo-Altaica [Publications of the
       Uralo-Altaica Society], 11).

Grammar with passages for reading and a Lapp-German vocabulary. An introduction
to the written language of North Lapp. In German.

The Sami culture.
See item no. 198.

Finno-Ugrian languages and peoples.
See item no. 466.

Literature

History and criticism

Histories and dictionaries

525 **Literature of Finland: an outline.**
Kai Laitinen. Helsinki: Otava, 1985. 160p. bibliog.
A brief but expert survey of literature in Finland (in Finnish and Swedish) from folk poetry, through the period of Swedish rule and the crucial developments of the 19th century, to the literary currents of the 1980s. Stresses the wide readership of poetry in Finland and notes the strength of reactions to literature, which is seen as a reflection of the nation's common heritage.

526 **Dictionary of Scandinavian literature.**
Virpi Zuck, editor-in-chief. New York; London: Greenwood Press, 1990. [xv] + 792p. bibliog.
Covers the five Nordic countries as well as Faroese, Lapp (Sami) and Greenland (Inuit) literature. Contains entries for authors and more general articles, such as 'Kalevala and Finnish folklore', by M. A. Branch, and 'Scandinavian literary journals', which includes a section on Finland. Finland is well represented among the literary authors and the biographical articles by such notable critics as Kai Laitinen, George C. Schoolfield and Pekka Tarkka are valuable sources of reference, providing also short bibliographies of works, translations and references to criticism. Finland fares less well in the more general articles such as 'Theater in Scandinavia', while the article on 'Scandinavian studies in North America and Britain' fails to mention Finnish studies in Britain. There is an index of authors and titles. Useful, in spite of some irritating editorial lapses.

527   **A history of Scandinavian literature, 1870-1980.**
Sven H. Rossel, translated by Anne C. Ulmer.   Minneapolis,
Minnesota: University of Minnesota Press, 1982. xi + 492p. bibliog.
(The Nordic Series, 5).

There are sections on Finnish and Finland-Swedish literature throughout this book, together with some separate chapters on the literature of Finland between the World Wars and on developments after the Second World War. The treatment concentrates on individual writers, giving brief characterizations of their development and of their principal works. The bibliography cites mainly general works in English and specific references (usually articles) in English about individual writers.

528   **A history of Finnish literature.**
Jaakko Ahokas.   Bloomington, Indiana: Indiana Research Center for
the Language Sciences, for the American-Scandinavian Foundation,
1973. ix + 568p.

Still to be found on library reference shelves, this is a personal approach to literature both in Finnish and Swedish, describing writers rather than writing, and arranged by period, with notes on individual authors and their works. There is very little on oral tradition. The notes compensate to some extent for the lack of a bibliography.

Criticism

529   **Features of the Finnish play today. Caracterisation de la pièce de
théâtre finlandaise moderne.**
Hilkka Eklund, translated by Philip Binham, Gabriel de Bridiers.
Helsinki: Suomen Näytelmäkirjailijaliitto; Suomen Teatteriliitto;
Työväen Näyttämöiden Liitto, in cooperation with the Finnish Centre
of the ITI, 1989. 27p.

This booklet gives a brief idea of the themes developed by Finnish playwrights in the 1960s-80s. Following up the individual works mentioned will, however, be difficult for the non-reader of Finnish since translations of Finnish drama are rare compared with those of prose and poetry.

530   **More equal than most. Essays on women in Finnish society and
culture.**
Edited by Celia Hawkesworth, Linda Edmondson.   London: School of
Slavonic and East European Studies, University of London, 1992.
vi + 64p. (SSEES Occasional Papers on Gender Issues in Central and
Eastern Europe, 1).

The contents include: 'The position of women in twentieth-century Finland', by Päivi Setälä; 'Language and language use: is Finnish a gender-neutral language?', by Auli Hakulinen; ' "I have a burning need to be alone sometimes": Finnish women writers at the turn of the century', by Eva Buchwald; and 'The message of *Enchanting Beasts* [see item no. 573]: observations on the role of women poets in Finland', by Kirsti Simonsuuri.

531 **A moving river of tears: Russia's experience in Finland.**
Temira Pachmuss.   New York: Peter Lang, 1992. xiii + 289p. bibliog.
(American University Studies. Series XII. Slavic Languages and
Literature, 15).
About the development of Russo-Finnish literary contacts between 1809 and 1940 and
particularly useful on Russian émigré culture in Finland after the Revolution of 1917.
Written from an intensely Russian nationalist viewpoint, lacking familiarity with
Finland, without understanding of Finnish literature and devoid of appreciation of the
intrinsic value of the Finns and Finnish culture, the book unintentionally exemplifies
why Russians can be so disliked by Finns.

532 **Suomen kirjallisuus.** (Finnish literature.)
Helsinki: Suomalaisen Kirjallisuuden Seura & Otava, 1963-70. 8 vols.
bibliog.
Finnish literature of all types is treated thematically as well as chronologically in this
massive and important collective work in Finnish, which is the only full account of its
subject. There is an extensive companion anthology, *Suomen kirjallisuuden antologia*
(Anthology of Finnish literature) (Helsinki: Otava, 1963-75. 8 vols.).

533 **The history of Finnish literary criticism 1828-1918.**
Yrjö Varpio.   Tampere, Finland: Societas Scientiarum Fennica, 1990.
243p. bibliog. (The History of Learning and Science in Finland
1828-1918, 15a).
Looks particularly at the influence of the most significant literary historians, critics
and essayists, both those with academic appointments and those without.

Sananjalka: Suomen kielen seuran vuosikirja. (Yearbook of the Finnish
Language Society.)
See item no. 473.

From folklore to applied arts: aspects of Finnish culture.
See item no. 638.

Finns in literature

534 **The image of the Finn in English and American literature.**
W. R. Mead.   *Neuphilologische Mitteilungen*, vol. 64, pt. 3 (1963),
p. 243-64.
Mead sorts the characters of Finns in English and American fiction into characteristic
types: the characters in occult; heroes in cardboard; prisoners of romance; and figures
of fun. He notes that the Finn was a negative character to writers of fiction until the
present century and shows how Finland has made its greatest impact on the outside
world at times of international and domestic stress.

Literature. History and criticism. Bio-bibliographical dictionaries

535   **Finland and the Finns as stereotypes.**
W. R. Mead. *Neuphilologische Mitteilungen*, vol. 83, no. 1 (1982),
p. 42-52.

Develops item no. 534. Mead concludes that the stereotype of the Finn presented in
the substantially increased volume of English-language fiction touching on Finland
retains the old-established characteristics – with alcoholism never far away – but with
some new features. A disproportionate number of plots deal with the relationship with
Russia.

536   **Raising the wind: the legend of Lapland and Finland wizards in
literature.**
Ernest J. Moyne, edited by Wayne R. Kime.   Newark, [Delaware]:
University of Delaware Press; London; Toronto: Associated University
Presses, 1981. [ix] + 212p. 2 maps. bibliog.

Aims first to trace the beginnings (in the 12th century) and progress of the legend that
Lapps and Finns were able to raise winds and storms and to sell them for money, and
secondly to show how writers, particularly English and American ones, used this
legend for artistic purposes. Good on Finns in literature. Published posthumously.

Bio-bibliographical dictionaries

537   **Suomen kirjailijat 1809-1916. Pienoiselämäkerrat.
Teosbibliografiat. Tutkimusviitteet. Finlands författare.
Kortbiografier. Verkförteckningar. Litteraturhänvisningar.
Writers in Finland. Concise biographies. Bibliographies. Research
references.**
Edited by Maija Hirvonen.   Helsinki: Suomalaisen Kirjallisuuden
Seura; Helsingfors: Svenska litteratursällskapet i Finland, 1993. 954p.
bibliog. (Suomalaisen Kirjallisuuden Seuran toimituksia [Publications
of the Finnish Literature Society], 570).

The last to be published of an essential series of bio-bibliographical dictionaries of
Finnish and Finland-Swedish literary authors (see also item nos. 538-39). The value of
the series is enhanced by the coverage of criticism as well as works. This volume
covers writers who began to publish between 1809 and 1916 together with a few who
began between 1800 and 1808. Includes also authors of Finnish origin writing in
Sweden and Russia. Contains an extremely helpful guide in English to the use of the
work which is applicable to all volumes of the series. Index of titles.

538 **Suomen kirjailijat 1917-1944. Pienoiselämäkerrat.**
Teosbibliografiat. Tutkimusviitteet. Finlands författare.
Kortbiografier. Verkförteckningar. Litteraturhänvisningar.
Writers in Finland. Concise biographies. Bibliographies. Research
references.
Editor-in-chief Hannu Launonen.   Helsinki: Suomalaisen
Kirjallisuuden Seura, 1981. 616p. bibliog. (Suomalaisen Kirjallisuuden
Seuran toimituksia [Publications of the Finnish Literature Society],
365).

An essential reference work about writers who began to publish between 1917 and
1944. The preface in English sets out the editorial principles. Includes an index of
titles. See also item nos. 537 and 539.

539 **Suomen kirjailijat 1945-1980. Pienoiselämäkerrat.**
Teosbibliografiat. Tutkimusviitteet. Finlands författare.
Kortbiografier. Verkförteckningar. Litteraturhänvisningar.
Writers in Finland. Concise biographies. Bibliographies. Research
references.
Edited by Maija Hirvonen, Hannu Launonen, Anna Nybondas, Inger
Bäcksbacka.   Helsinki: Suomalaisen Kirjallisuuden Seura, 1985.
873p. bibliog. (Suomalaisen Kirjallisuuden Seuran toimituksia
[Publications of the Finnish Literature Society], 402).

Invaluable information on modern Finnish and Finland-Swedish writers who began to
publish between 1945 and 1980, expanding and replacing the volume for 1945-70,
which was published in 1977. The preface is given in English as well as Finnish and
Swedish. Includes an index of titles. See also item nos. 537-38.

Periodicals

540 **Books from Finland.**
Helsinki: Helsinki University Library, 1967- . quarterly.

Originally published by the Publishers' Association of Finland, *Books from Finland*
changed completely in style and content with its change of publisher in 1976. It now
contains articles about Finnish literature and translations of creative writing as well as
reviews and a selective, annotated bibliography of new publications. *Books from
Finland* is the only periodical about Finnish literature in an international language and
as such is of considerable value both to those interested in that literature and in
Finnish publishing, and also to librarians concerned with the selection of Finnish
books.

541 **Parnasso.**
Helsinki: Yhtyneet Kuvalehdet, 1951- . eight issues per year.

Literary periodical in Finnish, containing creative prose and poetry in the original and
in translation as well as articles on literature and reviews of books, films and plays.

Oral tradition; *Kalevala*

Collections

542 **Finnish folk poetry – epic: an anthology in Finnish and English.**
Compiled by Matti Kuusi, Keith Bosley, Michael Branch. Helsinki:
Suomalaisen Kirjallisuuden Seura, 1977. 607p. map. bibliog.
(Publications of the Finnish Literature Society, 329).

Finnish oral tradition, particularly folk poetry, has immense significance in Finnish
literature. This collection of epic folk poetry, which is thematically arranged, gives a
selection of poems in Finnish and English. The extensive introduction and other
critical apparatus are in English. See also *A trail for singers* (item no. 544).

543 **The great bear: a thematic anthology of oral poetry in the
Finno-Ugrian languages.**
Lauri Honko, Senni Timonen, Michael Branch, poems translated by
Keith Bosley. Helsinki: Finnish Literature Society, 1993. 787p. map.
bibliog. (Finnish Literature Society Editions, 533).

Distinguished for its thematic approach, its scholarship and the quality of its
translations, this anthology sets a standard in its field. Finnish oral poetry forms only a
small proportion of the 450 poems in the anthology but the book forms an excellent
introduction to it, providing authoritative guidance on the Finno-Ugrian peoples and
on oral poetry generally. The poems (originals are given as well as English
translations) are grouped under such themes as the cosmos, hunting, festivities, love
and death, each theme with its own introduction and each poem with its own
commentary.

544 **A trail for singers. Finnish folk poetry: epic.**
Edited by Matti Kuusi, translated by Keith Bosley. Helsinki: Finnish
Literature Society, 1995. 309p. map. bibliog. (Publications of the
Finnish Literature Society, 601).

Derived from *Finnish folk poetry: epic* (item no. 542), this handy paperback provides
English translations of 148 Finnish oral poems, together with an introduction, name
index, motif index, *Kalevala* and *Kanteletar* concordance, and source, collection,
collection locality and collector indexes.

545 **Arvoitukset. Finnish riddles.**
Edited by Leea Virtanen, Annikki Kaivola-Bregenhøj, Aarre Nyman.
Helsinki: Suomalaisen Kirjallisuuden Seura, 1977. 287p. map. bibliog.
(Suomalaisen Kirjallisuuden Seuran toimituksia [Publications of the
Finnish Literature Society], 329).

An anthology of 1,248 true riddles known to Finnish tradition, taken from the Folklore
Archives of the Finnish Literature Society. Editorial principles and introductory
chapters are in English as well as Finnish. Also provides translations of the riddles and
an index of answers (in English).

546   **Finnish proverbs.**
Translated by Inkeri Väänänen-Jensen, calligraphy and illustrations by
Esther Feske.   Iowa City, Iowa: Penfield Press, 1990. [ix] + 51p.
A small selection of the many proverbs of the Finns, arranged in sections on such
topics as the 'Finnish spirit', 'Words of wisdom', 'Poverty and Plenty', and 'Nature
and the seasons', from which comes the appealing 'During the summer you don't have
time, and in winter it's too cold'.

547   **The maiden who rose from the sea and other Finnish folktales.**
Edited and translated by Helena Henderson, introduction by Pirkko-
Liisa Rausmaa.   Enfield Lock, England: Hisarlik Press, 1992.
xix + 172p.
These translations of fifty varied tales provide a good introduction to the oral tradition of
Finnish tales. Includes indexes of 'Narrators and Collectors', 'Tale Types', and 'Motifs'.

Criticism

548   **The narrative world of Finnish fairy tales: structure, agency, and
evaluation in Southwest Finnish folk tales.**
Satu Apo.   Helsinki: Academia Scientiarum Fennica, 1995. 322p.
bibliog. (FF Communications, 256).
A translation of a doctoral thesis which deals with methodological and empirical
questions in the little-studied field of Finnish fairy tales.

549   **Finnish folklore research 1828-1918.**
Jouko Hautala.   Helsinki: Societas Scientiarum Fennica, 1969. 197p.
map. bibliog. (The History of Learning and Science in Finland
1828-1918, 12).
A history of research into Finnish folklore by a leading authority. Includes an
extensive list of references.

550   **Mind and form in folklore: selected articles.**
Matti Kuusi, edited by Henni Ilomäki.   Helsinki: Suomalaisen
Kirjallisuuden Seura, 1994. 199p. 2 maps. bibliog. (Studia Fennica.
Folkloristica, 3).
A collection of articles by a leading Finnish folklorist, published in his honour. The
articles concentrate on *Kalevala* poetry and on proverbs.

551   **Folklore and nationalism in modern Finland.**
William A. Wilson.   Bloomington, Indiana: Indiana University Press,
1976. xii + 272p. 3 maps. bibliog.
An attempt to explain the influence of folklore on Finnish nationalism and its practical
consequences for Finnish politics.

Literature. Oral tradition; *Kalevala. Kalevala.* Texts

From folklore to applied arts: aspects of Finnish culture.
See item no. 638.

Kaunokirjallisuutemme käännöksiä: bibliografinen luettelo suomenkielisen kaunokirjallisuuden käännöksistä. Livres finnois en traduction: romans, nouvelles, poésies, pièces de théâtre. Guide bibliographique. (Finnish literature in translation: a bibliographical list of translations of Finnish-language literature: novels, short stories, poetry, plays. Bibliographical guide.)
See item no. 797.

Kalevala

Texts

552 **The Kalevala.**
An epic poem after oral tradition by Elias Lönnrot, translated from the Finnish with an introduction and notes by Keith Bosley.   Oxford; New York: Oxford University Press, 1989. lvi + 679p. map. (World's Classics).

Elias Lönnrot (1802-84) compiled *Kalevala* from oral poetry which he had recorded in north-east Finland and Russian Karelia. The first edition (the 'Old' *Kalevala*) was published in 1835 (see item no. 556) and the longer, definitive ('New') edition in 1849 (see also item nos. 553-55). This became known as the Finnish national epic, a symbol of Finnish language and culture, inspiring the nationalist movement in Finland and providing an impulse for much music, art, architecture and design as well as literature. Lönnrot worked as a district doctor but also devoted himself to the collection of oral poetry and literary work. A small number of *Kalevala* poems, the 'Proto-*Kalevala*', compiled originally in 1833, was published only in 1928 (see item no. 556). The poet Keith Bosley has provided a powerful modern translation of *Kalevala*.

553 **Kalevala: the land of the heroes.**
Translated by W. F. Kirby, introduced by M. A. Branch.   London; Dover, New Hampshire: Athlone Press, 1985. xxxv + 667p. map. bibliog.

This translation of the epic was originally published in Everyman's Library in 1907. The new introduction 'aims to throw some light on the nature and significance of Finnish oral poetry, and to show how the poems of a dying tradition were transformed into a work of literature that was to become a foundation stone of a Finnish national culture and identity'. There is a helpful guide to further reading in English, German and French.

554 **The Kalevala: epic of the Finnish people.**
Translated by Eino Friberg, edited and introduced by George C. Schoolfield, illustrated by Björn Landström.   Helsinki: Otava, 1988. 408p. bibliog.

'Perhaps a willingness to take chances, to be outrageously colloquial, is the most captivating aspect of Friberg's *Kalevala*' (Schoolfield, p. 35). Eino Friberg is an

152

American of Finnish origin, a poet and playwright. There is some introductory material, notes and a glossary.

555 The *Kalevala*, or poems of the Kalevala district.
Compiled by Elias Lönnrot, prose translation with foreword and appendices by Francis Peabody Magoun, Jr.   Cambridge, Massachusetts: Harvard University Press, 1963. Reprinted, 1970. xxiv + 413p. map. bibliog.

In addition to the translation itself, this volume includes appendices on Elias Lönnrot (1802-84), the original collector and creator of *Kalevala*, and translations of his prefaces, as well as appendices on the origin and influence of *Kalevala*, with the mention of various bibliographical references.

556 The *Old Kalevala* and certain antecedents.
Compiled by Elias Lönnrot, prose translations with foreword and appendices by Francis Peabody Magoun, Jr.   Cambridge, Massachusetts: Harvard University Press, 1969. xx + 312p. map.

This is a translation of *Kalevala* as printed by Lönnrot in 1835 (as distinct from the 'New' 1849 version). It includes a glossary of proper names and concordances linking the Old and New *Kalevala*, and the Proto-*Kalevala* of 1834 with the Old *Kalevala*. Important as a means of finding out about the Old *Kalevala* (see also item no. 552).

Criticism

557 The invention of a national epic.
Michael Branch.   In: *The uses of tradition: a comparative enquiry into the nature, uses and functions of oral poetry in the Balkans, the Baltic, and Africa.*   Edited by Michael Branch, Celia Hawkesworth. London: School of Slavonic and East European Studies, University of London; Helsinki: Finnish Literature Society, 1994, p. 194-211.

Considers the genesis of the two editions of *Kalevala* from the point of view of 'invented tradition'. Argues that *Kalevala* is a typical example of the cultural typology of 19th-century national movements.

558 Finnish folk poetry and the *Kalevala*.
Thomas A. DuBois.   New York; London: Garland, 1995. xiv + 328p. map. bibliog. (Publications of the American Folklore Society, New Series. New Perspectives in Folklore, 1. Garland Reference Library of the Humanities, 1895).

'The goal of this study ... is to read in the *Kalevala*, its source poetry, and the folk poetry which followed it, the signs of an aesthetic confrontation, one in which the traditional and aesthetic system of Baltic-Finnic singers became refigured according to literary standards current among European Romanticists ... I hope to sketch the world in which singers and authors lived, the worlds which shaped their songs' (p. 2-3).

559   **Hyperkalevala.**
Helsinki: Edita, 1996. CD-ROM + 16p.
An academically-sound collection of material on CD-ROM centred on *Kalevala* (and giving its complete text) as well as explanatory and critical apparatus. Also about Finnish mythology, early culture, and the reflection of *Kalevala* in modern Finnish culture. Includes text, sound, pictures and films.

560   **Kalevala 1835-1985: the national epic of Finland.**
Helsinki: Helsinki University Library, 1985. i + 82p. map. bibliog.
Edited by *Books from Finland* (see item no. 540) to mark the 150th anniversary of *Kalevala*'s first edition, this is a valuable introduction to the subject. Contributions include: Michael Branch, 'Kalevala: from myth to symbol'; Lauri Honko, 'The Kalevala process'; Senni Timonen, 'Lönnrot and his singers'; Robert Austerlitz, 'The poetics of the Kalevala'; and Kai Laitinen, 'The Kalevala and Finnish literature'. Also includes some of Keith Bosley's translations and essays by John Boulton Smith on 'Kalevala in Finnish art' and Robert Layton on 'The Kalevala and music'. Fine illustrations.

561   **Kalevala mythology.**
Juha Y. Pentikäinen, translated and edited by Ritva Poom.
Bloomington, Indiana: Indiana University Press, 1989. xix + 265p.
map. bibliog. (Folklore Studies in Translation).
A wide-ranging study of the origins, worldview and process involved in the creation by Elias Lönnrot of *Kalevala*, the Finnish national epic. The book's strength lies in its interdisciplinary character, with attention to comparative religion, anthropology, psychology, mythology and folkloristics. *Kalevala*'s roots are seen in shamanic poetry.

562   **Religion, myth and folklore in the world's epics: the Kalevala and its predecessors.**
Edited by Lauri Honko.   Berlin; New York: Mouton de Gruyter, 1990.
xi + 587p. bibliog. (Religion and Society, 30).
The contributors to this book range widely over epics from different times and different continents in a comparative approach. There is much on *Kalevala* in relation to epic tradition, on its interpretation, and on its reception and impact on the arts. 'Lönnrot's epic is, it seems, destined to totter like a tightrope walker between folk epic and literary epic' (Lauri Honko, p. 24). That in no way diminishes its impact or its continuing scholarly interest.

563   **Songs beyond the Kalevala: transformations of oral poetry.**
Edited by Anna-Leena Siikala, Sinikka Vakimo.   Helsinki:
Suomalaisen Kirjallisuuden Seura, 1994. 399p. map. bibliog. (Studia Fennica. Folkloristica, 2).
A collection of specialist articles on *Kalevala* metre, the reproduction, performance and variation of the 'runes', the mythical themes of the poems, their ritual associations, and 'the female perspective'.

564 **The Kalevala abroad: translations and foreign-language adaptations of the Kalevala.**
Compiled by Rauni Puranen. Helsinki: Suomalaisen Kirjallisuuden Seura, 1985. 48p.
'The list, in chronological order according to the year of publication of the first edition, consists of translations and foreign-language adaptations of the Kalevala that have appeared as independent works. An index of languages is given on p. 45' (p. 5). English is well represented among the 118 entries.

The Kalevala, Sallinen and 'Kullervo'.
See item no. 720.

Kanteletar

565 **The Kanteletar. Lyrics and ballads after oral tradition.**
Elias Lönnrot, selected and translated from the Finnish with an introduction and notes by Keith Bosley. Oxford; New York: Oxford University Press, 1992. xxxiv + 189p. (World's Classics).
This selection is the first from the *Kanteletar* (an anthology of folk poetry, originally published in 1840-41) to appear in English outside Finland.

Anthologies

General anthologies

566 **On the border: new writing from Finland.**
Edited by Hildi Hawkins, Soila Lehtonen. Manchester, England: Carcanet, 1995. xi + 164p.
An anthology of modern prose and some poetry, mostly from the late 1980s and 1990s. The selection reflects some of the new forms of expression and 'journeys of the imagination' which preoccupy Finnish writers at the present time. Twenty-four writers are represented and six translators. The pieces chosen were originally published in *Books from Finland* (see item no. 540) and mark not only the twentieth anniversary of its present form but also Finland's accession to the European Union.

567 **A way to measure time: contemporary Finnish literature.**
Edited by Bo Carpelan, Veijo Meri, Matti Suurpää. Helsinki: Finnish Literature Society, 1992. 435p.
An important anthology of post-Second World War Finnish writing, both poetry and prose, including a few extracts from novels, but no drama. Eighty-six writers are

represented. Pieces are mostly grouped according to themes, such as 'Childhood', 'Home', 'War' and 'Intimacy'.

568 **Territorial song: contemporary writing from Finland.**
Selected and translated by Herbert Lomas. London: Magazine Editions, 1981. xx + 157p.

Fourteen writers are represented, with more poetry than prose (short stories). Provides a good introduction and short notes on the authors.

569 **Snow in May: an anthology of Finnish writing 1945-1972.**
Edited by Richard Dauenhauer, Philip Binham. Rutherford, New Jersey: Fairleigh Dickinson University Press; London: Associated University Presses, 1978. 389p. bibliog.

The first major anthology of modern Finnish literature in English. Nine introductory essays – including an important contribution by Professor Kai Laitinen – precede sections on poetry, prose and drama. Postwar Finnish and Swedish writers are represented and there is an appendix of short biographies of those included as well as a short bibliography. The selection of material has been criticized as unbalanced and some of the translations have been faulted but this remains a notable and accessible collection.

570 **Voices from Finland: an anthology of Finland's verse and prose in English, Finnish and Swedish.**
Edited by Elli Tompuri. Helsinki: Sanoma, 1947. 296p.

Compiled with the aims of introducing English-speaking readers to the literature of Finland and of recalling it to Finns abroad. Poetry is reproduced in the original as well as in translation; prose in translation only. There are sections on *Kalevala* and *Kanteletar* (an anthology of folk poetry also produced by Lönnrot). Finnish writers in Finnish and Swedish are represented, including a selection of what were then recent works in addition to older poems and a selection of modern poetry and prose. There is a historical introduction. The anthology is still worth reading.

Poetry

General

571 **Contemporary Finnish poetry.**
Edited and translated by Herbert Lomas. Newcastle upon Tyne, England: Bloodaxe Books, 1991. 296p.

'Finnish poetry is a popular poetry ... its appeal is universal ... It is very spare' (Lomas, p. 9). Twenty-one Finnish-language poets are represented in this model anthology and their contributions to Finnish poetry are described and analysed in the extensive introduction and in biographical notes. The poets are: Risto Ahti, Tuomas Anhava, Paavo Haavikko, Pentti Holappa, Väinö Kirstinä, Eila Kivikk'aho, Kirsi Kunnas, Jarkko Laine, Eeva-Liisa Manner, Arto Melleri, Aila Meriluoto, Hannu Mäkelä, Lassi Nummi, Mirkka Rekola, Pentti Saarikoski, Pentti Saaritsa, Satu Salminiitty, Eira Stenberg, Ilpo Tiihonen, Sirkka Turkka and Caj Westerberg.

572 **Salt of pleasure: twentieth-century Finnish poetry.**
Translated by Aili Jarvenpa, with an introduction by K. Börje
Vähämäki. St Paul, Minnesota: New Rivers Press, 1983. 239p.
bibliog.

Provides translations of works by twenty-six Finnish poets, arranged chronologically
by year of their birth, from Eino Leino to Jukka Vieno, together with brief notes on
each poet and a longer general introduction.

Poetry by women

573 **Enchanting beasts: an anthology of modern women poets of
Finland.**
Edited and translated by Kirsti Simonsuuri. London; Boston,
Massachusetts: Forest Books, 1990. xiv + 126p.

Short introduction by the editor and brief personal prefaces by the poets themselves.
The poets – all notable – are: Marja-Liisa Vartio, Eeva-Liisa Manner, Mirkka Rekola,
Sirkka Turkka, Satu Marttila, Eira Stenberg, Kirsti Simonsuuri, Tua Forsström, Arja
Tiainen, Aune Hänninen and Annukka Peura.

574 **Thank you for these illusions. Poems by Finnish women writers.**
Edited and translated by Anne Fried. Porvoo, Finland; Helsinki:
Werner Söderström, 1981. 154p. bibliog.

The modern poets in question are Sirkka Selja, Eila Kivikk'aho, Helvi Juvonen,
Mirkka Rekola and Eila Pennanen. There is a short introduction.

Short stories

575 **From Baltic shores: short stories.**
Selected and edited by Christopher Moseley. Norwich, England:
Norvik Press, 1994. 264p.

An anthology of contemporary writing from Denmark, Estonia, Finland, Latvia,
Lithuania and Sweden. Four short stories from Finland are included, their authors
being Orvokki Autio, Bo Carpelan, Rosa Liksom and Eeva Tikka.

576 **Finnish short stories.**
Translated by Inkeri Väänänen-Jensen with K. Börje Vähämäki. Iowa
City, Iowa: Penfield Press, 1991. vii + 238p. bibliog.

First published in 1982, this book contains translations of thirty-two short stories from
nineteen Finnish (deliberately excluding Finland Swedish) writers, ranging over the
period 1859-1973 and arranged chronologically. Includes work by Aleksis Kivi,
Juhani Aho, Veijo Meri, Hannu Salama and Timo Mukka. Good notes on the authors.

Plays

577 **Modern Nordic plays: Finland.**
New York: Twayne, 1973. 304p. (Library of Scandinavian Literature, 17).
Reproduces four modern plays, with an introduction by Professor Kai Laitinen. The plays are: *The superintendent* by Paavo Haavikko, translated by Philip Binham; *Eva Maria* by V. V. Järner, translated by Dympna Connolly (the only one of the collection originally in Swedish); *Snow in May* by Eeva-Liisa Manner, translated by Philip Binham; and *Private Jokinen's marriage leave* by Veijo Meri, translated by J. R. Pitkin.

Finland-Swedish writing

578 **Swedish Book Review, 1992. Supplement. New Finland-Swedish writing.**
Guest editor: Tuva Korsström. Lampeter, Wales: Swedish Book Review, 1992. 112p.
An anthology, in English translation, of modern Finland-Swedish poetry and prose, together with several critical articles, mostly on recent literature, but also including some on modernism, notably on Edith Södergran. The mostly young writers represented are: Tua Forsström, Michel Ekman, Agneta Enckell, Tomas Mikael Bäck, Henrika Ringbom, Gungerd Wikholm, Eva-Stina Byggmäster, Anders Hed, Pia Ingström, Ulla-Lena Lundberg, Lars Sund, Pirkko Lindberg, Thomas Wulff, Trygve Söderling, Kjell Lindblad, Monika Fagerholm, Kjell Westö, Tuva Korsström and Oscar Parland.

579 **Swedish Book Review, no. 1, 1989. Finland-Swedish issue.**
Guest editor: George C. Schoolfield. Lampeter, Wales: Swedish Book Review, 1989. 116p.
An anthology, in English translation, of modern Finland-Swedish prose and poetry, together with some essays of criticism and evaluation. The authors represented are: Runar Schildt, Mirjam Tuominen, Solveig von Schoultz, Marianne Alopaeus, Bo Carpelan, Lars Huldén, Claes Andersson, Gösta Ågren, Gurli Lindén, Agneta Ara, Tua Forsström, Bodil Lindfors, Märta Tikkanen, Johan Bargum and Christer Kihlman. There are short biographical notes on each author.

580 **Ice around our lips: Finland-Swedish poetry.**
Translated and edited by David McDuff. Newcastle upon Tyne, England: Bloodaxe Books, 1989. 224p.
Extensive and helpful introduction to the work of ten poets who represent the development of the Finland-Swedish poetic tradition from the end of the 19th century to the 1980s. The poets are: Bertel Gripenberg, Arvid Mörne, Elmer Diktonius, Edith Södergran, Gunnar Björling, Rabbe Enckell, Solveig von Schoultz, Bo Carpelan, Claes Andersson and Gösta Ågren.

581 **Swedo-Finnish stories.**
Translated from the Swedish with an introduction by George C.
Schoolfield. New York: Twayne & the American-Scandinavian
Foundation, 1974. [viii] + 338p. (Library of Scandinavian Literature,
27).
A varied selection of stories from writers ranging (chronologically) from Sara
Wacklin to Johan Bargum. There is a general introduction on Swedish-language
literature in Finland and on the short story as well as notes on each author represented.

Individual authors

582 **A valley in the midst of violence: selected poems.**
Gösta Ågren, translated by David McDuff. Newcastle upon Tyne,
England: Bloodaxe Books, 1992. 110p.
Ågren (b. 1936), who writes in Swedish, 'has developed an intellectually austere and
laconic form of aphorism-lyric' (McDuff, p. 11).

583 **Sanoi Minna Canth.** (Minna Canth said.) **Pioneer reformer. Otteita
Minna Canthin teoksista ja kirjeistä. Extracts from Minna Canth's
works and letters.**
Edited by Ritva Heikkilä, English translation by Paul Sjöblom.
Porvoo, Finland; Helsinki: Werner Söderström, 1987. 281p. bibliog.
Minna Canth (1844-97) was a playwright (still performed), radical and feminist. This
book provides extracts (in Finnish and in English translation) which illustrate her style
and opinions.

584 **Axel: a novel.**
Bo Carpelan, translated by David McDuff. London: Paladin, 1991.
374p.
A fictional diary of the author's great uncle, Baron Axel Carpelan (1858-1919), a
friend of Sibelius. Bo Carpelan, a leading writer in Swedish, in poetry and prose, was
born in 1926.

585 **Homecoming.**
Bo Carpelan, translated from Finland-Swedish by David McDuff.
Manchester, England: Carcanet, 1993. 143p.
Three collections of poems, originally published in 1961, 1969 and 1989, showing
Carpelan's development as a poet.

586 **Elmer Diktonius.**
George C. Schoolfield.   Westport, Connecticut; London: Greenwood
Press, 1985. xvii + 243p. bibliog. (Contributions to the Study of World
Literature, 10).
A thorough assessment of Elmer Diktonius (1896-1967), whose poems (in Swedish)
'place him in the forefront of literary expressionism' and whose life 'has an unusual
drama, because of his ambiguous involvement with the politics of the left, his
hesitation between internationalism and a deep Finnish patriotism, and his somehow
unrequited passion for music' (p. vii).

587 **Snow leopard.**
Tua Forsström, translated by David McDuff.   Newcastle upon Tyne,
England: Bloodaxe Books, 1990. 55p.
Translation of the sixth collection of poems by an acclaimed Finland-Swedish poet
who was born in 1947.

588 **Selected poems.**
Paavo Haavikko, translated from the Finnish by Anselm Hollo.
Manchester, England: Carcanet, 1991. [ix] + 194p.
Haavikko (b. 1931) is a major Finnish poet and this is the first collection of his work
in English translation.

589 **The chain dance: selected poems.**
Lars Huldén, translated and with an introduction by George C.
Schoolfield.   Columbia, South Carolina: Camden House, 1991.
xiii + 231p. bibliog.
Lars Huldén (born 1926) is 'a central figure in Finland's Swedish culture' (p. 2), the
accessibility of whose verse, here presented in parallel Swedish text and English
translation, with a short introduction, 'can be misleading' (p. 1).

590 **Tale of the forest folk.**
Veikko Huovinen, photographs by Hannu Hautala, translated from the
Finnish by Tim Steffa, with Laura Mänki [and others].   Helsinki:
Otava, 1994. 2nd ed., reprint. 159p.
Prize-winning story, by a writer (born 1927) who trained as a forester, about the
changes wrought in a Finnish forest over many years, from the time of a major forest
fire, through regeneration, to marking trees for felling. The photographs are an
important and beautiful accompaniment to the text.

591 **My brother Sebastian.**
Annika Idström, translated from the Swedish by Joan Tate.   London;
Boston, Massachusetts: Forest Books, 1991. [v] + 130p. (UNESCO
Collection of Representative Works. European Series).
Novel about a lonely boy and his response to cruelty. Idström was born in 1947.

592   **Tove Jansson.**
W. Glyn Jones.   Boston, Massachusetts: Twayne, 1984. [xii] + 177p.
bibliog. (Twayne's World Authors Series, 716).
Though best known for her Moomin books for children and for her drawings, Tove
Jansson (born 1914) is more than just a children's writer and artist. This study
concentrates on her prose works, including the Moomin books, which are often more
subtle than they appear, and considers, too, her studies of old age and the changes that
affect people as they age.

593   **Moominland midwinter.**
Tove Jansson, translated by Thomas Warburton.   London: Black,
1994. 170p.
Included as representative of the numerous and charming Moomin books, which have
delighted adults as well as children, and which made Tove Jansson's name as a writer
and illustrator.

594   **The bride of life.**
Eeva Joenpelto, translated from the Finnish Elämän rouva, rouva Glad,
by Ritva Koivu.   New Paltz, New York: FATA, 1995. [iv] + iii +
376p.
This is a psychological novel about a businesswoman. Eeva Joenpelto (born 1921) is a
prominent representative of modern Finnish prose writing.

595   **The maiden who walks upon the water.**
Eeva Joenpelto, translated by Therese Allen Nelson.   Porvoo, Finland;
Helsinki: Werner Söderström, 1991. 460p.
This was Joenpelto's first work to be translated into English.

596   **Three novels.**
Aino Kallas, translated from the Finnish by Alex Matson.   Helsinki:
Otava, 1974. 219p.
Aino Kallas (1878-1956) wrote about Estonia in many of her works. This collection
comprises three of her best-known novels: *Barbara von Tisenhusen*; *The Rector of
Reigi*; and *The wolf's bride*.

597   **Sweet prince: a novel.**
Christer Kihlman, translated by Joan Tate.   London: Peter Owen,
1983. 232p. (UNESCO Collection of Representative Works. European
Series).
Christer Kihlman (b. 1930) is a major writer in Swedish whose treatment of Finnish-
Swedish life has a universal quality. *Sweet prince* (*Dyre prins*) was originally
published in 1975.

598 Tamara.
Eeva Kilpi, translated from the Finnish by Philip Binham. New York: Delacorte Press/Seymour Lawrence, 1978. 233p. (A Merloyd Lawrence Book).

A story of a woman's love and loves, originally published in 1972 by a leading modern woman writer (born 1928).

599 Heath cobblers (Nummisuutarit) and Kullervo.
Aleksis Kivi, translated by Douglas Robinson. St Cloud, Minnesota: North Star Press of St Cloud, 1993. xix + 216p.

Translations of two plays by the influential writer Aleksis Kivi.

600 Odes.
Aleksis Kivi, selected and translated with an introduction by Keith Bosley. Helsinki: Finnish Literature Society, 1994. 80p. (Finnish Literature Society Editions, 611).

The first translation into English of a selection of poems (principally lyrics) by the writer Aleksis Kivi (1834-72), well known as the author of the first Finnish novel, *Seven brothers*.

601 Seven brothers: a novel.
Aleksis Kivi, translated by Richard A. Impola. New Paltz, New York: Finnish American Translators Association, 1991. vi + 345p.

Aleksis Kivi's *Seven brothers* was first published in 1870; it was the first Finnish novel, and remains a classic, widely read and admired. This is a new translation, with a more modern, colloquial style than Matson's (item no. 602).

602 Seven brothers: a novel.
Aleksis Kivi, translated from the Finnish by Alex Matson, translation of 3rd edition revised by Irma Rantavaara. Helsinki: Tammi, 1973. 3rd ed. 342p.

Irma Rantavaara also contributed a short foreword about the book which for the non-Finnish readers is characterized as 'a key to the Finnish national character', by 'Finland's best-known author', Aleksis Kivi (1834-72).

603 Aukeavat sormenpäiden silmät. The eyes of the fingertips are opening.
Leena Krohn, photographs by Marja Pirilä, translated by Herbert Lomas. Helsinki: Musta Taide, 1993. 77p.

A mingling of poems (in Finnish with English translations) and photographs. Leena Krohn (born 1947) is the author of prose as well as poetry and has won the major Finnish literary award, the Finlandia Prize.

604 **Doña Quixote and other citizens. Gold of Ophir.**
Leena Krohn, translated from the Finnish by Hildi Hawkins.
Manchester, England: Carcanet, 1995. 226p.
Reproduces short stories, including *Doña Quixote*, the original of which was published in 1983. Leena Krohn, a prize-winning author, was born in 1947.

605 **Whitsongs.**
Eino Leino, translated from the Finnish by Keith Bosley, introduction
by Michael Branch. London: Menard Press, 1978. 79p.
An important introduction precedes a powerful translation of what is generally held to be Leino's poetic masterpiece, originally published in 1903.

606 **One night stands.**
Rosa Liksom, translated by Anselm Hollo. London; New York:
Serpent's Tail, 1993. [v] + 120p.
Short stories by a pseudonymous modern 'post punk' writer and artist (b. 1958).

607 **The unknown soldier.**
Väinö Linna. Porvoo, Finland: Werner Söderström, 1986. reprint.
xiv + 310p.
An immensely successful novel (first published in 1954) about a group of soldiers in the Continuation War of 1941-44. This translation published in Finland is a slight improvement on that published in London by Collins and in New York by Putnam in 1957.

608 **The song of the blood-red flower.**
Johannes Linnankoski. London: Gyldendal, 1920. [vi] + 285p.
The original, published in 1905, is a major prose work of the neo-romantic period, combining Shavian radicalism with Beardsley-like surrealism.

609 **Fog horses.**
Eeva-Liisa Manner, translated by Ritva Poom. Merrick, New York:
Cross-Cultural Communications, 1986. 40p. (Cross-Cultural Review
Chapbook, 18).
Contains the original Finnish and an English translation of eighteen short poems which were published in the author's collected poems, 1956-77. Manner (1921-95) was one of the leading Finnish-language modernist poets of the 1950s.

610 **The manila rope.**
Veijo Meri, translated from the Finnish by John McGahern, Annikki
Laaksi. New York: Knopf, 1967. [iv] + 140p. (A Borzoi Book).
Veijo Meri (born 1928) is a prominent and prolific writer who has been rather little translated into English. This novel is set in the Second World War.

611   **Statue of fire: the collected early poetry.**
       Aila Meriluoto, translated from the original Finnish by Leo Vuosalo
       and Steve Stone.   New Paltz, New York: Marathon Press, 1993.
       xiv + 77p.

Aila Meriluoto (born 1924) described her early volumes of poetry as 'visionary
books'; lyrical poems are relatively rare, some are outbursts, a few are deliberate self-
therapy (p. viii).

612   **The year of the hare.**
       Arto Paasilinna, translated from the Finnish by Herbert Lomas.
       London: Peter Owen; Paris: UNESCO, 1995. 135p. (UNESCO
       Collection of Representative Works).

The extraordinary, and often very funny, adventures of a journalist who adopts an
injured hare and abandons his settled life. Paasilinna was born in 1942.

613   **The year of the bull.**
       Oscar Parland, translated from the Swedish by Joan Tate.   London;
       Chester Springs, Pennsylvania: Peter Owen, 1991. 199p.

Novel about the time of the Civil War of 1918 as seen by a young boy. Parland was
born in 1912.

614   **My childhood.**
       Toivo Pekkanen, translated from the Finnish by Alan Blair, with an
       introduction by Thomas Warburton.   Madison, Wisconsin;
       Milwaukee, Wisconsin; London: University of Wisconsin Press, 1966.
       xvii + 250p. (Nordic Translation Series).

Lapsuuteni (My childhood) is one of the last works (published in 1953) of one 'of the first
writers to represent a "new" generation of the Finnish working class'. The novel is
characterized by Warburton as 'the book of a wise, understanding, and clear-sighted man'.

615   **The long distance patrol.**
       Paavo Rintala, translated from the Finnish by Maurice Michael.
       London: Allen & Unwin, 1967. 184p.

A translation of *Sissiluutnantti* (1963), a front-line story set in the Second World War.
Rintala (born 1930) has written extensively, often in a documentary form, about
Finland's recent history.

616   **J. L. Runeberg.**
       Tore Wretö, translated in collaboration with the author by Zalek S.
       Herman.   Boston, Massachusetts: Twayne, 1980. 186p. bibliog.
       (Twayne's World Authors Series, 503).

This introduction to Johan Ludvig Runeberg (1804-77) and his writing presents him in
his different literary roles, 'as critic, short story writer, epic poet, lyrist, poet of the
nation, and dramatist'. The author considers that 'as a creator of ideals and as a source
of style, Runeberg is one of the most significant Scandinavian authors'.

617 **The tales of Ensign Stål.**
John Ludvig Runeberg, illustrated by Albert Edelfelt, with an
introduction by Yrjö Hirn. Helsingfors: Söderström, 1952.
xxvi + 244p.
This is one of the most influential collections of poetry to be published in Finland.
Runeberg, who wrote in Swedish, inspired generations of Finns with his patriotic
poems. The translations here are by Charles Wharton Stork, Clement Burbank Shaw
and C. D. Broad. Edelfelt's illustrations are famous.

618 **Poems, 1958-1980.**
Pentti Saarikoski, edited and translated from the Finnish by Anselm
Hollo. West Branch, Iowa: Toothpaste Press, 1983. xii + 100p.
bibliog.
A collection of poems by Pentti Saarikoski (1937-83), a major and colourful modern
poet, who was also noted as a translator.

619 **The tale of Katrina.**
Sally Salminen, translated by Naomi Walford. London: Readers'
Union, with Thornton Butterworth, 1938. 384p.
The best work by Salminen (1906-76), a novel in Swedish about the hard life of a
sailor's wife.

620 **Heartwork: selected short stories.**
Solveig von Schoultz, translated from the Swedish by Marlaine
Delargy and Joan Tate. London; Boston, Massachusetts: Forest
Books, 1989. xii + 128p.
The author (born 1907) belongs to the followers of the Finland-Swedish modernists.
These seven short stories analyse human relationships.

621 **Snow and summers (poems 1940-1989).**
Solveig von Schoultz, translated from the Swedish by Ann Born.
London; Boston, Massachusetts: Forest Books, 1989. xviii + 107p.
'Solveig von Schoultz is the undisputed grande dame of Finland-Swedish literature'
(p. xi). She has published poetry and prose.

622 **Meek heritage: a novel.**
F. E. Sillanpää, originally translated by Alexander Matson, revised by
John R. Pitkin. Helsinki: Otava, 1971. 221p.
A translation of *Hurskas kurjuus*, originally published in 1919, and which uses
flashback technique to tell the story of a crofter whose eventual involvement on the
Red side in the Civil War of 1918 cost him his life. The translation by Matson was
first published in London (Putnam, 1938. [vii] + 280p.) and New York (Knopf, 1938.
[vii] + 274p.).

623 **People in the summer night: an epic suite. Ihmiset suviyössä.**
F. E. Sillanpää, translated from the Finnish by Alan Blair, with an
introduction by Thomas Warburton.   Madison, Wisconsin;
Milwaukee, Wisconsin; London: University of Wisconsin Press, 1966.
xviii + 158p. (Nordic Translation Series).
'Sillanpää's last work of undiminished strength', published in 1934, is a collection of
episodes about people held together by a fight and manslaughter. Helpful introduction
and bibliography. Sillanpää received the Nobel prize for literature in 1939.

624 **Edith Södergran: modernist poet in Finland.**
George C. Schoolfield.   Westport, Connecticut; London: Greenwood
Press, 1984. 177p. bibliog. (Contributions to the Study of World
Literature, 3).
A study of the life and work of the poet (1892-1923), whose considerable reputation is
posthumous.

625 **Edith Södergran: nine essays on her life and work.**
Edited by W. Glyn Jones, M. A. Branch.   London: School of Slavonic
and East European Studies, University of London; Helsinki: Finnish
Literature Society, 1992. xiii + 138p. (SSEES Occasional Papers, 17).
These papers from a symposium on Södergran fall into three groups which examine
her present standing, matters of textual interpretation and her personality.

626 **Two women writers from Finland: Edith Södergran (1892-1923)
and Hagar Olsson (1893-1978). Papers from the Symposium at
Yale University, October 21-23, 1993.**
Edited by George C. Schoolfield, Laurie Thompson, Michael
Schmelzle.   Edinburgh: Lockharton Press, 1995. 224p.
Sixteen essays (eight in English) on aspects of two Finland-Swedish modernists:
Södergran, a poet; and Olsson, a critic and prose writer.

627 **Complete poems.**
Edith Södergran, translated by David McDuff.   Newcastle upon Tyne,
England: Bloodaxe Books, 1992. 2nd ed. 201p.
Translations of the Swedish poems of Edith Södergran (1892-1923), whose early
poetry was written in German. 'Her poetry, though imagistic in expression, is
primarily a poetry of ideas' (McDuff, p. 50).

628   Poet under black banners: the case of Örnulf Tigerstedt and
extreme right-wing Swedish literature in Finland 1918-1944.
Göran O:son Waltå.   Uppsala, Sweden: University of Uppsala,
Department of Literature; Stockholm: Almqvist & Wiksell
International (distributor), 1993. 347p. bibliog. (Skrifter utgivna av
Litteraturvetenskapliga institutionen vid Uppsala universitet
[Publications of the Department of Literature, University of Uppsala],
31).
A dissertation which concentrates on the worldview of the Finland-Swedish author
and essayist Örnulf Tigerstedt (1900-62) and the literary manifestation of that view.
Tigerstedt was a leader in a group of extreme right-wing authors. The book shows
how, like others, he was a man of tradition, order and refined civilization who was
also captivated by radical right-wing impulses. He blended these different views into a
totalitarian whole though remaining essentially a romantic whose thinking was based
on emotions and tradition. Particularly interesting on various aspects of Finland-
Swedish culture.

629   Black and red: selected poems.
Ilpo Tiihonen, translated from the Finnish by Herbert Lomas.
Guildford, England: Making Waves, 1993. 41p.
Translations of a contemporary poet (b. 1950).

630   Snobs' Island.
Henrik Tikkanen, translated from the Swedish by Mary Sandbach.
London: Chatto & Windus, 1980. xvii + 122p.
A translation of Tikkanen's autobiographical novel *Brandövägen 8 Brandö Tel. 35*
(1976), set in the 1920s and 1930s, which established his reputation as a writer. Also
published as *A winter's day* (New York: Pantheon, 1980).

631   Love story of the century.
Märta Tikkanen, translated by Stina Katchadourian.   Santa Barbara,
California: Capra Press, 1984. 132p. (Rhodora Books).
A novel in poem form about the life of an alcoholic's wife, originally published in
Swedish in 1978, and awarded the Nordic Women's Literary Prize the following year.
Märta Tikkanen was born in 1935.

632   The Sea King's gift and other tales from Finland.
Zacharius Topelius, retold by Irma Kaplan.   London: Frederick
Muller, 1973. 137p.
Taken from a collection of stories, poems and fairy tales, *Läsning för barn* (Readings
for children), originally published by Topelius (1818-98) in 1865-96. This selection of
eight stories conveys the author's power as a storyteller, though he was much more
than just a writer for children.

Literature. Individual authors

633 Selected writings.
Mirjam Tuominen, translated by David McDuff. Newcastle upon Tyne, England: Bloodaxe Books, 1994. 155p.
A selection of poetry and stories by the Swedish-language writer and literary critic Mirjam Tuominen (1913-67).

634 The spring of the moonstone.
Kaari Utrio, translated by Hildi Hawkins, photographs by Marja Vehkala. Helsinki: Otava; Kalevala Koru, 1995. 95p.
A historical novel, set in the 11th century. The photographs feature nature, often adorned with examples of the traditional-style jewellery produced by Kalevala Koru, the co-publisher.

635 The dark angel.
Mika Waltari, translated by Naomi Walford. London: New English Library, 1964. 302p. (Four Square Books).
Perhaps Waltari's greatest success after *Sinuhe*. Originally published as *Johannes Angelos* (1952), this is a historical novel dealing with the siege of Constantinople in 1453. Various editions have been issued.

636 Sinuhe, the Egyptian: a novel.
Mika Waltari, translated by Naomi Walford. Bath, England: Cedric Chivers, 1973. [v] + 503p. (Portway Reprints).
A translation of *Sinuhe, egyptiläinen* (published in 1945), the most successful universal best-seller in Finnish literature. It is a historical novel set in ancient Egypt. There are numerous editions and the book has also been published in translation as *The Egyptian*.

637 A stranger came to the farm.
Mika Waltari, translated from the Finnish by Naomi Walford. London: Brown, Watson, [1960]. 157p. (Digit Books).
Set in Finland, this novel (*Vieras mies tuli taloon*, published in 1937), with its tragic theme, caused a considerable stir when it first appeared. Other editions have been issued.

Books from Finland.
See item no. 540.

The Kalevala, Sallinen and 'Kullervo'.
See item no. 720.

Kaunokirjallisuutemme käännöksiä: bibliografinen luettelo suomenkielisen kaunokirjallisuuden käännöksistä. Livres finnois en traduction: romans, nouvelles, poésies, pièces de théâtre. Guide bibliographique. (Finnish literature in translation: a bibliographical list of translations of Finnish-language literature: novels, short stories, poetry, plays. Bibliographical guide.)
See item no. 797.

168

Culture, Cultural Policy and the Arts

Culture and cultural policy

638 **From folklore to applied arts: aspects of Finnish culture.**
Edited by Päivi Molarius. Lahti, Finland: University of Helsinki,
Lahti Research and Training Centre, 1993. 224p. bibliog. (Profiles of
Finland – a Study Program. Teaching Monographs, 20).
An admirable survey of Finnish art and culture, paying particular attention to
international influences. The contents include: Leea Virtanen, 'Folklore'; Vilhelm
Helander, 'Architecture'; Aimo Reitala, 'The visual arts'; Paavo Helistö, 'Music';
Maria-Liisa Nevala, 'Literature'; Pirkko Koski, 'The dramatic arts'; Seppo Väkevä,
'Applied arts, crafts and design'; Jukka Sihvonen, 'Cinema'; and Pekka Gronow,
'Popular culture'. All chapters have helpful lists of further reading in English. There is
an index of names and a subject index which includes titles of works.

639 **Cultural policy in Finland: national report. Prepared at the
request of the Finnish Ministry of Education by a group of
researchers working under the auspices of the Arts Council of
Finland, its Research and Information Unit.**
Helsinki: Arts Council of Finland, Research and Information Unit,
1995. 396p. (European Programme of National Cultural Policy
Reviews. Council of Europe).
Designed to serve as a source of information for the panel of European experts who
reviewed Finnish cultural policy (see item no. 640), this is an extensive survey of
cultural policy in Finland, how it evolved, its development and objectives, its
financing and the dissemination of culture. Contains numerous statistics. Appendices
list major cultural and arts associations and organizations and the principal legislation
pertaining to cultural policy and cultural administration. A major starting point for
consideration of Finnish cultural life.

640 **Cultural policy in Finland: report by the panel of European experts.**
Compiled by Jacques Renard. Strasbourg, France: Council for Cultural Co-operation, 1995. 188p. (European Programme of National Cultural Policy Reviews).

An examination of the existing system for cultural policy which also takes account of recent and imminent changes. Chapters deal with: the institutional and financial framework; promoting artistic creation (including the 'culture industries' – books, cinema, TV and radio, video and record industries); cultural institutions at the national and local level; and participation in cultural life. Makes recommendations.

641 **Handbook of cultural affairs in Finland.**
Edited by Ritva Mitchell. Helsinki: Arts Council of Finland; Finnish Library Services, 1991. 190p. (Handbooks Published by the Arts Council of Finland, 3).

'Culture' in the context of the handbook covers the arts, cultural heritage, information and documentation, adult education and libraries. 'The Handbook deals with the administrative and organizational aspects of Finnish cultural life' (p. 13). Inevitably somewhat dated, this is nevertheless useful as a list of organizations, their objectives and addresses. Contains indexes of names of organizations, English-Finnish and Finnish-English (Finnish also including Swedish names).

642 **The impact of American culture. Proceedings of an international seminar in Turku, April 17-18, 1982.**
Edited by Eero Kuparinen, Keijo Virtanen. Turku, Finland: University of Turku, Institute of History, General History, 1983. 146p. bibliog. (Institute of History, General History, University of Turku. Publications, 10).

Short papers on various aspects of the influence of American culture in Finland, including films, popular music and jazz, technology, and even language (the impact of English, which is not by any means exclusively American).

643 **Festival fever: Finland festivals.**
Kaija Valkonen, Markku Valkonen. Helsinki: Otava, 1994. 157p.

Describes the history of Finnish summer festivals, going back to choral festivals at the end of the 19th century. The modern festival movement began in the 1960s and there are now more than fifty 'festival' events, from the internationally-known Savonlinna Opera Festival to the Accordion Festival at Ikaalinen. Gives details of the festivals of 1994, mostly music of various kinds, but also cinema, dance, theatre, literature and heritage events (mostly folk music and dance).

Finland: a cultural outline.
See item no. 4.

The climate of Finland in relation to its hydrology, ecology and culture.
See item no. 27.

Finland: people, nation, state.
See item no. 96.

Cultural minorities in Finland: an overview towards cultural policy.
See item no. 188.

Finnish Institute Yearbook.
See item no. 454.

Culture of the everyday: leisure and cultural participation in 1981 and 1991.
See item no. 734.

Visual arts

Art in general

644 **Finnish art over the centuries.**
Markku Valkonen, translated by Martha Gaber Abrahamsen.
Helsinki: Otava, 1992. 159p. bibliog.
A short but broad and rich chronological survey of Finnish art (painting and sculpture) from prehistoric times to the 1980s.

645 **Apollo: the Magazine of the Arts.**
Vol. 115, no. 243 (May 1982).
Most of this issue is devoted to art in Finland, with well-illustrated articles on Finnish medieval art, Helsinki's neo-classical centre, old masters and modern paintings in Helsinki (in the Sinebrychoff and Ateneum collections), Finnish painting from 1840 to 1940, art nouveau and national romanticism in Finland, and currents and undercurrents in Finnish architecture.

646 **Art history in Finland before 1920.**
Sixten Ringbom. Helsinki: Societas Scientiarum Fennica, 1986.
115p. bibliog. (The History of Learning and Science in Finland 1828-1918, 15b).
The survey also includes a chapter on research on art and antiquities before 1828.

Kalevala 1835-1985: the national epic of Finland.
See item no. 560.

From folklore to applied arts: aspects of Finnish culture.
See item no. 638.

Suomen taidemuseot. Finlands konstmuseer. Art museums in Finland.
See item no. 757.

Ateneum guide from Isak Wacklin to Wäinö Aaltonen.
See item no. 758.

The Finnish National Gallery.
See item no. 759.

Art in particular periods

647 **Early Finnish art from prehistory to the Middle Ages.**
István Rácz, introduction by C. F. Meinander, notes on the illustrations
by Pirkko-Liisa Lehtosalo. Helsinki: Otava, 1967. 176p.
Originally published in Finnish as *Kivikirves ja hopearisti: Suomen esihistorian
taideaarteita* (Stone axe and silver cross: art treasures of Finnish prehistory) (Helsinki:
Otava, 1961). Contains 'A review of Finnish prehistory' by C. F. Meinander (p. 7-19),
plates, some coloured (p. 21-164), and notes on the plates (with museum references
and dimensions of the objects), (p. 165-76). Fine photographs and a useful introduction
and notes.

648 **Art treasures of medieval Finland.**
István Rácz, introduction and notes on the pictures by Riitta
Pylkkänen, translated from Finnish by Diana Tullberg, Judy Beesley.
New York; Washington, DC; London: Praeger, 1967. 3rd ed. 253p.
Contains excellent photographs, mostly black-and-white, a short introduction (but
longer than that in the original edition published in Finland in 1961) and useful notes.

649 **Mercy and justice: miracles of the Virgin Mary in Finnish
medieval wall-paintings.**
Helena Edgren. Helsinki: Suomen muinaismuistoyhdistys, 1993.
235p. bibliog. (Suomen muinaismuistoyhdistyksen aikakauskirja
[Journal of the Society of Antiquaries of Finland], 100).
Sets the paintings of the miracles of the Virgin Mary in Finnish medieval churches
into their European context and acts as a reminder not only of the quality of art in
medieval Finland but also of the country's Catholic past, when Finland was specially
placed under the protection of the Virgin Mary and where her cult was particularly
strong.

650 **Treasures of Finnish renaissance and baroque art.**
István Rácz, introduction and notes on the illustrations by Nils Cleve.
Helsinki: Otava, 1969. 229p.
Originally published as *Suomen renessanssin ja barokin taideaarteita* (Helsinki:
Otava, 1967). Covers the period 1550-1721. The short introduction (p. 5-15) surveys
the period in general. There are 209 illustrations of a high quality and useful notes on
the plates (p. 217-29).

651   **The golden age: Finnish art, 1850-1907.**
Markku Valkonen, translated by Michael Wynne-Ellis.   Porvoo,
Finland; Helsinki: Werner Söderström, 1992. 311p. bibliog.
A handsomely-illustrated volume on Finnish art from the 1850s to the 1900s, with an
introduction on art in Finland during the autonomy period, followed by reproductions
of the paintings or sculptures of thirty-eight artists, from the von Wrights, through
Albert Edelfelt and Akseli Gallen-Kallela to Eero Järnefelt and Verner Thomé.

652   **The golden age of Finnish art: art nouveau and the national spirit.**
John Boulton Smith.   Helsinki: Otava, 1985. 2nd revised ed. 237p.
bibliog.
A very well illustrated account, by a British authority on the period, of the various
branches of art in Finland at the end of the 19th and the beginning of the 20th century
when Finnish art burgeoned. The bibliography (p. 231-34) of works in English or with
summaries in English is partially annotated and most valuable.

653   **Modern Finnish painting and graphic art.**
John Boulton Smith.   London: Weidenfeld & Nicolson, 1970.
48 + 62p.
Covers the period from the 1890s to the 1960s, concisely and with well-chosen
illustrations.

654   *Finnish vision: modern art, architecture and design.*
Jaakko Lintinen, Kirmo Mikkola, Matti Rinne, Pekka Suhonen.
Helsinki: Otava, 1983. 128p.
On art, architecture and design from the 1960s to the early 1980s, with plenty of
illustrations, some in colour. Attempts to see the influence of nature, folk tradition and
international movements such as functionalism.

Sculpture

655   **Suomalaista veistotaidetta. Finnish sculpture.**
Editorial committee: Kari Juva, Ukri Merikanto, Heikki Nieminen,
Anneli Sipiläinen, Ulla Sinkkanen.   [Helsinki]: Association of Finnish
Sculptors; Porvoo, Finland; Helsinki: Werner Söderström, 1980. 267p.
'The aim of the book is to provide a picture of the main stylistic streams to be seen in
our sculpture today, seen from the perspective of past Finnish sculpture' (p. 5). Fifty
sculptors are represented, with black-and-white illustrations of some of their works.
There is a useful 'Review of Finnish sculpture 1910-80' by Leena Ahtola-Moorhouse
(p. 6-47). Parallel text in Finnish and English and picture captions in both languages.

Individual artists

656 **Akseli Gallen-Kallela: national artist of Finland.**
Timo Martin, Douglas Sivén, English adaptation by Keith Bosley,
Satu Salo.   Helsinki: Watti, 1996. 4th printing. 255p. bibliog.
A handsome volume, first published in 1985, on one of Finland's most important
artists, Akseli Gallen-Kallela (1865-1931).

657 **Helene Schjerfbeck.**
Edited by Leena Ahtola-Moorhouse.   Helsinki: Finnish National
Gallery Ateneum, 1992. 334p. bibliog.
Catalogue of an exhibition, 'Helene Schjerfbeck: Finland's Modernist Rediscovered',
held in Washington and New York in 1992-93, and which represented all aspects of
the work of this important figure in Finnish art. A 'memorandum' (p. 303-28) sets out
the life and works of Helene Schjerfbeck (1862-1946) and subsequent exhibitions.
Various essays deal with aspects of her art and there is a catalogue of her works, well
illustrated, which represents about half of her output.

Design

Design in general

658 **Finland: living design.**
Elizabeth Gaynor, photographs by Kari Haavisto.   New York: Rizzoli,
1984. 250p. bibliog.
'This book is a record through pictures and impressions of a lifestyle, at its best, from
which the design sense evolved' (p. 9). The spread of interests and of periods is wide,
with Gustavian, art nouveau and modern interiors (and exteriors), and the depiction of
objects made of wood, ceramics, textiles and glass. The value of the book lies in the
breadth with which it exemplifies the subject.

659 **Images of Finnish design 1960-1990.**
Edited by Juliana Balint.   Espoo, Finland: Tietopuu, 1991. 279p.
bibliog.
A volume in celebration of the eightieth anniversary of Ornamo, the Finnish
Association of Designers. A rich feast of fashion, furniture, interiors, glass and
porcelain, arranged by decade and designer.

660   **Design in Finland. 1995.**
      Helsinki: Helsinki Media Company Special Magazines, 1995. 82p.
A glossy review of design, including architecture, telephones and other products. Intended for the promotion of trade. Has been published since 1961 with varying titles. Seemingly annual.

661   **Form Function Finland.**
      Helsinki: Finnish Society of Crafts and Design/Design Forum Finland, 1980- . four issues per year.
On design, architecture, arts and visual culture. Contains information about, and reviews of, relevant exhibitions.

From folklore to applied arts: aspects of Finnish culture.
See item no. 638.

Bookplates

662   **Ex libris Suomi Finland.**
      Helmiriitta Honkanen.   [Espoo, Finland]: Frederika, 1987. 92p.
Charmingly illustrated book on the bookplate in Finland. The introductory text and alphabetical list of artists (giving brief biographical details) are in English as well as Finnish.

Firearms

663   **Arma Fennica. Suomalaiset aseet. Finnish firearms.**
      Timo Hyytinen, English translation by Tony Melville, Erja Melville.
      Jyväskylä, Finland: [T. Hyytinen], 1985. 304p.
'This book contains information about old Finnish firearms as well as sporting and hunting guns manufactured on an industrial scale. In addition the most important basic models of military arms are also presented' (p. 3). The text and captions are not completely translated but the English-language user would have no problems with the book since it is richly illustrated. There is a second volume: *Arma Fennica, 2. Sotilasaseet* (Military firearms) (Jyväskylä, Finland: [T. Hyytinen], 1987. 429p.) but unfortunately this has no English translation. It is a thorough account of the muskets, rifles, pistols, sub-machine guns, machine guns and anti-tank rifles used in Finland, systematically arranged and excellently illustrated.

Glass

664　**Suomen lasi – Finnish glass. A Ceolfrith Gallery, Sunderland Arts Centre Touring Exhibition 1979.**
Sunderland, England: Ceolfrith Press, 1979. [69]p.
Contains a short historical essay on the Finnish glass industry and the artists working with it. There are brief biographies (and notes on their exhibitions) of fifteen notable modern artists, together with photographs of their work, some in colour.

Knives

665　**Suuri puukkokirja. Finnish knives and bayonets.**
Timo Hyytinen, translated by Ulla Lauri, Anthony Melville, J-P. Peltonen.　Jyväskylä, Finland: Gummerus, 1988. 286p. bibliog. (Arma Fennica, 3).
Finland is noted for its knives – the *puukko* being a good working knife as well as nowadays an object to sell to tourists. This book on Finnish knives and on bayonets used in Finland is chiefly in Finnish but there are some English summaries and numerous illustrations. For *Arma Fennica* 1-2 see item no. 663.

Silver

666　**Finnish silver.**
Edited by Tuula Poutasuo, English text by Michael Wynne-Ellis.
Helsinki: Kirjayhtymä, 1989. 127p. bibliog.
A history of Finnish silver, from the middle ages (or, more properly, the 17th century) to the 1980s, and emphasizing the period after 1948. Includes a chapter on Finnish silversmiths in St Petersburg.

Textiles

667　**The *ryijy*-rugs of Finland: a historical study.**
U. T. Sirelius.　Helsinki: Otava, 1926. [xii] + 251p. 93 plates. map.
The standard history and description of the *ryijy* rug in Finland, written by one of Finland's leading ethnographers. Has notes but no bibliography. The *ryijy*, a pile-woven woollen textile, was originally used as a bed cover but is now used as a decorative wall hanging.

668　**Art – craft – design? Reflections on past Finnish textiles.**
Marjo Wiberg.　*Finnish Institute Yearbook*, 1995, p. 108-21.
Focuses on the characteristics of the 'textile culture' of Finland which the author, as a designer, considers important.

Architecture

General works

669   **Architecture and landscape: the building of Finland.**
Riitta Nikula, translated by Timothy Binham.   Helsinki: Otava, 1993.
160p. bibliog.
Develops the worthwhile idea of explaining why Finland looks as it does, starting with
the landscape and moving chronologically through Finnish architecture of all types to
the present day. Good black-and-white illustrations.

670   **800 years of Finnish architecture.**
Sir James M. Richards.   Newton Abbot, England: David & Charles,
1978. 191p. map. bibliog.
This admirable and judiciously balanced survey of Finnish architecture superseded the
author's *A guide to Finnish architecture* (London: Evelyn; New York: Praeger, 1967.
112p.). The short, annotated bibliography is mostly of works in English.

From folklore to applied arts: aspects of Finnish culture.
See item no. 638.

Castles

671   **Suomen vanhat linnat. The castles of Finland.**
Vesa Mäkinen.   Porvoo, Finland; Helsinki: Werner Söderström, 1978.
2nd rev. ed. 192p. maps. bibliog.
This combined picture-book and guidebook imparts a great deal of information about
ancient fortifications in Finland, the medieval castles (including that of Viipuri
[Vyborg], now in Russia), and fortified manor houses. The text itself is in Finnish only
but there is an English 'Commentary on the contents' on p. 185-88 and the captions to
the fine colour illustrations and castle plans also appear in English.

Churches

672   **The stone churches of the medieval diocese of Turku: a systematic
classification and chronology.**
Markus Hiekkanen, translated by Jüri Kokkonen.   Helsinki: [Suomen
Muinaismuistoyhdistys], 1994. 412p. 4 maps. bibliog. (Suomen
Muinaismuistoyhdistyksen aikakauskirja [Journal of the Society of
Antiquaries of Finland], 101).
Finland's economic resources permitted the construction of stone churches – with few
exceptions – only from the 1420s. The period of their building, following a diocesan

plan and generally adopting a uniform design, ended in the 1550s. This detailed and well-illustrated study concludes that, for the above reasons, 'the medieval stone churches of the Diocese of Turku came to form a coherent chronological and geographical body of architecture unparalleled in other countries' (p. 256).

673 **Suomalainen puukirkko. Finnish wooden church.**
Expert: Lars Pettersson. Translations: Jüri Kokkonen. Helsinki:
Otava, 1992. 2nd ed. 160p. map. bibliog.
A superb study of the history and construction of the wooden church in Finland, with plans, drawings and photographs (some in colour); even the types of tools used by the builders are illustrated. Parallel text in Finnish and English.

Architecture by period

674 **Suomalainen puukaupunki. Trästaden i Finland. The Finnish wooden town.**
Henrik Lilius. Rungsted Kyst, Denmark: Anders Nyborg; Helsinki:
Akateeminen Kirjakauppa (distributor), 1985. 219p. map. bibliog.
Provides a scholarly but accessible account of the development of the Finnish wooden town from the 16th century to the end of the 19th century. Covers town planning and in particular dwelling houses. The text and captions are trilingual, in Finnish, Swedish and English.

675 **Architecture in Finland in the 20th century.**
Kimmo Mikkola, translated by David Miller. [Helsinki]:
Finnish-American Cultural Institute, 1981. 80p.
An admirably concise but wide-ranging illustrated account and critique of Finnish architecture from national romanticism, through classicism, more romanticism and rationalism to constructivism.

676 **The Finland pavilions: Finland at the Universal Expositions 1900-1992.**
Peter B. MacKeith, Kerstin Smeds. [Helsinki]: City, 1993. 184p.
Looks at the Finland pavilions as architectural works and also at their contribution to the image of Finland abroad.

677 **Sankaruus ja arki. Suomen 50-luvun miljöö. Heroism and the everyday. Building Finland in the 1950s.**
Editor-in-chief: Riitta Nikula. Helsinki: Museum of Finnish
Architecture, 1994. 207p.
This is the catalogue of an exhibition held at the Museum of Finnish Architecture in 1994. There are seventeen articles in Finnish grouped into sections on 'Thought and place' (including public buildings and building techniques), 'Housing and environment', 'Home and objects' (on design), and 'Images and reflections' (on painting, sculpture, cinema and architectural photography). Much of the book consists

of photographs, the captions to which are in English as well as Finnish. Gives a good impression of a somewhat neglected period.

678   **Suomalainen rakennustaide. Modern architecture in Finland.**
Vilhelm Helander, Simo Rista.   Helsinki: Kirjayhtymä, 1987. 208p.
map.
A richly-illustrated and rewarding volume with parallel text in Finnish and English. Begins by considering the 'Origins of the Finnish environment', providing a survey of trends in Finnish architecture and noting that 'Quick and abrupt changes of ideals have ... been evident in Finnish 20th century architecture' (p. 31). Chapters are devoted to the architecture of particular styles and periods, concluding with business and industrial buildings and 'Interior and natural light'.

679   **Suomalainen arkkitehtuuri 1900-luvulla. Finnish architecture in the 20th century.**
Photographs by Ilpo Okkonen, text by Asko Salokorpi.   Jyväskylä, Finland; Helsinki: Gummerus, 1988. 2nd ed. 204p.
A large-format book consisting principally of very fine photographs but which also contains some explanatory text in Finnish and English. Covers national romanticism, rationalism, the classicism of the 1920s, functionalism, the 1940s, the golden age of the 1950s, and the functionalist tradition and the search for new expression.

680   **The new Finnish architecture.**
Scott Poole.   New York: Rizzoli, 1992. 224p.
Richly-illustrated study of thirteen modern Finnish architects or architectural partnerships with an introduction by Colin St. John Wilson on 'Finland and the tradition of modernism'.

681   **Finnish architecture and the modernist tradition.**
Malcolm Quantrill.   London: Spon, 1995. xii + 242p. bibliog.
'In this study of Finnish architecture in the twentieth century, I have attempted a more-or-less blow-by-blow account of how modernism came into being in Finland and how it made its mark on Finnish culture and life' (p. ix). A fine work accompanied by excellent illustrations (chiefly black-and-white) and plans.

Architects

682   **Alvar Aalto: a critical study.**
Malcolm Quantrill.   Helsinki: Otava, 1983. xii + 307p. bibliog.
A major study of the architect, setting his work in its context, and considering his major buildings and furniture designs in some detail. Includes a chronological list of Aalto's main works.

683 Alvar Aalto: the early years.
Göran Schildt, translated by Timothy Binham.   New York: Rizzoli, 1984. 292p.

The first volume of the standard work on Aalto (1898-1976), covering both life and works. Takes the story to the mid-1920s and includes a list of all Aalto's works between 1912 and 1927.

684 Alvar Aalto: the decisive years.
Göran Schildt, translated by Timothy Binham.   Helsinki: Otava, 1986. 282p.

Schildt's second volume on Aalto's life and work covers the period between 1927 and 1939. Contains numerous illustrations and drawings. Ends with a 'List of works from 1928 to 1939', also illustrated with plans, and which contains references to the buildings mentioned in the main part of the book.

685 Alvar Aalto: the mature years.
Göran Schildt, translated by Timothy Binham.   New York: Rizzoli, 1991. 328p.

The third volume of the standard biography of Aalto describes the architect's life and work until his death in 1976 and emphasizes not his architecture but his personal history and the political, social and economic circumstances of his life. Based, like the other volumes, on written sources and interviews and on the author's personal relationship with Aalto.

686 Alvar Aalto: the complete catalogue of architecture, design and art.
Göran Schildt, translated from Swedish by Timothy Binham.
London: Academy Editions, 1994. 317p. bibliog.

A catalogue of the works of the leading Finnish architect and designer and the final volume of Schildt's biography of Aalto. Contains chapters on: 'Planning'; 'City and district centres'; 'Religious buildings and facilities'; 'Buildings for physical health'; 'Cultural buildings'; 'Office buildings'; 'Industrial and commercial buildings'; 'Housing'; 'Interior design'; 'Design and art'; and 'Aalto exhibitions'.

687 Alvar Aalto.
Richard Weston.   London: Phaidon, 1995. 240p. bibliog.

A clear work which sets out Aalto's architectural achievement in its national Finnish context. Attractively illustrated with photographs and plans, and accompanied by a list of Aalto's works.

688   **Classicism and history. Anachronistic architectural thinking in Finland at the turn of the century: Jac. Ahrenberg and Gustaf Nyström.**
Ville Lukkarinen.   Helsinki: Suomen Muinaismuistoyhdistys, 1989. 197p. bibliog. (Suomen Muinaismuistoyhdistyksen aikakauskirja [Journal of the Society of Antiquaries of Finland], 93).
An academic study of 'historicism' in architecture which considers two neglected Finnish architects. Ahrenberg is characterized as a representative of 'esthetic historicism' and Nyström as a genuine classicist.

689   **Carl Ludwig Engel.**
Nils Erik Wikberg.   Helsinki: City of Helsinki, 1973. [76]p.
Carl Ludwig Engel (1778-1840) was the architect who created the new centre of Helsinki after the city had become Finland's new capital in 1819. This short but excellent study was originally produced in a fuller form for an exhibition about Engel in Berlin in 1970. It concentrates on Engel's work in Helsinki. Fine illustrations (mostly black-and-white) of plans and buildings.

690   **Writing architecture.**
Roger Connah.   Cambridge, Massachusetts; London: MIT Press, 1989. 463p. bibliog.
A distinctly unconventional book about the work of the architect Reima Pietilä (1923-93) set in a broad cultural context. Numerous sketches and other illustrations.

691   **Reima Pietilä: architecture, context and modernism.**
Malcolm Quantrill.   Helsinki: Otava, 1985. 250p. bibliog.
'This study offers the first comprehensive analysis of Pietilä's ideas and buildings' (p. 7). Reima Pietilä was initially overshadowed by Alvar Aalto and has followed Aalto's tradition of modern architecture. Includes a chronological list of Pietilä's works and projects.

692   **Eliel Saarinen: projects, 1896-1923.**
Marika Hausen, Kirmo Mikkola, Anna-Liisa Amberg, Tytti Valto. Helsinki: Otava, 1990. 355p. bibliog.
This is a comprehensive account of Saarinen's life, work and projects during his time in Finland, including his contribution to town planning and his subsequent influence. Saarinen (1873-1950) subsequently moved to the USA. Contains a comprehensive catalogue of his architectural and town planning works, from well-known buildings like the railway station in Helsinki to the Munkkiniemi and Haaga Tram Lines Transformer Station. Saarinen's work has both national romantic charm and considerable grandeur.

693   **Lars Sonck, 1870-1956. Arkkitehti. Architect.**
Helsinki: Museum of Finnish Architecture, 1981. 156p. bibliog.
(Monographs by the Museum of Finnish Architecture).
This is the catalogue of an exhibition about Lars Sonck which provides a thorough
overview of the architect's life and work. The text and the captions to the numerous
illustrations are in English as well as Finnish.

694   **Innovation versus tradition: the architect Lars Sonck. Works and projects 1900-1910.**
Pekka Korvenmaa.   Helsinki: Suomen Muinaismuistoyhdistys, 1991.
169p. bibliog. (Suomen Muinaismuistoyhdistyksen aikakauskirja
[Journal of the Finnish Society of Antiquaries], 96).
Lars Sonck (1870-1956) was one of the leading Finnish architects of his time. This
book analyses various buildings or designs during the period in which, the author
argues, Sonck's means of expression became standardized.

Architecture as a profession

695   **The work of architects: the Finnish Association of Architects, 1892-1992.**
Edited by Pekka Korvenmaa.   Helsinki: Finnish Association of
Architects [and] Finnish Building Centre, 1992. 320p.
Several essays (well illustrated in black-and-white) published to commemorate the
centenary of the Finnish architects' professional association. Covers from the
beginning of the 19th century to the present, looking particularly at the opportunities
and limitations of architectural work, including urban planning, and with a history of
the Association.

696   **The fringe of a profession: women as architects in Finland from the 1890s to the 1950s.**
Renja Suominen-Kokkonen, translated by Jüri Kokkonen.   Helsinki:
[Suomen Muinaismuistoyhdistys], 1992. 138p. bibliog. (Suomen
Muinaismuistoyhdistyksen aikakauskirja [Journal of the Society of
Antiquaries of Finland], 98).
'Reviews women architects from the perspectives of education, practical work and its
experiences of femininity, and the place of women in the field of architecture' (p. 14).

Architecture of the Helsinki region

697   **Helsinki, Espoo, Kauniainen, Vantaa: an architectural guide.**
Arvi Ilonen.   Helsinki: Otava, 1990. 195p. 13 maps.
An attractively-produced and highly informative guide to the architecture of Helsinki
and its surroundings, arranged geographically. Has a chronological index of buildings

and indexes of building types and architects. The photographs are mostly black-and-white and small but very clear.

698   Helsinki Jugendstil architecture, 1895-1915.

Jonathan Moorhouse, Michael Carapetian, Leena Ahtola-Moorhouse.
Helsinki: Otava, 1987. 352p. maps. bibliog.

Helsinki is rich in art nouveau architecture and this book is an admirable (though not exactly portable) guide to it. A general introduction is followed by sections on particular parts of the city, with admirable photographs, plans and local maps. There are indexes of architects (with biographical details), names of buildings and of streets.

699   Linna: the presidential palace.

Tellervo Koivisto, Yrjö Blomstedt, Riitta Nikula, Sirkka Peisa.
Helsinki: Otava, 1992. 198p. bibliog.

The modest presidential palace by the South Harbour in Helsinki began as a merchant's house before becoming first the imperial and then the presidential palace. The book is not just an architectural description but is also about life in the palace, the first author being the wife of President Koivisto.

700   Mäntyniemi. Pohjoinen timantti. Diamond of the north.

Jorma Marttala, Seppo Hilpo, English text by Michael Wynne-Ellis.
Porvoo, Finland; Helsinki: Werner Söderström, 1994. 119p.

Generously illustrated (photographs by Seppo Hilpo) book about the new official presidential residence designed by Reimo Pietilä (1923-93) and built beside the sea near Helsinki between 1989 and 1993 at a cost of 198.5 million Finnish marks. Gives details of the materials and suppliers used. The text is in Finnish and English.

701   Tango Mäntyniemi: the architecture of the official residence of the president of Finland. Tasavallan Presidentin virka-asunnon arkkitehtuuri.

Edited by Roger Connah.   Helsinki: Painatuskeskus, 1994. 224p.

About the recently-built presidential residence, designed by Reima Pietilä. See also item no. 700.

702   Ooperatalo. The Opera House. Das Opernhaus. Helsinki.

Edited by Tapani Eskola.   Helsinki: Projektilehti, 1995. 120p.

A description, with good photographs, of the new Opera House in Helsinki, now home of the Finnish National Opera and the National Ballet.

703 **Sveaborg, Viapori, Suomenlinna: the island fortress off Helsinki. Linnoituksen rakennushistoria. Fästningens byggnadshistoria. An architectural history.**
Olof af Hällström.   Rungsted Kyst, Denmark: Anders Nyborg;
Helsinki: Akateeminen Kirjakauppa (distributor), 1986. 204p. bibliog.

Suomenlinna, as it is now known, is one of the finest examples of an artillery fortification in the world. It was built by the Swedes in the second half of the 18th century to protect the south coast of Finland against Russian attack. Surrendered to the Russians in 1808, it became an important Russian fortress up to Finland's independence. It only recently ceased to be a Finnish garrison. This book, beautifully illustrated with colour reproductions of original plans and paintings, provides an expert description of its architecture and a useful account of its history. The text and captions are in Finnish, Swedish and English.

704 **Yliopiston Helsinki. University architecture in Helsinki.**
[Edited by] Eea Pekkala-Koskela, translated by Jüri Kokkonen.
Helsinki: Helsingin yliopisto; Sanomaprint, 1989. 218p. bibliog.

Describes the buildings of the University of Helsinki individually and in some detail with excellent illustrations. Provides a cross-section of Finnish architecture from Engel's classicism to modernism. The text and captions are in English as well as Finnish.

705 **Tapiola: a history and architectural guide.**
Timo Tuomi, translated by Jüri Kokkonen.   Espoo, Finland: Espoo
City Museum, 1992. 192p. bibliog.

Much has been written on the garden city of Tapiola (just outside Helsinki), which has been recognized as an important piece of post-Second World War town planning. This little guide concentrates (though not exclusively) on residential areas and looks in detail at particular buildings. Well illustrated and indexed.

Carl Ludwig Engel.
See item no. 689.

Music and Dance

General works

706 Music of Finland.
Edited by Inkeri Aarnio, Kauko Karjalainen, Valdemar Melanko.
Helsinki: Finnish Music Information Centre, 1983. 82p.
Brief text and lively pictures on the history of Finnish music, music education, folk music, jazz, light music, popular music and rock.

707 Scandinavian music: Finland and Sweden.
Antony Hodgson.   Rutherford, New Jersey: Fairleigh Dickinson
University Press; London: Associated University Presses, 1984. 224p.
Useful general survey from Bernhard Henrik Crusell (1775-1838) and Fredrik Pacius (1809-91) to Leif Segerstam (b. 1944). Provides some musical examples and an extensive discography.

708 Finnish orchestral music.
Kimmo Korhonen, translated by Timothy Binham.   Helsinki:
Foundation for the Promotion of Finnish Music, Finnish Music
Information Centre, 1995. 2 vols.
Two little volumes, the first on Finnish orchestral music up to the 1920s and 1930s, including a brief history of the symphony orchestra in Finland, the second on post-Second World War Finnish music. A handy introduction to the subject.

709   **Finnish concertos.**
      Kimmo Korhonen, translated by Philip Binham.   Helsinki: Foundation
      for the Promotion of Finnish Music, Finnish Music Information Centre,
      1995. 88p.
On Finnish concertos from Crusell (1775-1838) onwards. Arranged chronologically,
followed by sections on concertos for particular instruments or types of instrument.

710   **Finnish jazz.**
      Matti Konttinen.   [Helsinki]: Foundation for the Promotion of Finnish
      Music, Finnish Music Information Centre, 1982. [2nd ed.] 72p.
First published in 1974, this booklet provides a brief historical survey, biographical
notes on musicians and a discography.

711   **Finnish Music Quarterly.**
      Helsinki: Performing Music Promotion Centre, 1985- . quarterly.
Varied and attractive illustrated articles on Finnish music and musical life, including
contemporary artists, musical history, composers and their works, and folk and
popular music.

Kalevala 1835-1985: the national epic of Finland.
See item no. 560.

From folklore to applied arts: aspects of Finnish culture.
See item no. 638.

Festival fever: Finland festivals.
See item no. 643.

**Culture of the everyday: leisure and cultural participation in 1981 and
1991.**
See item no. 734.

Music by period

712   *Harmoniemusik* **in Finland – on military music in eighteenth-
      century Savo.**
      Kari Laitinen.   In: *Balticum – a coherent musical landscape in 16th
      and 18th centuries.*   Edited by Irma Vierimaa.   Helsinki: Department
      of Musicology, University of Helsinki, 1994, p. 103-16. (Studia
      musicologica Universitatis Helsingiensis, 6).
An unusual piece about the music played by the band of the Savo Light Infantry
Regiment at the end of the 18th century and the beginning of the 19th century based
on catalogues of the band's music.

713 **Finnish Viennese classical composers and Europe.**
Seija Lappalainen.   In: *Balticum – a coherent musical landscape in 16th and 18th centuries.*   Edited by Irma Vierimaa.   Helsinki: Department of Musicology, University of Helsinki, 1994, p. 91-102. (Studia musicologica Universitatis Helsingiensis, 6).
About various Finnish composers in the Viennese classical style and their travels to Sweden, Estonia, St Petersburg and Central Europe. The composers are the well-known Bernhard Henrik Crusell (1775-1838) and the lesser known Thomas Byström (1772-1839) and members of the Lithander family from the same period.

714   **From Sibelius to Sallinen: Finnish nationalism and the music of Finland.**
Lisa de Gorog with the collaboration of Ralph de Gorog.   New York: Greenwood Press, 1989. [xi] + 253p. bibliog. (Contributions to the Study of Music and Dance, 16).
Considers Finnish music before Sibelius, has much on Sibelius and his legacy, and finishes with chapters on post-Sibelian instrumental music and stage and vocal music in Finland. Concludes that nationalism in the Sibelian sense is not dead as a force in Finnish music although its manifestations are very different. Includes musical examples and a discography.

715   **Finnish composers since the 1960s.**
Kimmo Korhonen, translated by Timothy Binham.   Helsinki: Foundation for the Promotion of Finnish Music, Finnish Music Information Centre, 1995. 158p. bibliog.
'The purpose of the book is to present Finnish composers who have come to the fore after the second modernist wave' (p. 6). Includes a selected list of works by thirty-four of them.

Sibelius

716   **Sibelius.**
Erik Tawaststjerna, translated by Robert Layton.   Volume I. 1865-1905.   London: Faber & Faber, 1976. xv + 316p. bibliog.
Volume II. 1904-1914.   Berkeley, California: University of California Press, 1986. 302p. bibliog.
Jean Sibelius (1865-1957) has dominated Finnish music. Professor Tawaststjerna's biography – in five volumes – is a monumental work on the man and on the composer and his music, widely acclaimed as a combination of scholarship and warmth. This translation by Robert Layton (who wrote the biography *Sibelius* [item no. 717]) is an abridged and as yet incomplete version of the original. Volume I of the translation covers volumes 1 and 2 of the original, with revisions by the author. Volume II

represents volume 3 of the original 'together with a few pages of Volume 4'. The book contains musical examples and has an excellent index.

717 **Sibelius.**
Robert Layton. London: Dent, 1992. viii + 247p. bibliog. (The Master Musicians Series).

Originally published in 1965, the book has been revised to take account of Tawaststjerna's biography (item no. 716) and research on the catalogue of Sibelius's works. Contains relatively little biographical information but much on the works, which are often analysed in some detail, with musical examples. Catalogue of works and a considerable bibliography.

718 **The works of Jean Sibelius.**
Fabian Dahlström. Helsinki: Sibelius-Seura, 1987. 154p.

A preliminary but extensive catalogue of Sibelius's works. Arranged in three parts: a list of compositions, with opus numbers; a systematic list (e.g. orchestral works, chamber music with piano) of all known finished works; and an alphabetical index by the titles of works. Gives publishers.

719 **The Jean Sibelius musical manuscripts at Helsinki University Library: a complete catalogue. Die Musikhandschriften von Jean Sibelius in der Universitätsbibliothek Helsinki: ein vollständiges Verzeichnis.**
Kari Kilpeläinen. Wiesbaden, Germany: Breitkopf & Härtel, 1991. xxxii + 487p.

Helsinki University Library possesses the largest collection of Sibelius manuscripts, including those that belonged to the composer himself, with many drafts and sketches. The catalogue revises some of the dating given by Fabian Dahlström, *The works of Jean Sibelius* (see item no. 718). This immensely detailed catalogue is essential for the musicologist. Gives copyright information. There are indexes of titles and names of works, of persons, and of opus numbers. The introductory material is in German as well as English; the catalogue descriptions are in English only.

Opera

720 **The Kalevala, Sallinen and 'Kullervo'.**
John Allison. *Opera*, vol. 43, no. 2 (February 1992), p. 163-70.

Gives the background (in *Kalevala* and Aleksis Kivi's tragedy) to Aulis Sallinen's opera 'Kullervo', the première of which took place in Los Angeles in February 1992. Sallinen (born 1935) is a leading contemporary Finnish composer, noted for his operas.

721   **Jorma Hynninen.**
      Hilary Finch.   *Opera*, vol. 46, no. 7 (July 1995), p. 768-73.
On the Finnish baritone, who is also artistic director of the Savonlinna Opera Festival,
and in particular about his work with the Finnish composers Aulis Sallinen and
Einojuhani Rautavaara.

Ooperatalo. The Opera House. Das Opernhaus. Helsinki.
See item no. 702.

Folk music and songs

722   **Song of Finland. Tuhansien laulujen maa. Lauluja Suomesta.**
      (Land of thousands of songs.)
      Edited by Einari Marvia.   Porvoo, Finland; Helsinki: Werner
      Söderström, 1990. 3rd ed. 92p.
An agreeable selection of songs with colourful illustrations. Includes patriotic songs
(among them the national anthem), folk songs (the largest category), sea shanties and
various other well-known Finnish songs. Gives the music and the words in English
and Finnish (occasionally in English and Swedish or in all three languages).

723   **Suomalaisia kansanlauluja. Finnish folk songs.**
      Edited by Esko Rahikainen, Heikki Uusitalo.   Helsinki: Musiikki
      Fazer, 1984. 78p. bibliog.
Contains sixty-eight folk songs, with music, and words in the original Finnish (or
occasionally Swedish) and in English translation.

724   **Finnish Christmas songs.**
      Edited by Marjatta Bell, translated by J. J. Mary Hatakka.   London:
      Finnish Church Guild, 1988. 36p.
Includes the music and words (in English, Finnish and Swedish) for twelve well-
known Christmas songs, some religious, some secular. Also contains the music for the
'Christmas entertainment' of 'The Star Boys', which has a Swedish (and ultimately a
German) origin. The directions and words for this are given only in English.

Music education

725 **Aspects of musical life and music education in Finland.**
Osmo Palonen. Helsinki: Sibelius Academy, 1993. 2nd rev. ed.
[iv] + iii + 65p. bibliog. (Sibelius Academy. Series of Educational
Publications, 8).

On government policy towards the arts, musical organizations and, above all, on
music education at all levels, particularly the Sibelius Academy (the country's music
university). Notes that much attention has been paid to music education, and that the
standards of music making and contemporary music are high.

Dance

726 **Suomen Kansallisbaletti tänään. The Finnish National Ballet
today.**
Auli Räsänen, Kari Hakli, translated by Michael Wynne-Ellis.
Porvoo, Finland; Helsinki: Werner Söderström, 1995. 94p.

Primarily a picture-book but with a brief parallel Finnish and English text on the
history of the Finnish ballet, its present role, the National Ballet Company, its
director, ballet school, and repertoire.

727 **Old Finnish folk dances.**
Edited by Sari Heikkilä. Helsinki: Suomalaisen kansantanssin
ystävät; Finnish Folklore Association, 1988. 47p.

Aims 'to provide folk dancers all over the world with accurate and easy-to-understand
descriptions of some of the most typical and most popular dances' of Finland (p. 6). A
brief introduction on the history of Finnish folk dances is followed by twenty-one
dances, with music, words (where appropriate) and descriptions.

Theatre and Film

Theatre

728   **Finnish theatre: a northern part of world theatre.**
Maija Savutie, English translation by Philip Binham.   Helsinki:
Otava, 1980. 64p.
A plentifully illustrated little book on the special characteristics of the Finnish theatre,
trends in repertoire, and the Finnish drama.

729   **Finnish theatre finlandais.**
Helsinki: Finnish Theatre Information Centre, 1981- . two issues per
year.
Informative bilingual (English and French) magazine on various aspects of the theatre
in Finland. Has had several changes of title.

730   **Suomen Kansallisteatteri. The Finnish National Theatre.**
Edited by Ritva Heikkilä.   Porvoo, Finland: Werner Söderström,
1972. 2nd rev. ed. 279p.
First published to mark the ninetieth anniversary of the foundation of the Finnish
National Theatre and revised for the centenary. Contains a very brief introduction,
numerous illustrations of actors and productions, and lists of the company's tours,
visiting companies and the most popular productions. The text is in Finnish and
English.

From folklore to applied arts: aspects of Finnish culture.
See item no. 638.

Film

731   Finnish cinema.
Peter Cowie.   Helsinki: VAPK, 1990. 223p.

Considers the development and history of the Finnish cinema, identifying particular themes and examining modern films more closely. Notes the lack of a film-making tradition in Finland which has helped to reduce the international impact of Finnish films. Contains an index of film titles (in English translation). The original version of the book was published in 1976.

732   K/K a couple of Finns and some Donald Ducks: cinema in society.
Roger Connah.   Helsinki: VAPK Publishing, 1991. 505p.

This is a highly individual (some might say odd) look at Finnish cinema in Finnish society and especially at the films of Aki and Mika Kaurismäki.

733   Suomen kansallisfilmografia. (National filmography of Finland.)
Helsinki: Valtion painatuskeskus [and] Suomen elokuva-arkisto, 1989- .

When complete, the ten volumes of this work will provide a filmography of Finnish films from 1907 (the date of the first dramatic film) to the present (1996). The following have been published: vol. 2, 1936-41 (1995); vol. 3, 1942-47 (1993); vol. 4, 1948-52 (1992); vol. 5, 1953-56 (1989); and vol. 6, 1957-61 (1991). Each volume includes a 'Guide to the use of the filmography' in English and a list of the headings used, making the work moderately accessible to the English reader. Details of each film include, *inter alia*, director, original work, music, cast, summary of contents, criticism, notes and sources. The indexes include film titles and persons. Each volume has an introductory essay on the films of the period covered, and some illustrations. Essential for the study of Finnish films.

From folklore to applied arts: aspects of Finnish culture.
See item no. 638.

Finnish mass media.
See item no. 760.

Leisure, Recreation and Sport

Leisure and recreation

734   **Culture of the everyday: leisure and cultural participation in 1981 and 1991.**
Edited by Mirja Liikkanen, Hannu Pääkkönen.   Helsinki: Statistics Finland, 1994. 135p. bibliog. (SVT [Official statistics of Finland], Culture and the Media, 1994:3).
A detailed report on leisure activities in Finland, based on interviews with several thousand respondents, and providing a comparison with a corresponding survey in 1981. Covers leisure activities (hobbies), the reading of books, newspapers and magazines, TV viewing, radio listening, home computers, music consumption [sic], sports and physical culture and participation in cultural events, religious activities, clubs and societies. A valuable picture of how Finns spend their spare time.

From folklore to applied arts: aspects of Finnish culture.
See item no. 638.

Sport

735   **Flying Finns: story of the great tradition of Finnish distance running and cross country skiing.**
Matti Hannus.   Helsinki: Tietosanoma, 1990. 179p.
A sports writer's view of Finnish running and cross-country skiing from the 1910s to the 1980s. Here are the great names, such as Paavo Nurmi and Lasse Viren, and descriptions of their achievements, often recounted in the breathless style of the commentary box.

736 **Every second counts.**
Ari Vatanen, Vesa Väisänen, translated into English by S. K. Kusnierz.
Harrow, England: SAF Publishing, 1988. 287p.
Finns have been particularly successful as rally drivers. This is the autobiography of
the champion rally driver Ari Vatanen.

737 **Motion: Sport in Finland.**
Helsinki: Finnish Society for Research in Sport and Physical
Education, 1990- . two issues per year.
A popular magazine on sports of all kinds, containing a calendar of sporting events.

Culture of the everyday: leisure and cultural participation in 1981 and 1991.
See item no. 734.

Sauna

738 **The world of the sauna.**
Caj Bremer, Antero Raevuori, English translation and adaptation by
Tim Steffa. Porvoo, Finland; Helsinki: Werner Söderström, 1986.
192p.
A series of photographs and descriptions of saunas of different types from various
parts of Finland, rural and urban, private, public and institutional, which build up an
impression of the sauna as a part of the Finnish way of life. Concludes with some
drawings of garden and indoor saunas, giving details of their manufacturers.

739 **Sauna as symbol: society and culture in Finland.**
L. M. Edelsward. New York: Peter Lang, 1991. [xii] + 267p. bibliog.
(American University Studies, Series XI. Anthropology and Sociology,
53).
An anthropologist's view of the role and significance of the sauna in Finnish culture
and life.

740 **Finnish sauna: design, construction and maintenance.**
Helsinki: Building Information Institute, Finnish Building Centre,
1995. 2nd ed. 152p.
A clearly set out practical handbook on how to build and maintain a sauna.

741   **Smoke sauna.**
Risto Vuolle-Apiala.   Helsinki: RAK; Sarmala, 1993. 112p.
A well-illustrated volume on the traditional Finnish smoke sauna together with information about how to build one.

Food and drink

742   **Finnish cuisine à la Eero Mäkelä.**
Eero Mäkelä, translated by Martha Gaber Abrahamsen.   Helsinki: Otava, 1992. 206p.
A wide selection of Finnish recipes.

743   **The best of Finnish cooking.**
Taimi Previdi.   New York: Hippocrene Books, 1995. 242p.
A good selection of recipes with notes on what foods are served on particular festive occasions.

744   **Food from Finland.**
Anna-Maija Tanttu, Juha Tanttu.   Helsinki: Otava, 1993. 5th ed. 96p.
Not just a cookery book, although there are recipes in plenty. Provides a lot of information about Finnish eating and drinking habits which is very useful for the visitor.

Libraries, Archives, Museums and Art Galleries

Libraries

745 **Suomen tieteellisten kirjastojen opas. Vetenskapliga bibliotek i Finland. Guide to research libraries and information services in Finland.**
Edited by Matti Liinamaa, Eija Niemelä. Helsinki: Suomen tieteellinen kirjastoseura, 1993. 9th rev. and enl. ed. 208p.
This is an alphabetical list of Finnish research libraries and information services, giving basic information about addresses, hours of opening, collections, etc. There is a combined index to subjects and to libraries, including entry words in Finnish, Swedish and English. An English-language key is provided to the information given under each library.

746 **Finland.**
Anneli Äyräs. *Scandinavian Public Library Quarterly*, vol. 27, no. 1 (1994), p. 10-15.
On legislation relating to libraries in Finland and the Åland islands, including extracts from the texts of relevant laws.

747 **The Finnish library – a dynamic 200-year old.**
Tuula Haavisto. *Scandinavian Public Library Quarterly*, vol. 27, no. 3 (1994), p. 7-9.
On the history of public library development and how the bicentennial year of Finnish public libraries was commemorated.

748 **The Helsinki University Library: an architectural jewel.**
Esko Häkli, translated by Rachel Kirkwood.   Helsinki: Helsinki
University Library, 1995. [16]p.
An attractively-produced illustrated booklet about the beautiful building of Helsinki
University Library, the national library of Finland.

749 **Kirjastolehti.** (Library Journal.)
Helsinki: Suomen Kirjastoseura, 1908- . monthly.
The journal of the Finnish Library Association (Suomen Kirjastoseura), which was
entitled *Kansanvalistus ja kirjastolehti* (Public Education and Library Journal) from
1921 to 1947. Publishes articles in Finnish on librarianship and libraries, with an
emphasis on public libraries, together with some material of a more general cultural
character. Some abstracts in Swedish.

750 **Signum.**
Helsinki: Suomen tieteellinen kirjastoseura, 1968- . 8 issues per year.
Published by the Association of Scientific Libraries in Finland. Contains articles and
notices (in Finnish and Swedish) about information science and about specialized
aspects of the work of research libraries.

Handbook of cultural affairs in Finland.
See item no. 641.

Archives

751 **Guide to the public archives of Finland.**
Helsinki: National Archives, 1980. 50p. map. bibliog.
'The aims of this Guide ... are to provide foreign scholars with an introduction to the
National Archives and the provincial archives as research institutes and to give
practical advice about their use to those undertaking research.' The guide outlines the
development of archive administration in Finland, the establishment of the National
Archives and, later, of the provincial archives. It lists their functions, provides
information about their services and facilities and indicates the main type of records to
be found in the public archives. A new law relating to archives was enacted in 1994
but in essential respects this guide retains its value.

752 **Guide to the Military Archives of Finland.**
Edited by Risto Ropponen.   Helsinki: Military Archives, 1977.
[iv] + 56p. bibliog.
This is not simply a practical guide to the holdings of the Military Archives and how
to use them; it also includes (on p. 1-9) a most convenient historical outline of the
organization of the Finnish defence forces up to 1966.

Quellenkunde zur Geschichte Finnlands. (Sources for the history of Finland.)
See item no. 105.

Finnish onomastics. Namenkunde in Finnland.
See item no. 475.

Museums

753   **Suomen museot. Finnish museums.**
[Helsinki]: Suomen museoliitto, 1990. 467p.
Provides basic information (including opening hours) about the museums of Finland, arranged by place, together with brief characterizations of the museums in English. The index of museums is in Finnish and (separately) in English. A new edition was due in the autumn of 1996.

754   **The Finno-Ugric collections at the National Museum of Finland.**
Ildikó Lehtinen.   [Helsinki]: National Board of Antiquities, 1990. 57p. 2 maps. bibliog.
The National Museum of Finland has not revised its English-language guide, *National Museum of Finland: guide* (Helsinki: National Board of Antiquities and Historical Monuments, 1978. 3rd ed. [112]p.) but instead has begun to publish in English a series of guides to its collections. This one describes, with good illustrations, some of the rich materials held by the Museum relating to the Finno-Ugric peoples living outside Finland.

755   **Seurasaari. Kuvakirja ulkomuseosta. The Open-Air Museum in pictures.**
Raija Järvelä-Hynynen.   Helsinki: National Board of Antiquities, 1992. 88p.
Founded in 1909, Seurasaari is a remarkable open-air museum in Helsinki comprising wooden buildings representing different types of Finnish farmhouses and outbuildings as well as a manor house and a church. The introduction and picture captions appear in English as well as Finnish.

756   **Treasures of the Orthodox Church Museum in Finland.**
Kristina Thomenius, translated by Erja Melville, Tony Melville. Kuopio, Finland: Kustannuskiila, 1985. 124p.
The Orthodox Church Museum in Kuopio houses a magnificent collection of objects of Orthodox church art, many coming from the Russian monastery of Valamo which lay within the borders of Finland until the Second World War. The Museum reflects the cultural heritage of the Orthodox Church in Finland.

Art galleries

757 **Suomen taidemuseot. Finlands konstmuseer. Art museums in Finland.**
Edited by Jaana af Hällström.   Helsinki: Finnish Museums Association, 1995. 80p. (Suomen museoliiton julkaisuja [Publications of the Finnish Museums Association], 41).
A list of over sixty art museums arranged by place with brief descriptions in Finnish, Swedish and English, addresses, telephone numbers and opening hours. There is a regional index.

758 **Ateneum guide from Isak Wacklin to Wäinö Aaltonen.**
Marjatta Levanto, English translation by Harald Arnkil.   [Helsinki]: Otava [for] the Fine Arts Academy of Finland, the Art Museum of the Ateneum, 1987. 191p. bibliog.
An illustrated guide to the basic collections – rather than to the rooms – of the Finnish national gallery, arranged by period, from the 18th century, through the Biedermeier and national romanticism, to symbolism, expressionism and abstract art. Valuable as an introduction to Finnish painting and sculpture.

759 **The Finnish National Gallery.**
Susanna Laitala, translated by Martha Gaber Abrahamsen.   Helsinki: The Finnish National Gallery, 1992. 64p. bibliog.
Not a guide but a brief history and description of the different components of the Finnish National Gallery, published after the reopening of the Ateneum building in 1991. The National Gallery comprises the Museum of Finnish Art, Ateneum; the Museum of Foreign Art, Sinebrychoff; the Museum of Contemporary Art; and the Central Art Archives. There are also conservation, educational and administrative departments. Good photographs of premises and of a few exhibits. A curious piece of large-format book production with corrugated paper covers.

Apollo: the Magazine of the Arts.
See item no. 645.

The Media and Books

Mass media

760 **Finnish mass media.**
Helsinki: Statistics Finland, 1994. 292p. bibliog. (SVT [Official Statistics of Finland], Culture and the Media, 1994:1).
Begins with six articles on topical issues concerning the media (e.g. changes in reading habits) but the bulk of the book consists of statistics which provide a valuable comprehensive view of the mass media in Finland. Each section of statistics is preceded by a helpful summary article. Covers the mass media economy and consumption, television, radio, phonograms, video films, books and libraries, newspapers, magazines and periodicals, government subsidies for the mass media, and gives some international comparisons.

Books and publishing

761 **The book in Finland, 1488-1988.**
Editor-in-chief Kai Laitinen; editor Soila Lehtonen. Helsinki: Helsinki University Library, 1988. 64p.
This special issue of *Books from Finland* (see item no. 540) marked the 500th anniversary of the printing of the first book intended for use in Finland, the *Missale Aboense* (Turku missal). The articles cover not only early printing in Finland, but also include a brief history of Finnish publishing, by Pekka Tarkka, and a survey of reading in Finland, by Heikki Hellman, which discusses publishing and reading patterns in the 1970s and 1980s.

762 **Jäsenluettelo. List of members. 1996.**
Helsinki: Suomen Kustannusyhdistys; Finnish Book Publishers'
Association, 1996. 58p.
Contains information in a standardized format about seventy-nine Finnish publishers,
including all the large commercial ones but few learned societies. Gives a note in
Finnish (or Swedish) and English of the type of books they publish, as well as contact
names, telephone and fax numbers and e-mail addresses.

Books from Finland.
See item no. 540.

Culture of the everyday: leisure and cultural participation in 1981 and 1991.
See item no. 734.

Finnish mass media.
See item no. 760.

The press

763 **Press directory Helsinki, Finland, 1996.**
Ministry for Foreign Affairs.   [Helsinki]: Ministry for Foreign
Affairs, Department for Press and Cultural Affairs, 1996. 137p.
A small-format reference book which is broader in content than its title would suggest.
Gives basic information (including the names of key staff) about Finnish news and
photograph agencies, the principal newspapers, weekly magazines and a selection of
periodicals. Gives circulation figures. Shows how Finland has an extensive range of
newspapers, with a strong local base, and of many (and no) political affiliations. There
is also information about radio and television (including correspondents abroad), a list
of foreign news agencies represented in Finland and foreign correspondents there,
details of various organizations of journalists and publishers, parliamentary and
government information units, and the Department of Press and Cultural Affairs of the
Foreign Ministry, including the names and addresses of press and cultural officers at
Finnish embassies abroad.

764 **Press media in Finland.**
Helsinki: Finnish Newspaper Publishers Association, [1992?]. 12p.
map.
Provides brief information, including statistics, about the press in Finland and its
special characteristics, such as the sale of most newspapers through subscription.

765 **Finnish press laws.**
Edited by Lars Bruun. Helsinki: Ministry for Foreign Affairs, Press and Cultural Centre, 1984. 45p.
Publishes extracts from or complete laws relating to the freedom of the press, the deposit of free copies, broadcasting, the availability of official documents, and defamation of character. Also gives the Guidelines for Good Journalistic Practice of the Union of Journalists in Finland.

Broadcasting

766 **Radio Finland. 31.3.-96-24.10.-96.**
Helsinki. YLE Radio Finland, 1996. folding leaflet.
Radio Finland broadcasts not only within Finland in Finnish and Swedish but also transmits abroad in those languages and also in English, German, French and Russian. In addition, it broadcasts the unique and highly-acclaimed Nuntii Latini – News in Latin. This regularly-published leaflet (the latest seen covered the spring and summer of 1996) gives the times and frequencies of broadcasts to Europe, the Middle East, North America, Asia and Australia. It is obtainable from: YLE Radio Finland, P.O. Box 78, FIN-00024 Yleisradio, Helsinki. *Yleisradio 1926-1996: a history of broadcasting in Finland*, edited by Rauno Endén (Helsinki: Finnish Historical Society, 1996. 279p. 2 maps) was published while this bibliography was being edited.

The north European exception: political advertising on TV in Finland.
See item no. 264.

Culture of the everyday: leisure and cultural participation in 1981 and 1991.
See item no. 734.

Finnish mass media.
See item no. 760.

Periodicals and Newspapers

Periodicals

767 **Finsk tidskrift.** (Finnish Review.)
   Åbo, Finland: Föreningen Granskaren, 1876- . 10 issues per year.
This Swedish-language publication on cultural, economic and political topics is the oldest cultural periodical in Scandinavia.

768 **Hiidenkivi. Suomalainen kulttuurilehti.** (Finnish Cultural Magazine.)
   Helsinki: Painatuskeskus, 1994- . six issues per year.
Hiidenkivi (the title is the popular name for the type of boulder worn down and left by the retreating glaciers) was formed from the amalgamation of three older journals. It has quickly established itself as a lively and high-quality source of information and discussion on Finnish national culture (widely interpreted) and history. Includes news, articles, book reviews and a calendar of forthcoming events. Good illustrations. In Finnish.

769 **Kanava.** (Channel.)
   Helsinki: Yhtyneet Kuvalehdet, 1973- . nine issues per year.
A periodical in Finnish which publishes articles on social, cultural, political and historical topics as well as reviews. It succeeded the older-established *Suomalainen Suomi* (Finnish Finland) and *Aika* (Time).

770 **Nya Argus.** (New Argus.)
   Helsingfors: Nya Argus, 1980- . ten issues per year.
Originally published as *Argus*, 1908-11, this is a Swedish-language periodical on cultural, social and economic topics.

771 **Suomen kuvalehti.** (Finnish Picture Post.)
Helsinki: Yhtyneet Kuvalehdet, 1916- . weekly.
An illustrated weekly in Finnish which contains news and feature articles on Finnish and world events and issues.

772 **Suomen silta. Finlandsnytt. Suomi Bridge.**
Helsinki: Suomi-Seura, 1937- . six issues per year.
Published by the Suomi-Seura (Finland Society), whose aim is to keep Finns abroad in touch with Finland, and currently supported financially by the Finnish Ministry of Labour, *Suomen silta* provides information about the Finnish government, foreign policy and matters concerning employment, pensions and education as well as some cultural items. Each issue distributed outside Scandinavia contains special 'English pages' giving translations or summaries of selected articles. Useful as a source of information for non-Finns as well as for its intended readership.

Culture of the everyday: leisure and cultural participation in 1981 and 1991.
See item no. 734.

Finnish mass media.
See item no. 760.

Suomen aikakauslehti-indeksi. 1803-1863. Index to Finnish periodicals.
See item no. 800.

Suomen aikakauslehti-indeksi. Index to Finnish periodicals. 1959-81.
See item no. 801.

Suomalaisia aikakauslehtiartikkeleita uutuusindeksi. Finländska tidskrifts-artiklar nyhetsindex. (Index to current Finnish periodical articles.)
See item no. 802.

Newspapers

773 **Aamulehti.** (Morning Post.)
Tampere, Finland: Aamulehti-yhtymä, 1882- . daily.
A daily Finnish-language, politically independent newspaper with a large circulation outside its native Tampere.

774 **Demari.** (Democrat.)
Helsinki: Kustannus Oy Demari, 1895- . 5 issues per week.
The newspaper of the Finnish Social Democratic Party, originally *Työmies* (Worker), then from 1918 to 1988 *Suomen Sosialidemokraatti* (Finnish Social Democrat). It is produced in a tabloid format, with few pages. Not published at the weekend.

775   **Helsingin Sanomat.** (Helsinki News.)
       Helsinki: Sanoma, 1890- . daily.
A Finnish-language daily, with no party affiliation and the largest circulation of any
Finnish newspaper. Originally *Päivälehti* (Daily Post), 1890-1904. Unusual in that it
retains advertisements on the front page.

776   **Hufvudstadsbladet.** (News of the Capital.)
       Helsingfors: Hufvudstadsbladet, 1864- . daily.
A Swedish-language newspaper, with the largest circulation of any such paper in the
country.

**Culture of the everyday: leisure and cultural participation in 1981 and
1991.**
See item no. 734.

Finnish mass media.
See item no. 760.

Encyclopaedias, Yearbooks and Biographical Dictionaries

Encyclopaedias

777 **Nykysuomen tietosanakirja.** (Modern Finnish encyclopaedia.)
Porvoo, Finland; Helsinki: Werner Söderström, 1992-93. 4 vols. maps.
Volume 1 (Henkilöt) is a biographical dictionary of some 12,000 notable persons, with brief entries. There are indexes grouping people by historical period and by occupation or activity, as well as an index of literary, musical and other works, with references to their authors, composers, etc. Finns are well represented. Volume 2 (Maat ja paikat) is about countries and places, again with a good emphasis on Finland. Volumes 3-4 (Yleistieto) are a general knowledge encyclopaedia containing brief articles, alphabetically arranged. In Finnish.

778 **Suomalainen tietosanakirja.** (Finnish encyclopaedia.)
Espoo, Finland: Weilin & Göös, 1988-93. 11 vols. maps.
The work is divided into two parts. Vols. 1-8 form a general encyclopaedia with articles arranged in alphabetical order. There is a generous treatment of Finland and Finnish topics and persons. Some articles have bibliographies. Vols. 9-11 comprise a three-volume 'rapid information' reference work containing some 120,000 entry words with brief definitions or explanations. In Finnish.

779 **Uppslagsverket Finland.** (Finland encyclopaedia.)
Helsingfors: Schildt, 1982-85. 3 vols. maps.
This Swedish-language encyclopaedia is an admirable source of reference on Finland in all respects although its emphasis on information about the Finland Swedes gives it special value as far as their life and culture are concerned. The work is easy to use and sensibly illustrated. Its bibliographical references to works in Finnish as well as Swedish demonstrate the cultural unity of the country.

780 **WSOY iso tietosanakirja.** (Werner Söderström's great
encyclopaedia.)
Porvoo, Finland; Helsinki: Werner Söderström, 1995- . Vol. 1- .
maps.
An extensive new Finnish general encyclopaedia, planned in ten volumes, following a
conventional alphabetical arrangement. Has a good emphasis on Finland. Well
illustrated but with no bibliographies. The first four volumes cover from 'A' to 'Ko'.
In Finnish.

Yearbooks

781 **Mitä – missä – milloin: kansalaisen vuosikirja.** (What – Where –
When: the Citizen's Yearbook.)
Helsinki: Otava, 1951- . annual.
An informative annual containing articles and surveys on a wide range of topics on
Finland and elsewhere. *Mitä, missä, milloin hakemisto 1951-90* (index to 1951-90)
was published in 1990.

782 **Suomen valtiokalenteri. Finlands statskalender. Julkaissut
Helsingin yliopisto. Utgiven av Helsingfors universitet.** (The Official
Yearbook of Finland. Published by Helsinki University.)
Helsinki; Helsingfors: Lakimiesliiton kustannus; Juristförbundets
förlag, 1869- . annual.
This important work lists government departments and subordinate organizations,
including universities, with their senior officials. There is information about the
churches, political parties, the press, societies and organizations of various types. A
Swedish-language version, *Finlands statskalender*, was published 1810-1981.

Finland handbook: 1996.
See item no. 81.

Yearbook of Population Research in Finland.
See item no. 193.

Economic survey: Finland.
See item no. 325.

Bank of Finland Yearbook.
See item no. 334.

Yearbook of Finnish Foreign Policy 1973- .
See item no. 335.

Encyclopaedias, Yearbooks and Biographical Dictionaries. Biographical
dictionaries

Sininen kirja 28. Talouselämän suurhakemisto. Finlands affärskalender.
Business directory of Finland.
See item no. 397.

The Finnish Timber and Paper Directory 1994-95.
See item no. 413.

Suomen tilastollinen vuosikirja. Statistisk årsbok för Finland. Statistical
Yearbook of Finland.
See item no. 418.

Finland in figures.
See item no. 419.

Finnish Institute Yearbook.
See item no. 454.

Sananjalka: Suomen kielen seuran vuosikirja. (Yearbook of the Finnish
Language Society.)
See item no. 473.

Design in Finland, 1995.
See item no. 660.

Press directory Helsinki, Finland 1996.
See item no. 763.

Biographical dictionaries

783 Kuka kukin on. Who's who in Finland. Henkilötietoja nykypolven
suomalaisista. 1994. (Personal information about Finns of the present
generation.)
Helsinki: Otava, 1994. 1,119p.

Has entries for 4,240 living Finns. In the case of certain retired individuals and
persons who did not respond to the compilers' questionnaire, reference is made to
fuller entries in previous volumes. A table of 'English equivalents of some words and
abbreviations' makes some use of the work just possible without a knowledge of
Finnish. *Kuka kukin on* was published in 1964, 1966, 1970, 1974, 1978, 1982, 1986
and 1990. For older entries see *Kuka kukin oli* (Who was who in Finland), item no.
785.

784 Vem och vad? Biografisk handbok 1992. (Who and what?
Biographical handbook 1992.)
Edited by Henrik Ekberg. Esbo, Finland: Schildts, 1992. 572p.

The fourteenth in a series of biographical reference books about notable living Finns,
with an emphasis on Swedish Finns. Contains 2,646 biographies.

785 **Kuka kukin oli. Who was who in Finland. Henkilötietoja 1900-luvulla kuolleista julkisuuden suomalaisista.** (Personal information about Finns in public life who died in the 20th century.) Helsinki: Otava, 1961. 593p.

Comprises 2,614 biographies of prominent Finns who died after 1 January 1900 and thus includes many persons active in the 19th century. May be complemented by the older volumes of *Kuka kukin on* (Who's who in Finland), item no. 783.

786 **Kansallisbiografia. Näytevihko.** (Dictionary of national biography. Sample fascicule.) Edited by Aulikki Litzen. Helsinki: Suomen Historiallinen Seura, 1994. 71p.

This sample fascicule, published by the Finnish Historical Society and containing several entries, is the forerunner of an extensive new dictionary of Finnish national biography. It will appear first on CD-ROM and then, in 2000, as a book in eight volumes.

Dictionary of Scandinavian history.
See item no. 85.

Dictionary of Scandinavian literature.
See item no. 526.

Suomen kirjailijat 1809-1916. Pienoiselämäkerrat. Teosbibliografiat. Tutkimusviitteet. Finlands författare. Kortbiografier. Verkförteckningar. Litteraturhänvisningar. Writers in Finland. Concise biographies. Bibliographies. Research references.
See item no. 537.

Suomen kirjailijat 1917-1944. Pienoiselämäkerrat. Teosbibliografiat. Tutkimusviitteet. Finlands författare. Kortbiografier. Verkförteckningar. Litteraturhänvisningar. Writers in Finland. Concise biographies. Bibliographies. Research references.
See item no. 538.

Suomen kirjailijat 1945-1980. Pienoiselämäkerrat. Teosbibliografiat. Tutkimusviitteet. Finlands författare. Kortbiografier. Verkförteckningar. Litteraturhänvisningar. Writers in Finland. Concise biographies. Bibliographies. Research references.
See item no. 539.

Nykysuomen tietosanakirja. (Modern Finnish encyclopaedia.)
See item no. 777.

Bibliographies

General bibliographies and bibliographical guides

787 **Finland and the Finns: a selective bibliography.**
Elemer Bako. Washington, DC: Library of Congress, 1993.
xvi + 276p.
Lists, often with annotations, 2,108 publications (1,716 monographs and 392 serials)
on Finland held by the Library of Congress. A strength is the inclusion of material in
Finnish and Swedish as well as in English and other languages. Thanks to the extent
of the Library of Congress collection, this gives a rounded impression of the literature.
A weakness is the frequent arrangement of several items under one reference number,
making unnecessarily difficult the use of the index of personal names and the topical
guide to chapter contents, which acts as a subject index. Arranged in broad chapters,
e.g. history, legislative system, foreign and international affairs. Good explanation and
listings of national bibliographies and series of statistics. Contains little published
after 1989.

788 **Finlands bibliografiska litteratur: kommenterad förteckning.**
(Finnish bibliographical works: an annotated list.)
Henrik Grönroos. Ekenäs, Finland: Ekenäs tryckeri, 1976. 388p.
The aim of this annotated bibliography of Finnish bibliographies is to assist users in
Scandinavia. The inclusion of a brief summary in English has facilitated its use
elsewhere – fortunately, since despite its age this remains an essential Finnish
bibliographical reference book. It covers general bibliographies, Finland in foreign
writing and foreign countries in Finnish writing, subject bibliographies and
bibliographies of individuals. The indexes include Swedish-Finnish and Finnish-
Swedish subject indexes. There are over 1,400 entries, cross-referencing is good, and
the work is clearly arranged and easy to use. It is a revision of an earlier work: Henrik
Grönroos, *Suomen bibliografisen kirjallisuuden opas. Guide des bibliographies
finlandaises* (Guide to Finnish bibliographies) (Helsinki: Suomalaisen Kirjallisuuden

Seura, 1965. 219p.) which has its table of contents and an abridgement of its introduction translated into French.

789 **Books in English on Finland: a bibliographical list of publications concerning Finland until 1960, including Finnish literature in English translation. Appendix: a selected list of books published from 1961 to 1963 inclusive.**
Hilkka Aaltonen. Turku, Finland: Turku University Library, 1964. 276p. (Publications of Turku University Library, 8).

Contains over 5,000 unannotated entries, comprising both books and periodical articles, arranged in a classified order and with indexes of persons and of anonymous publications. Most items have been examined *de visu*. Very useful.

790 **Finland: sources of information. A selective list of publications 1960-1977.**
Kyllikki Ruokonen, Erkki Vaisto. Helsinki: Helsinki School of Economics Library, 1979. 224p. map. (Helsingin kauppakorkeakoulun julkaisuja [Publications of Helsinki School of Economics], D-39).

Some 4,000 references (unannotated), arranged in UDC classified order, to Finnish and foreign material, mainly on economics and business. Most items are in English, except for some bibliographies and journals. Author and subject indexes are provided.

791 **Finland: sources of information. A selective list of publications 1978-1986.**
Kyllikki Ruokonen. Helsinki: Helsinki School of Economics Library, 1988. [v] + vii + 193p. (Helsingin Kauppakorkeakoulu. Selvityksiä [Helsinki School of Economics Reports], E-54).

792 **Finland: sources of information. 2. A selective list of publications 1978-1988.**
Kyllikki Ruokonen. Helsinki: Helsinki School of Economics Library, 1989. [v] + 112p. (Helsingin Kauppakorkeakoulu. Selvityksiä [Helsinki School of Economics Reports], E-56).

These items continue item no. 790, containing 2,926 and 1,793 entries respectively, with the emphasis on economic and business information but with greater attention to history and culture in the second volume. Includes no annotations but careful classification – including the separation within sections of Finnish from foreign material – and good subject indexing make these exceedingly useful for identifying material in English on Finland. Unfortunately, no more are to be published.

Finland: a country study.
See item no. 1.

The Finnish National Bibliography

793 **Suomen kirjallisuus. Finlands litteratur. The Finnish National Bibliography. 1972- .**
Helsinki: Helsinki University Library, 1972- . monthly.
This is the currently published Finnish national bibliography, with nine issues a year, three being double numbers. An annual cumulation ceased publication with the volume for 1994: *Suomen kirjallisuus: vuosiluettelo. Finlands litteratur: årskatalog. The Finnish National Bibliography: Annual Volume.* This bibliography was preceded by *Suomen kirjallisuus* (Finnish bibliography), 1949-66 (in three-year periods), while 1967-71 was covered in a five-year period. For bibliographies covering the period to 1948, and for details of their contents, see Henrik Grönroos, *Finlands bibliografiska litteratur* (item no. 788), p. 35-44. The contents of the bibliography, including books published outside Finland but with a Finnish author or translator, and books in Finnish published abroad, are to be found on the national bibliography database Fennica-CD-ROM. Data is being extended back through a retrospective conversion programme and the CD-ROM now covers material from 1945 onwards. The earliest literature is covered in *Suomen kansallisbibliografia. Finlands nationalbibliografi. Finnische Nationalbibliographie* (Finnish national bibliography) *1488-1700*, edited by Tuija Laine, Rita Nyqvist (Helsinki: Helsingin yliopiston kirjasto; Suomalaisen Kirjallisuuden Seura, 1996. 2 vols. [Suomalaisen Kirjallisuuden Seuran toimituksia (Publications of the Finnish Literature Society), 642-43; Helsingin yliopiston kirjaston julkaisuja (Publications of Helsinki University Library), 59-60]). The introductory material is in Finnish, Swedish and German.

Specialized bibliographies

794 **Finland's war years 1939-1945: a list of books and articles concerning the Winter War and the Continuation War, excluding literature in Finnish and Russian.**
Kristina Nyman, preface by K. J. Mikola. Helsinki: Sotahistoriallinen Seura, 1973. XXXII + 259p. 4 maps. (Publications of the Society of Military History, 4).
This still useful, unannotated classified list of books and articles is arranged in five sections: 1, the Winter War; 2, the Continuation War; 3, a miscellaneous section of books and articles touching on Finland in the period described but not exclusively about it; 4, Mannerheim; and 5, the Åland islands question (1938-39). Contains 3,410 numbered entries of material published to 1970, an appendix of about seventy items published in 1970-72, and an index. The preface by the military historian Colonel K. J. Mikola, 'Finland's wars during World War II (1939-1945)', p. IX-XXXII, is a handy short account of the subject.

795 **A select list of books and articles in English, French and German on Finnish politics in the 19th and 20th century.**
Compiled by Martti Julkunen, Anja Lehikoinen. Turku, Finland: Institute of Political History, 1967. 125p. (Institute of Political History, University of Turku Publications, B: 1).
A list, classified by period, of material on politics interpreted in a wide sense. Contains an index of authors. There are no annotations but the work is very serviceable. Continued by item no. 796.

796 **A select list of books and articles in English, French and German on Finnish politics in the 19th and 20th century. Volume II: Publications 1968-89.**
Compiled by Ilse Vähäkyrö, Antti Uusitalo. Turku, Finland: Department of Political History, University of Turku, 1990. 82p. (University of Turku. Political History, B:4).
A supplement to item no. 795. Interprets politics widely and includes international relations.

797 **Kaunokirjallisuutemme käännöksiä: bibliografinen luettelo suomenkielisen kaunokirjallisuuden käännöksistä. Livres finnois en traduction: romans, nouvelles, poésies, pièces de théâtre. Guide bibliographique.** (Finnish literature in translation: a bibliographical list of translations of Finnish-language literature. Finnish books in translation: novels, short stories, poetry, plays. Bibliographical guide.)
Sulo Haltsonen, Rauni Puranen. Helsinki: Suomalaisen Kirjallisuuden Seura, 1979. 150p. (Suomi [Finland], 122:4).
This is a revised and expanded edition of Haltsonen's bibliography *Suomalaista kaunokirjallisuutta vierailla kielillä ... Livres finnois en traduction* (Finnish literature in foreign languages ... Finnish books in translation) (Helsinki: Suomalaisen Kirjallisuuden Seura, 1961. 138p.). The new edition adds information about translations from Finnish-language literature for 1961-75, plus some subsequently published works, amounting to about 700 additions to the original work's 1,168 entries. English (p. 10-14) is one of thirty-eight languages represented. The selection of anthologies (p. 114-26) includes material in Western languages; *Kalevala* and folk poetry in English appear on p. 127-28. The table of contents is in Finnish and French. Regrettably, the work has not been continued to cover more recent translations.

Historical dictionary of Finland.
See item no. 95.

Finland: people, nation, state.
See item no. 96.

Historisk tidskrift för Finland. (Finnish Historical Journal.)
See item no. 107.

Revue Internationale d'Histoire Militaire: Edition Finlandaise. (International Review of Military History: Finnish Edition.)
See item no. 308.

The Kalevala abroad: translations and foreign-language adaptations of the Kalevala.
See item no. 564.

Official publications

798 **Valtion virallisjulkaisut. Statens officiella publikationer. Government publications in Finland. 1961- .**
Helsinki: Eduskunnan kirjasto, 1962- . annual.
The Library of Parliament publishes this annual list of government publications: vol. 33 covering 1993 came out in 1995. Includes the publications of government offices, institutions and committees but excludes maps and various small-scale and pamphlet publications. The preface and list of government departments are in Finnish, Swedish and English. Arranged by department with an alphabetical index of authors (personal and corporate) and a subject index (using Finnish terms only).

799 **Finland.**
Henrik Schauman, Kaarina Puttonen. In: *Official publications of Western Europe.* I. *Denmark, Finland, France, Ireland, Italy, Luxembourg, Netherlands, Spain and Turkey.* Edited by Eve Johansson. London: Mansell, 1984, p. 27-44. bibliog.
Basic information about the principal central and local government publications.

Indexes to periodicals

800 **Suomen aikakauslehti-indeksi. 1803-1863. Index to Finnish periodicals.**
Turku, Finland: Turun yliopiston kirjasto, 1974. VII + 211p.
An index to forty-six serials published between 1803 and 1863. Classified arrangement, with the headings in the list of contents also given in English. Contains an index of authors.

801 Suomen aikakauslehti-indeksi. Index to Finnish periodicals. 1959-81.
Turku, Finland: Turun yliopiston kirjasto, 1961-84. annual.
This annual index covered about 150 scholarly and popular periodicals. Classified arrangement (with the headings in the list of contents also given in English). Index of authors. Continued by *Suomalaisia aikakauslehtiartikkeleita uutuusindeksi* (item no. 802).

802 Suomalaisia aikakauslehtiartikkeleita uutuusindeksi. Finländska tidskriftsartiklar nyhetsindex. (Index to current Finnish periodical articles.)
Helsinki: Kirjastopalvelu, 1982- . five issues per year.
An index to about 15,000 articles in nearly 200 current periodicals, arranged in classified (UDC) order. Continues *Suomen aikakauslehti-indeksi* (item no. 801). Indexes the English-language periodicals *Books from Finland*, *Finnish Music Quarterly* and *Form Function Finland*.

Index

Title entries are italicized and refer either to the main titles, or to many of the other works cited in the annotations. The numbers refer to bibliographical entry rather than page number. Individual index entries are arranged in alphabetical sequence.

225

Mathematics
history of 460
Matiskainen, H. 70
Matson, A. 596, 602, 622
Maude, G. 95, 328
Mead, W. R. 5-7, 17, 26,
28, 408, 534-35
Medals 313
Media 2, 640, 760, 763-64
see also Press; Radio;
Television
Medicine
history of 461
see also Folk medicine
Meditz, S. W. 1
Meek heritage: a novel 622
Meinander, C. F. 647
Melanko, V. 706
Melin, H. 223
Melleri, A. 571
Melville, A. 663, 665, 756
Melville, E. 663, 756
Melville, Tony see
Melville, A
Memoirs 176, 180, 186
see also
Autobiographies;
Biographies; Names
of individuals
Memoirs of Marshal
Mannerheim 180
Men 222, 228, 233, 423
mortality 222
Mercy and justice:
miracles of the Virgin
Mary in Finnish
medieval wall-
paintings 649
Meri, V. 567, 576-77, 610
Merikanto, U. 655
Meriluoto, A. 571, 611
Merita Group (bank) 371
Mettälä, K. 390
Michael, M. 615
Migration from Finland to
North America in the
years between the
United States Civil
War and the First
World War 208
Mikkola, Kimmo 675
Mikkola, Kirmo 654, 692
Mikola, K. J. 794

Military Archives of
Finland 752
Military history see
History, military
Military law see Law,
military
Miller, D. 675
Mind and form in folklore:
selected articles 550
Mineralogy
history of 458
Ministry for Foreign
Affairs 239, 326, 336,
427, 763
Ministry for Foreign
Affairs. Press and
Cultural Department
3, 763
Ministry of Agriculture
and Forestry 430
Ministry of Education 433,
437, 440, 639
Ministry of the
Environment 427
Ministry of Finance 374
Ministry of the Interior
301, 430
Ministry of Labour 772
Ministry of Social Affairs
and Health 234-35
Ministry of Trade and
Industry 388, 427
Minorities 1, 188, 221
Missale Aboense 761
Mitä, missä, milloin
hakemisto 1951-90
(Index to What,
Where, When,
1951-90) 781
Mitä – missä – milloin:
kansalaisen vuosikirja
(What – Where –
When: the Citizen's
Yearbook) 781
Mitchell, R. 641
Modeen, T. 195, 279, 443
Modern Finnish painting
and graphic art 653
Modern language studies
history of 462
Modern language studies
in Finland 1828-1918
462

Modern Nordic plays:
Finland 577
Molarius, P. 638
Monetary policy in
Finland 359
Money 244, 312-13
Money and economic
activity in Finland,
1866-1985 363
Moominland midwinter
593
Moorhouse, J. 698
More equal than most.
Essays on women in
Finnish society and
culture 530
Moring, T. 264-65
Mörne, A. 580
Moseley, C. 575
Motion: Sport in Finland
737
Möttölä, K. 387
Moving river of tears:
Russia's experience in
Finland 531
Moyne, E. J. 536
Mukka, T. 576
Munch-Petersen, T. 91
Muodin vuosikymmenet.
Dress and fashion
1810-1910. Suomen
kansallismuseo.
National Museum of
Finland 79
Murray, J. 52
Murtorinne, E. 214
Museum of Contemporary
Art 759
Museum of Finnish
Architecture 677
Museum of Finnish Art,
Ateneum 645, 758-59
Museum of Foreign Art,
Sinebrychoff 645, 759
Museums 753-59
Music 560, 638, 706-15,
725
periodicals 711
see also Folk music
Music education 706, 725
Music of Finland 706
My brother Sebastian 591
My childhood 614

S

241

242

Map of Finland

This map shows the more important towns and other features.

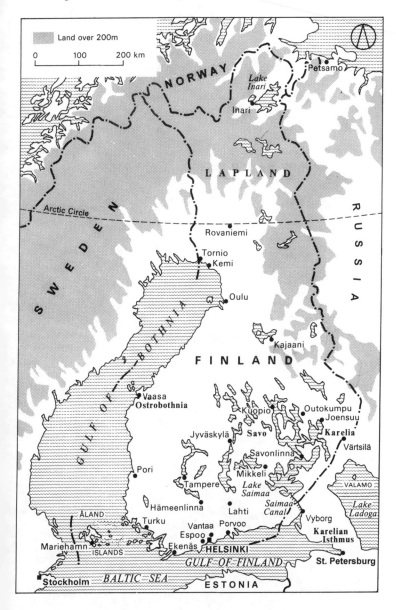

ALSO FROM CLIO PRESS

INTERNATIONAL ORGANIZATIONS SERIES

Each volume in the International Organizations Series is either devoted to one specific organization, or to a number of different organizations operating in a particular region, or engaged in a specific field of activity. The scope of the series is wide-ranging and includes intergovernmental organizations, international non-governmental organizations, and national bodies dealing with international issues. The series is aimed mainly at the English-speaker and each volume provides a selective, annotated, critical bibliography of the organization, or organizations, concerned. The bibliographies cover books, articles, pamphlets, directories, databases and theses and, wherever possible, attention is focused on material about the organizations rather than on the organizations' own publications. Notwithstanding this, the most important official publications, and guides to those publications, will be included. The views expressed in individual volumes, however, are not necessarily those of the publishers.

VOLUMES IN THE SERIES